NEW CLASSIC WINEMAKERS OF CALIFORNIA

NEW CLASSIC WINEMAKERS OF CALIFORNIA

CONVERSATIONS WITH **STEVE HEIMOFF** FOREWORD BY **H. WILLIAM HARLAN**

UNIVERSITY OF CALIFORNIA PRESS   BERKELEY LOS ANGELES LONDON

University of California Press, one of the most distinguished university presses in the United States, enriches lives around the world by advancing scholarship in the humanities, social sciences, and natural sciences. Its activities are supported by the UC Press Foundation and by philanthropic contributions from individuals and institutions. For more information, visit www.ucpress.edu.

University of California Press
Berkeley and Los Angeles, California

University of California Press, Ltd.
London, England

Library of Congress Cataloging-in-Publication Data
Heimoff, Steve.
    New classic winemakers of California : conversations with Steve Heimoff / foreword by H. William Harlan.
        p.   cm.
    Includes index.
    ISBN 978-0-520-24722-2 (cloth : alk. paper)
    1. Vintners—California—Biography.   2. Wine and wine making—California—History.   I. Title.
TP547.AIH45   2008
641.2'20922794—dc22   2007005166

Manufactured in the United States of America
17   16   15   14   13   12   11   10   09   08
10   9   8   7   6   5   4   3   2   1
This book is printed on Natures Book, which contains 50% post-consumer waste and meets the minimum requirements of ANSI/NISO Z39.48-1992 (R 1997) (Permanence of Paper). ♾

FOR MOM, AS PROMISED

CONTENTS

1 Ceàgo Vinegarden (Javier Tapia Meza)
2 Rosenblum Cellars (Kent Rosenblum)
3 Morgan Winery (Dan Morgan Lee)
4 Pisoni Vineyards & Winery (Gary, Mark, and Jeff Pisoni)
5 Saxum Vineyards (Justin Smith)
6 Talley Vineyards (Brian Talley)
7 Alban Vineyards (John Alban)
8 Brewer-Clifton (Greg Brewer)
9 Melville Vineyards and Winery (Greg Brewer)
10 Richard Longoria Wines (Rick Longoria)
11 Foxen Winery & Vineyard (Bill Wathen)
12 Fiddlehead Cellars (Kathy Joseph)
13 Gallo Family Vineyards (Gina Gallo)
14 Seghesio Family Vineyards (Ted Seghesio)
15 Tandem Winery (Greg La Follette)
16 De Loach Vineyards (Greg La Follette)
17 Merry Edwards Wines (Merry Edwards)
18 Siduri Winery (Adam and Dianna Lee)
19 Kendall-Jackson (Randy Ullom)
20 La Sirena Wines (Heidi Peterson Barrett)
21 Colgin Cellars (Mark Aubert)
22 Aubert Wines (Mark Aubert)
23 Beckstoffer Vineyards (Andy Beckstoffer)
24 Showket Vineyards (Heidi Peterson Barrett)
25 Robert Mondavi Winery (Genevieve Janssens)
26 Harlan Estate (Bob Levy)
27 Paradigm Winery (Heidi Peterson Barrett)
28 Chateau St. Jean (Margo van Staaveren)
29 Hanzell Vineyards (Michael Terrien)
30 Baldacci Family Vineyards (Rolando Herrera)
31 Shafer Vineyards (Doug Shafer and Elias Fernandez)
32 Mi Sueño Winery (Rolando Herrera)
33 Etude Wines (Tony Soter)

FOREWORD

H. WILLIAM HARLAN

Much of American effort involves the quest for new frontiers. Each generation discovers for itself the character of place in the context of time. Each individual does the same. That process is inexorable—and inseparable from the land, for gravity grounds us all.

So do roots, and memories, and the need for congress with nature, whether immediate or at a refined remove. However advanced America becomes technologically, it remains at its heart a nation of farmers. In California, this is especially true: from one valley to the next, from one region to the next, life exists at both the speed of the microchip and the pace of the seasons. A fortunate combination of terrain, climate, and geology endows the earth here with the capacity for great bounty. It provides also the potential for great art, made from the fruit of the vine, coaxed by man—subject to nature.

The grape has long been central to California's culture and its agriculture, yet generations of winegrowers in the West have struggled to find the fullest means of its expression. In the six score–plus years since the industry first blossomed here, California wines have followed progress on a cyclical forward march, with great moments and fallow periods. Two devastating bouts with phylloxera, one in the 1880s and one in the 1980s, frame a century of winemaking interrupted almost to extinction by the 1906 earthquake, Prohibition, the Depression, and two world wars. But between the Civil War and the end of the nineteenth century, a few California vintners produced wines that would have been comfortable on the grand tour. In the 1970s, several California vintners claimed elite prizes in international competitions. Today, California's finest wines habitually keep company with Europe's aristocracy of vintages.

This latest rebound began in the postwar boom, when Ernest and Julio Gallo began their tireless efforts to improve soundness and consistency, and to introduce the habit of wine with meals into a culture of cocktails and beer. Then, as now, California's universities advanced the science of viticulture, training class after class of competent winegrowers in the laboratory. Iconoclasts, too, existed, as always: John Daniel and a few of the old-line vintners, along with their wines, are still the stuff of legend. Through the force of his own passion, André Tchelistcheff swayed still others to pursue the ideal of fine wine, improved by experimentation and research.

Robert Mondavi shifted the paradigm in 1966. In enthusiasts like me, who visited the winery in its earliest days, Mondavi instilled the pioneering spirit by demonstrating that passion, discipline, and daring make it possible to do something new, and that the aspiration to excellence produces something of consequence. To fledgling vintners then migrating to California's winegrowing regions from other places and other lives, he also passed along values common to agricultural communities from time immemorial—sharing information, making introductions, offering help. Due largely to his efforts, and the successes of the 1970s—the Paris tasting and the emergence of a superb indigenous cuisine (thanks to Julia Child, M. F. K. Fisher, and Alice Waters)—California began to achieve parity with the world's leading winegrowing regions.

As the past thirty years of winegrowing here attest, and as each of Steve Heimoff's fascinating conversations confirms, generational shifts produce many things—above all, enormous potential. Today's winegrowers and winemakers, so many more than before, and more and more women among them, proceed with the confidence and clarity accruing to them from the accumulated experience, technological expertise, and craft of their predecessors. If this flourishing new crop maintains its focus, it will distill even further the essence of individual vision, recalibrating its sense of purpose while pursuing new regions and grape varieties to plant.

As grape growing and winemaking integrate even further, and as growers and vintners continue to expand their understanding of each specific parcel of land and its capabilities, the chance becomes ever greater of making wine that is, in fact, the art of man and nature. As the refinement of established winegrowing regions into smaller appellations goes on to designate specific vineyards, and even blocks within vineyards, and as smaller wineries proliferate because of the direct relationship between the vintner and the public, wine of balance and finesse, wine that captures a year, in a particular place, in a bottle, becomes more and more a likelihood. This is the ideal that every winemaker strives for: wine that has much to give to connoisseur and casual enthusiast alike.

The viability of vines in California spans from twenty-five to fifty years, from a generation to a life's work. During the past half century, the quality of life in America, and particularly at the American table, has improved profoundly. Today, no winegrowing area surpasses California's in hospitality. We all play a role in this: the growers and winemakers, the chefs and sommeliers who commit themselves to education and to encouraging lives of warmth and hospitality, and, of course, the ever-expanding community of wine lovers. The power of the critics fuels all of this, as does the enormous positive influence of the media.

Wine is global and local, a tradition and an art form with ancient roots and cross-cultural reach. Its pleasures involve the senses and the table, and the warmth and welcome shared between host and guest—as well as other joys purely intellectual. Wine has always been integral to good health, and to the life well lived. Europeans, of course, have long known this. Asians are just now learning it. Americans have recently taken it very much to heart.

That fact alone makes shepherding our extraordinary fertile areas, vineyards among them, safely into the future a cultural and social imperative, even as preserving our agricultural heritage becomes ever more difficult amid the constant economic pressure for growth and change. Precedents, however, do exist: Napa Valley's Agricultural Preserve, created in 1968, provides a useful model.

If future residents of California's winegrowing regions cleave fast to what our forebears cultivated so tenaciously, they will conserve places of exceptional promise, remarkable beauty, and a way of life still tied closely to the seasons. Should coming generations of California vintners strive, like their predecessors, for constant improvement, they will ensure that California's wines go on closing the legacy gap to achieve the kind of distinction that once belonged solely to the Europeans by virtue of their long history. A century from now, and more, the land will abide, potent, here for further discovery— and this era will be but a beginning.

ACKNOWLEDGMENTS

Many individuals contributed to the making of this book. Of course, it would not have been possible without the cooperation of the winemakers (and one grower) who let me into their lives—pleasurably, I hope, for them. I would like also to thank my editor at University of California Press, Blake Edgar, who has been so helpful and kind in so many ways. And a word of appreciation to Bill Harlan for graciously writing the foreword. Finally, I lift a glass to the great wine industry, which makes our sometimes sorry world a better place.

INTRODUCTION

This book owes inspiration to an earlier book. *Great Winemakers of California: Conversations with Robert Benson* was published in 1977 by Capra Press. Sometime in the mid 1980s, I bought a used copy at a San Francisco bookstore. It instantly became one of my favorite wine books, and, when I became a working wine writer, it was a trusted source for historical information.

Benson's book consisted of a series of conversations—twenty-eight in all—between him and California winemakers (only one of whom was a woman; we've come a long way since then). Each conversation was published in question-and-answer form. That enabled the reader to get inside the winemaker's head, follow a train of thought, and pick up a little of the winemaker's personality.

A conversation is different from an interview. Usually, when writers interview subjects, only isolated quotes survive, scattered here and there in the resulting publication, sometimes out of context. Subjects, moreover, tend to be guarded during interviews. An interview has something of the feel of a third-degree grilling.

A conversation, by contrast, is a more natural context for human beings, who are, after all, social creatures. Conversation implies sharing, exchanging, interacting. We converse with friends; we don't interview them. I've done plenty of interviewing in my checkered career, but the conversations—the things you have when you're just hanging out—I've had with winemakers have been among the most satisfying aspects of my job, in both a personal and a professional sense. I wanted to share that experience with readers.

In his conversations, Benson delivered up the complete winemaker, so to speak: that mixture of intellect, temperament, and soul, heart and opinion, emotion and quirky individuality that constitutes everyone we know, including ourselves—what makes us, when you think about it, worth knowing. In an era when American wine writing already was becoming formulaic and breathy, *Conversations* was that rarity, a smartly readable (and rereadable) wine book.

Benson captured the California wine industry at a most interesting time. It was just after the beginning of the boutique winery era of the 1960s, when the radical experimentalism of that decade was bearing fruit. The excitement generated by Robert Mondavi's opening of his winery in 1966 seemed to symbolize the period, but there was so much more going on than that. Innovation ran rampant throughout wine country, guided by high-minded ambitions. The modern California wine industry was born in a flash of collective brilliance. By the time *Conversations* was published, the shock wave had spread across America and was being felt in Europe. (The Paris tasting had occurred in May 1976.) American (which is to say California) wine had clambered onto the global stage, and Benson caught his vintners in this heady, optimistic moment.

———————

When Benson wrote, wine enthusiasts were interested in different sorts of things than they are today. They gravitated toward the more technical aspects. I've never been quite sure why; most movie lovers don't concern themselves with the minutiae of film technology, or book readers with the ins and outs of manufacturing paper. Benson's questions tended to be about fining, filtering, centrifuging, gondolas, crushers, and that sort of thing. Perhaps technique was something Americans, a race of tinkerers, could relate to; maybe that early in their wine learning curve, they needed the steadying effect of formula to latch on to.

I decided to take a different approach. It seems to me there's a limit to how much today's wine readers care to wade through deep trenches of technology. (The modern popular wine press, too, has drifted away from extensive reporting on hard-core viticulture and enology.) I couldn't see asking dozens of winemakers seriatim at how many pounds per square inch they press their grapes. When technique seemed a fruitful or appropriate area to investigate, I did, and as it turned out, technique crept into all of these conversations to a greater or lesser degree. But I also wanted stories, personal histories, opinions, viewpoints—to know not only *what* these people did and *how* they did it, but *why*. For me, *terroir* includes above all the winemaker's vision.

Why include the human element in a definition of *terroir?* Most writers, as far as I can tell, don't. To me it's obvious, but this impossible-to-translate French term has been the subject of so much obfuscation and controversy that perhaps I ought to explain more fully. The easiest way is by a silly example. If you agree that, say, the Harlan estate vineyard is a great natural source of Cabernet Sauvignon because of the climate of the Oakville foothills, the soils, exposures, and so on, then consider this question: If you or I made the wine instead of Bob Levy, would it be "Harlan Estate"? Obviously, no. It might not even be drinkable.

Granted, you and I are not winemakers. Let's say, instead, that you plucked, for example, Justin Smith out of Paso Robles and shipped him north to make Harlan wine. Would it then be Harlan Estate? I don't think so. It would be a good wine, because Justin Smith is a good winemaker, but it would reflect *him* and *his* choices, not Bob Levy's and Bill Harlan's. So this line of reasoning suggests that mere technical aspects of place can begin to, but not completely, explain the totality of great wine.

Another thought-experiment way of looking at it is to imagine a winemaker known for mastering a particular estate working somewhere else under far different circumstances. I asked Mark Aubert if he thought he could make great wine in Lodi—an appellation not known for great wine—and he answered, "I could elevate Lodi!" which, broken down, is Aubert's way of suggesting the primacy of the winemaker over place. His reply made me think of Baron Philippe de Rothschild elevating Château Mouton-Rothschild from second growth to first. Did Mouton's *terroir* change when it leaped a level? No. But the vision imposed upon it by the baron forced a transformation that, ultimately, even the hidebound authorities of the INAO (Institut national des appellations d'origine) had to recognize. Baron de Rothschild became an indispensable part of Mouton's *terroir.*

When Benson hit the road, there weren't that many winemakers around, so his options were limited. He snagged most of the big names: Robert Mondavi, André Tchelistcheff (who wrote his preface), Louis P. Martini, Paul Draper, Richard Arrowood, and so on. When I began my selection process, the choices were vastly greater. I don't know how many winemakers worked in California when I wrote this book, but it had to be a lot. There were 1,605 bonded wineries in the state in 2004, according to the Alcohol and Tobacco

Tax and Trade Bureau. (And keep in mind that many brands produce under someone else's bond.)

So how to choose? My foremost parameter was that the winemaker be making consistently excellent wine. I wanted, obviously, to include more women than Benson had, and I did. But in the period I wrote, there still was gender inequity in California winemaking, and of my twenty-seven winemakers, only seven are female. (But the University of California, Davis, recently announced that women now account for 50 percent of the students in the Department of Viticulture & Enology, so we should soon achieve parity.)

I also wanted diversity from a production point of view: small wineries and large ones, specialists and generalists. You'll find in these pages Randy Ullom, presiding over five million cases annually of many different varieties at Kendall-Jackson Vineyard Estates, and Justin Smith, whose Saxum winery produced, when I spoke with him, only a thousand cases of red Rhône wines from the western hills of Paso Robles.

I wanted geographic balance. Benson had sought this, too, but in a way that strikes us today as anachronistic. His three regional divisions were "South of San Francisco Bay" (but nothing of San Luis Obispo County or Santa Barbara County; neither made it onto his radar), "North of San Francisco Bay" (Napa, Sonoma, and Mendocino counties), and "South Coastal Mountains," which consisted of a single interview with the founder of Callaway Vineyard and Winery, in Temecula (!).

Today's realities dictate greater, more precise geographic diversity, but the reader will note that there is no one in this book from inland areas: no Lodi, Sierra foothills, Central Valley, or Temecula. I agonized over this, but my foremost parameter, consistent quality, unfortunately precluded them. Nor was it ultimately convenient to divide the book into a geographic scheme of any sort.

I decided too against categorizing the book by wine type or variety. Too many winemakers are making too many different kinds of wines to be pigeonholed. Where would you put, say, Ullom in a varietally organized book?

So I have split up the book by the decade in which the winemaker first began his or her career: the 1970s, 1980s, and 1990s. We Americans are a decade-minded people anyway; I admit to thinking that winemakers who came of age in the 1970s (and thus have a few decades of experience under their belts) differ in outlook and temperament from those who came in during the 1990s. But I don't want to overemphasize divisions. The winemakers in this book, in their devotions and talents, are united far more than anything that differentiates them.

"My method was simple," Benson writes in his introduction. "Between the summers of 1975 and 1976, I tramped through vineyards and wineries with a tape recorder, and questioned vintners face to face." I did the same, thirty years later. His intentions, Benson explained, were threefold: to craft a record of "lasting value"; to record, through "oral history," information about the California wine industry's "most important era"; and to appeal to both "the casual wine drinker" and "the true wine buff." These are my intentions, too.

Benson thought he was recording California's most important wine era. Granted, the 1970s was an exciting time to be making wine in California, but so were the 1960s, and so for that matter were the 1880s, when California wines were winning medals in Europe. (Prohibition, of course, wiped out whatever progress had been made.) California wine is always in a state of ferment (no pun intended), always evolving from what it was to what it will be—like California itself. So what will historians say of our wine era?

After its razzle-dazzle, paparazzi-ed vault to stardom over the past thirty years, California wine no longer has a reputation to build; it has one to protect. There is no longer anything to prove (except to extreme skeptics), but plenty to enhance. Ensconced at the highest levels of world fame, California wine has entered its Golden Age, akin, perhaps, to glorious prephylloxera-era France. Bordeaux has endured, often supremely, for more than three hundred years, through ups and downs, trials and tribulations, peace and war. There is no reason California wine should not do the same—unless something drastic happens to end it, and us, all.

Yet all is not rosy. There are speed bumps in the road; California wine is not without challenges. High alcohol is a concern among many writers, sommeliers, restaurateurs, consumers, and even (when they will admit it) growers and winemakers, who worry that the resulting wines are not in balance and may not age. Related to high alcohol is residual sugar, or at least the perception of sweetness, which in a table wine is offensive to some people, including me. During the years I wrote this book, 2004–2006, these were red-hot topics of conversation in wine circles, guaranteed to prompt a debate. California winemakers are going to have to figure out how to deal with these things, which may involve factors beyond their control, such as global warming.

Then, too, pricing has become problematic, especially among the so-called cult wines. How high can they go? (As I write, Screaming Eagle's retail price has been boosted to more than five hundred dollars, which is bound to have a ripple effect on everyone else.) And in today's fiercely competitive, internationalized market, vintners also face challenges of marketing, promotion, public relations, and selling. The rest of the globe is coming online, not just

Australia and New Zealand, Chile and Argentina, and "old" Europe. In southeastern Europe and some of the former Soviet republics, entrepreneurs are working overtime to perfect their indigenous wine industries—and it should not be forgotten that this is the ancestral home of *Vitis vinifera*. We have recently heard reports of a massive wine industry in the making in, of all places, China. When these wines hit the market, duck; the grape and wine market will have to make serious adjustments. Even the most famous winemakers sometimes worry about their jobs; even the wealthiest owners understand that if they don't relentlessly pursue quality, history may pass them (or their children) by. The best winemakers spend sleepless hours trying to figure out how to stay ahead of the game, knowing full well that nothing can be taken for granted.

What does it take to make great wine? Good grapes, of course. Beyond that, if it were simply a matter of technical correctness, there would be more great wine in California than in fact there is. In the end, it all comes down to the person, and while every great winemaker I've known—well, most of them—states humbly that he or she is a mere steward of the land, the truth is this: the greatest vineyard in the world would be reduced to raw acreage in the hands of the inexpert. What the vintners in these pages share is a tendency to view life as a quest, a do-or-die mentality; ultimately, a great, crazy-making passion. Money greases the wheels; if you're a multimillionaire, you have what it takes to hire and buy the best. But as we see over and over (thankfully), wealth is not a necessity. Indeed, most of the winemakers in this book were born without it and succeeded through sheer zeal.

Which, come to think of it, suggests what may be the signal achievement of this era: winemaking has become, not the quaint eccentricity it was thirty years ago when Benson wrote, but a noble profession.

1970s

It was a great time to be alive and making wine in California, maybe to be doing anything in California. The scent of the 1960s still hung in the air of a state not yet thronged with newcomers and paved over by subdivisions and freeways. Winemaking no doubt seemed a fairly exotic career for a young man or (far less likely) a young woman. But for those who for whatever reason were attracted to it, the allure was immense. Imagine living on the land, out in the country, in a place of idyllic beauty, doing honest work with one's hands, work that resulted in the creation of such a pure, wonderful product—not to mention following in the footsteps of Mondavi, Ray, Draper, Martini, Heitz, the immortal Tchelistcheff.

Winemakers who began their careers in the '70s were like the young hopefuls who'd always made their way from across America to Hollywood. Driven by their dreams, they didn't know how it would happen, or where they might work, or how to make ends meet. It was one big adventure. Often young, and with families to support, they could not possibly have known how long and arduous the path might be. But they knew what they wanted: to make wine, great wine, in the fabled Golden State.

As well known today as the names in this section of the book are, we ought not to forget the challenges they faced. In the years leading up to the '70s, Prohibition remained a living memory for many older adults, and its effects, so damaging, continued to be felt throughout California wine country, and America at large. Whatever progress had been made in the nineteenth century and past the turn of the twentieth had been largely wiped out.

Sweet wines continued to outsell dry table wines, as they had for a generation; a cola drink or cocktail was more likely to be drunk at the dinner table than wine. In such vineyards as there were, grape varieties were planted willy-nilly, in places ill suited for them—and often as not, the vines were diseased. The typical vineyard might contain Riesling and Gewürztraminer—cool-climate grapes—side by side with Zinfandel and Petite Sirah, not to mention inferior types like Carignan and Thompson Seedless. An absence of federally mandated labeling laws meant that almost any grape variety could be (and was) called by almost any name the packager wanted. This was still a time when the biggest-selling wines were "Burgundy," "Moselle," and the similar purloined coinages salvaged from a bygone age.

Vine trellising systems were at best primitive. What today is called, disparagingly, "California sprawl"—in which the vine throws huge, uncontrolled canopies—was the norm, with the effect that grapes were prevented from achieving ripeness or, more correctly, ripened unevenly. Not that quality mattered; there was virtually no market for fine wine anyway. Those few individuals who understood fine wine understood (or thought they did) that it came from Europe, not California. This undermined efforts to perfect California wine, whose quality was controlled to a great extent by growers—farmers more interested in the profits that came from high yields than in the production of premium wine. The nation's wine (and alcoholic beverage) distribution system, such as it was, was a shambles. Even if a vintner could make fine wine, he was likely to encounter huge difficulties selling it.

But good things were happening in quiet ways. By the '60s, the Bay Area's economy had produced a class of men and women, small in number but influential as tastemakers, who could appreciate fine wine. A sort of neighborhood pride sent them looking around for local products, mainly to Napa Valley, and when they found them, they told their friends, who in turn told theirs. It was the emergence of this class, centered in and around Berkeley and San Francisco but with connections to Los Angeles, New York City, and even Europe, that provided not only the inspirational support but also, in some cases, the financial backing for some of Napa's earliest, serious start-ups. The era of the "boutique winery"—the small, family-owned estate that aimed for the very top—culminated in, or was symbolized by, the launch in 1966 of Robert Mondavi's eponymous winery, but was not limited to that event.

Names like Chappellet, Freemark Abbey, Mayacamas, Souverain, Hanzell, and Sterling, now having joined the stellar veterans Inglenook, Charles Krug, Beaulieu, and Louis M. Martini, had established themselves as reference points by which the newcomers of the '70s—the Tony Soters, Rick Longorias, Margo van Staaverens, and others in this section—could steer, and steer reliably, secure in the knowledge that great wine could be made, provided one were serious and implacable. Hard work was what it took: hard land-clearing, hard viticulture, hard enology, and hard sales, all of it fueled by hard cash. If these winemakers ever had moments of doubt (and it would be surprising if they didn't), they were cheered by the increasing plaudits given to California wine by connoisseurs who counted. Especially inspiring was the now-famous "Paris tasting" of 1976, in which American wines, both red and white, bested their Bordeaux and Burgundy analogues, in a blind tasting held by French wine critics.

The 1970s marked the eruptive beginnings of the rise of California wine to worldwide fame. With so little actually known or accomplished, either in the vineyard or in the winery, everything was raw, tantalizing possibility. The men and women in this section of the book created templates where previously there had been none, and when rules did exist, which was seldom enough, they had few compunctions about breaking them when they had to. To the extent that California wine today possesses elegance, balance, and harmony, it is because these men and women envisioned those qualities in the wines they made, and insisted they be manifest in the bottle.

BILL WATHEN

FOXEN WINERY & VINEYARD

Foxen is one of those wineries that makes great wine year after year, but is probably better known to sommeliers than to the general public. Located in Santa Barbara County's hilly, picturesque Foxen Canyon region, it has been the province of winemaker Bill Wathen and his partner, Dick Doré, who does the marketing, since 1985. Wathen is a simple, natural kind of guy who's happiest cheering on his kids' ball teams or making wine. We chatted outdoors on a cold day in February 2006, since there was no space inside the ramshackle winery building except the tasting room, which was mobbed with tourists doing the local wine trail.

Locate us geographically.
We're in the Santa Maria Valley, nine miles from the Santa Ynez Valley appellation.

Who is Dick Doré?
His great-great grandfather [William] Benjamin Foxen was the first white settler in the county. Had his own ship; pulled into Goleta Harbor in 1835 with a broken mast and never set foot on a ship again. [Doré's family has owned the land on which the vineyards grow ever since.]

This was Mexico at the time?
Yes. He was escorted to the local governor's house, and the lady that opened

the door became his wife. He became a Mexican citizen and came onto the Tinaquaic land grant, which was all of [what is now] Foxen Canyon, ten thousand acres. The family still owns two thousand acres of the original land grant.

How did you meet Dick?
I was a viticulturalist, graduated in '75 from Cal Poly San Luis Obispo, came down to Santa Maria Valley to farm 250 acres of vines for a partnership out of Los Angeles. It was everything: Cabernet [Sauvignon], Riesling, Merlot, Napa Gamay. I was there for three years, then went to work for [vineyard developer] Dale Hampton, who had come over from Delano. Dale knew my food and wine interest, and he says, "You know, there's an opening at a place called Chalone [Vineyard]." Well, I knew Chalone. I was up there every spring as a kid.

You mean the area, not the winery?
Yes, but I knew of the winery. So I went up and interviewed with Dick Graff and took the job as their viticulturalist, managing two hundred acres and putting in more.

Was that your first exposure to Pinot Noir?
It was.

How long did you stay?
Four vintages. I had met Dick [Doré] when I came out of Cal Poly. So I left, came back here, thinking, "You know what? After learning the ins and outs of Pinot Noir, Chardonnay, and Chenin Blanc at Chalone, I thought I could make wine."

Had you made wine at Chalone?
No, but I'd observed, and done the manual work. Nobody made decisions up there, because Dick Graff was the decision maker. He was tough to work for, a taskmaster. So Dick and I started making wine here, in '85.

What was the first Foxen wine?
The '85 Cabernet, from Rancho Sisquoc [fruit], followed by the '86 Cabernet.

At that time, did you see Foxen specializing in Cabernet?
That was the original plan. And we kind of, after '86, said, "You know what? We need to branch out."

Why?
Well, you know, it was good, but it was classic Santa Maria Valley Cabernet.

Which is . . . ?
Herbal. The climate is Region I. So we jumped into Pinot Noir and Chardonnay.

Where did you get those grapes?
Chardonnay from Nielsen and Pinot from Sierra Madre [vineyards], both in Santa Maria Valley. But over the years, we've done a lot of migration, in and out, playing the field. Because I knew all the growers down here, we'd source fruit from different places. We had a huge learning curve over fifteen years, and finally got locked into what I think are the best vineyards in each appellation in Santa Barbara County.

When did you start planting your own grapes?
Eighty-nine, up on top of the canyon. It's our estate vineyard, Tinaquaic, a quarter mile from here. Dick and I own it, on leased land. It's ten acres: seven Chardonnay, one and a half Syrah, one and a half Cabernet Franc.

Why no Pinot Noir?
As soon as you turn the corner from the river down here, all those nice things about Pinot Noir start washing away, aromatically and flavorwise. It's a little too warm up there. These other varietals do better in these side canyons.

So all your Pinot is purchased?
Yes. We have a lease at Bien Nacido [vineyard], and we selected the clones and rootstocks, our Block Eight. We also have Julia's [vineyard], which is owned by Jess Jackson, or actually [Jackson's wife] Barbara Banke. That's Santa Maria, too. We get a percentage of Sea Smoke['s vineyard], in Santa Rita Hills. I was instrumental in finding that property for the owner, Bob Davids. We'd spent two years looking for Pinot Noir property. We were sitting just east of the old Sanford & Benedict vineyard, kind of bummed out, and I looked across and said, "You know what, Bob? That's the piece. But it's not for sale." And he said, "Well, we'll see about that." He made it happen, and as a thank-you, he said, "Bill, you're going to be the only outside winery that gets Sea Smoke."

What do you look for in an undeveloped piece of land?
It's just a feeling. You'd look at that, even when it was virgin, and say, "You know what? That's the south slope over there." You could just see. Bruno [D'Alfonso, Sanford Winery's winemaker] and I used to do that all the time; we'd sit up there and go, "God, would I like to have that piece!" And it just happened. There was a really good feeling about the site.

So Sea Smoke, Julia's, Bien Nacido, who else?
Sanford & Benedict. Well, we've been in a—I didn't like the way it was being farmed. But it's changed; Coastal Vineyard Care has taken it over, and we're going back to S&B this year.

Can you contrast the Pinot Noirs from Santa Maria Valley and Santa Rita Hills?
Yeah. Santa Rita: dark fruit, heavier, bolder. Santa Maria: spicy, red fruit, little bit lighter texture. Really a lot of hard spice that you don't get in Santa Rita.

To what do you attribute those differences?
There's a little more, believe it or not, heat summation in Santa Rita, because of all the little turns the river and the hills take. And Santa Maria is just this funnel from [Highway] 101, wide open to the sea.

The Santa Rita people say the same thing.
It's not as wide open, especially when you get into the heart of the appellation—Sanford & Benedict, Rinconada, Sea Smoke, Fiddlestix.

Has your Pinot Noir–making technique changed over the years?
It's still changing. We went into this bold, tightwire without a safety net. There was a lot of guessing. We're so tarp-and-bungee here, this old barn, and I've got fermenters outside. We're planning a new facility now, on the property, but it's hard to make wine outside; it really is.

To keep it from getting too hot?
Or too cold. We've been able to add jackets to the fermenters, and that helped.

What Brix do you pick Pinot at?
It depends on the vineyard and the vintage. A lot of times, what happens is you're just on the verge of ripeness, and you get that heat wave that comes in, and it's just, all of a sudden, 27, 28 . . .

Can you pick exactly when you want? Do you run into a lack of field hands?
No. No. We're comfortable with my picks. I've never had an issue where they told me they couldn't pick for me. I love all the guys. If I'm not growing, I'm trusting them to grow. They're really good people. As soon as we hit 24, I start visiting the vineyard every day to taste. I look for that almost-over-the-top [stage], and try not to get too much shrivel. I'm not favorable to watering down Pinot Noir; it's something I hate to do. But winemaking, you do what you have to do.

You would water down to lower alcohol?
Yeah.

What [percent alcohol] do Foxen Pinot Noirs tend to run?
High 14s to mid 15s.

When was your first Pinot?
Eighty-seven.

What was the alcohol on that?
Thirteen.

So what's different?
Oh, the learning curve. I don't like any of those old Pinot Noirs.

Did you like them back then?
For a year or two. But they just kind of fall off. They're green, and we were using stems. All of us making Pinot Noir in the '80s went through this big experimental period of stems. But it's hard to get the clusters ripe in Santa Barbara County. They add too much stemminess. You see that more as the wine ages than initially. Santa Maria–wise, I've been completely whole-berry fermentation for the last ten years. Some of the Sea Smoke stuff, I will use partial whole clusters.

Do you feel you're making Pinots to age?
They seem to do best the first five or six years. I like drinking them young. They're beautiful in their youth.

Do you use natural yeast?
I'm a little afraid of fermentations breaking down using wild, uninoculated [yeast]. I've got certain favorite yeasts, and they've been consistent for me, so I stick with it. But these superyeasts now that'll ferment bone-dry, 30 Brix— I don't know if it's a good tool or not.

What do you think of the high alcohol level of so many California wines?
I think there's just the beginning of a movement going back. I'm kind of in the middle of the road. I've liked some of these wines with real high alcohol, but then I also am a real foodie, and I don't like those wines on the table.

Sometimes they pall after a sip.
Right. There are two different wines: your social wines and your dinner wines.

You said you're a big foodie. What do you mean?
I've been cooking since I left home, at eighteen. Early in life, Dick Graff was great, into food; and Julia Child, I got to hang out with her a bit, and that was a big part of my life.

So moving into that Chalone milieu, Dick was very cultured. He was gay, and led a refined life—played the harpsichord, into philosophy. Did that rub off on you?
Just kitchen work rubbed off. We'd cook dinner and sit down and eat good food and drink good wine. I think it was the beginning, for me, of dinner with wine matchups. My parents did not drink wine; my mom was the cook, and made big pots of stuff.

> We were making a lot of Santa Barbara County[–appellated] wine, and it just wasn't right. So we said, "Who do we want to do business with and who *don't* we want to do business with? Let's work with the people we want to do business with forever."

So what do you cook?
Just about anything. I can do—with preparation—French, Thai, Indonesian, Mexican.

Do you design dinners around specific bottles of wine? Is it always a Foxen wine?
I do a lot of trade. I've got [this] great bunch of winemaker friends down here. Sea Smoke, Au Bon Climat, Qupé, Longoria . . .

Tell me a dinner you might design around a bottle.
Oh, we could do what I call California food.
We make a really nice dry Chenin Blanc here, a wine that ages. This was a vineyard that was planted by Dick's cousin in '66. So maybe oysters in the broiler, on the half shell, with the Chenin. And then one of Jim [Clendenen]'s Chardonnays, Au Bon Climat, a real nice one, with a scallop and lobster tamale and vanilla butter. And then I'll do a chorizo corn bread and set it down on the plate and just put a chipotle quail on top, with Syrah.

I am getting hungry! Now, I see you at events a fair amount, like Hospice du Rhône [an annual wine tasting event held in Paso Robles that focuses on Rhône varieties].
Right. Because we make all these varietals. We're not just at Pinot Noir events, we're at Syrah events. But I don't like to go out very much. I like to hang out here. I like to farm, I like to make wine.

Why don't you like going out?
Because it's always during sporting events that my son or daughter are involved in, and that's a priority for me. Last year for Hospice, I was going to stay up there, but no, I had to come home for the baseball games, so I had to commute back and forth!

Will your kids do anything with the winery?
They're welcome to. They know it's here. I'd love them to. I told them, "It's there, it's a family business."

You told me you used to work in your tasting room and no longer do.
Well, in the early days, Dick would work Saturdays, I'd work Sundays. That worked for a couple years, but it started getting old. I wanted to be home on weekends. One day, I was getting ready to close when this limo pulls up, and these drunks come in, just obnoxious; it was a bad, bad experience. They didn't even buy anything. So the next morning I go, "You know, Dick, I had this deal happen yesterday, and because of it, I quit the tasting room." And he goes, "You can't do that!" And I go, "Well, I'm doing it!" "Well! Then I quit, too!" *[laughs]* So we had to hire people, and that was our first employees.

Is Foxen where you want it to be?
The lineup is, and our vineyard sources. We were making a lot of Santa Barbara County[–appellated] wine, and it just wasn't right. So we said, "Who do we want to do business with and who *don't* we want to do business with? Let's work with the people we want to do business with forever." And we have all our sources now, and they're really good. We've been making Cabernet Sauvignon for twenty years, and it's always been a migration. Now we're sourcing Cabernet in Happy Canyon, from Vogelzang vineyard, this beautiful, new, what's going to be an appellation. It's completely different from anything we've ever had from Santa Barbara County. More ripe, less marine layer out there.

Do you see any new projects for yourself?
I would like to have my own vineyard someday. My own personal vineyard. I don't have that; I don't have my own piece of property.

Where would this vineyard be?
Oh, you know, I'm dreaming, but either Santa Rita or Central Otago [in New Zealand].

How much would it cost?
Well, you're talking—if you had enough money to get the property, it would cost you about twelve thousand dollars an acre to plant.

You already own half of Tinaquaic.
I have half of it, but it's leased. And I can't hand that down to anybody.

DAN MORGAN LEE

MORGAN WINERY

Dan Morgan Lee has made wine in a warehouse, in a gritty industrial district of Salinas, since launching his brand back in 1984. It may not be the most aesthetically pleasing facility, but that hasn't stopped Morgan's wines from soaring to the top as his Monterey-grown Pinot Noirs, Chardonnays, and Syrahs have garnered awards. Morgan is another of those winemakers who started with little in the way of resources, then used sheer tenacity to achieve his vision. A few years before this conversation, which took place in August 2005, he'd been jazzed about the new winery he was finally building, at his Double L vineyard in the cool, northwest Santa Lucia Highlands, so I began by asking him about it.

––––––––––

How's the winery doing?
We were ready to go in 2001, but it became moot with the dot-com bust and then 9/11. All of a sudden, our sales dropped off the edge of the earth. Things were pretty bad, and we put the winery on hold. But we're talking again with the builder; we're back on track.

You've been in Monterey since when?
I came down in 1978, out of UC Davis, to work at Jekel. I worked for five harvests there.

Why did you leave?

When I came, Bill Jekel wanted something small, quality-oriented. But then there was this shift in game plan. They wanted to expand, but they didn't want to buy more barrels and things. So Bill started telling me, "We want to make more, but we don't have the budget to buy new barrels." That was the handwriting on the wall.

Did you always intend to have your own brand?

Well, when I first went to Jekel, I was just happy to get a job. I was new to Monterey. I don't think I'd ever even been in the Salinas Valley. Then I met [my future wife] Donna and we became serious. I saw what was happening at Jekel, I didn't like it. I wanted to stay small, so we started talking about doing our own gig. One thing led to another, we put some numbers down, and Donna put a budget together. We sold the idea to my parents, who cosigned the first loan and invested. I sold my motorcycle, one of my main transportation vehicles at that time!

How much money did you need?

About fifty grand, for equipment, grapes, barrels. There was no salary, no fluff at all. And we had to rent a facility. I was still at Jekel when we did the first two harvests for Morgan, the '82 and '83. I'd work at Jekel during the day, and at Morgan in the evening.

Was Jekel your last hired job?

No. I worked at Durney [Vineyards, now Heller Estate], in Carmel Valley, for two years.

What were your first wines at Morgan?

Chardonnay, half from hillside vineyards in the Santa Lucia Highlands and half from Cobblestone vineyard, in the Arroyo Seco. All purchased fruit. It became clear the hillside fruit had more character. But it was also problematic, because the acids were so high—pure Santa Lucia Highlands. At that point, it was unusual to go past 24 Brix. Once you got there, you picked, no matter what. But the hillside vineyards a lot of times still had a tenth of a gram per liter acidity. Just crazy. So we decided we're going to have to wait [to pick]. We were renegades for the growers. I mean, 24 sugar was their magic number.

Weren't there ways to deacidify wine?

Yes. You'd use calcium carbonate. But it's not as desirable as getting the fruit right in the first place.

So you came up with this idea of letting the fruit hang longer to drop acids? Nobody had been doing that?
No. Most of the fruit was going to larger wineries, and they mixed it with stuff they could blend out [to reduce the acidity].

How did the growers react to longer hang time?
They were used to working with big wineries. They were like, "Hey, we picked this whole vineyard two weeks ago, and now you want us to pick your little bit?" So you had that subtle pressure, like, "Are you guys nuts?" They were just wanting to get done. A lot of these managers have different ranches. They pick and then move all the machinery out, and they didn't like to bring everything back in for a little ten tons or whatever.

What was your first Pinot Noir?
The '86, from two vineyards in Monterey: Vinco and Lone Oak, both Santa Lucia Highlands, both purchased fruit. There was no other winery in Monterey County producing Pinot Noir, other than Chalone. So we had nothing to go on, no neighbors, just shooting in the dark.

Why did you want to make Pinot Noir?
I'd liked it at Davis. We had a student tasting group with Steve Kistler, and Dick Ward and David Graves from Saintsbury.

Did you feel you knew how to make Pinot Noir?
I think it was a crapshoot. Dick and David were at Saintsbury, and Carneros was the hotbed of Pinot Noir, so I went up and got some fruit from what is now Stanly Ranch, and got this Monterey fruit, and did an experiment. I didn't care if I released a wine, but I wanted to see the differences. I made the wines identical to each other. And it was obvious, the Monterey vineyards were old clones, just California sprawl, nothing like what we do now. But we could see that in the Vinco stuff, they'd let more sun in [the cluster], while the Lone Oak was just a massive bush, everything was shaded, no sunlight. The Vinco clone was lacking in color, but had nice fruit. The Lone Oak was this herbal, tomato-juice character, because there wasn't any sunlight coming in. So the first year, the Lone Oak we didn't like at all. And the Carneros stuff was darker, with some nice fruit-berry characteristics, but monochromatic. It didn't have a lot of interest. So we were messing around one day, and we dumped them all together, and it was a pretty good wine.

What are the two or three biggest changes that you've adopted, in the winery, in making Pinot Noir since '86?
You know, I'd have to be truthful, the winemaking end has not changed a whole bunch.

Really? Cold soak, destemming, maceration times, cap management? None of that has changed?
Well, for our area, we realized that stems were not a friend, because we were trying to get away from that green character. Especially with the fruit back then, they weren't canopy-managed very well. Now, the people in Carneros, due to the fact that it was more family-farmed, smaller plot and so forth, were already getting into the quality thing of leaf removal early on. After that first year, we tried some Paraiso [vineyard] fruit, and we didn't do Lone Oak again, we did Vinco and Paraiso; and then we started liking the Paraiso fruit, it became our favorite vineyard.

What was it about Paraiso you liked?
Well, [owner] Rich Smith's vines weren't healthy, so by natural conditions it let more sunlight into the clusters, and I think that was a big reason. Then, in '87, '88, I told Rich, "Hey, these guys up in Carneros, they leaf-pull right after [the clusters] set, you know? Would you do that for me?" That had never been done in Monterey County.

This is back when people were afraid to leaf-pull because they were afraid the grapes would get sunburned.
Right. But sunburn was not likely in Santa Lucia. In a normal vintage, we have maybe two hot days, so there's a possibility, but not much. Anyway, Rich looked at me like, "You want us to pick leaves? That's expensive! I've gotta send my crew back in!" I said, "Yeah, but it's gonna pay off in the long run." I said, "What do you want? I'll pay extra." So I paid him extra to have his crew go in and pull leaves. We did an experiment, some with pulled leaves, some without, and showed Rich the difference. Next year, he was in there, pulled all our stuff. Year after that, he was pulling all his own stuff off!

> There was no way we were going to compete with the big boys on volume, so our niche from the very beginning was quality.

Were you seeking all this time to compete with the most expensive Pinot Noirs?
Yeah. We knew early on there was no way we were going to compete with the big boys on volume, so our niche from the very beginning was quality.

But you didn't own a vineyard. When did you finally—?
Our Double L, the first year of production was '99.

What took you so long?
We were saving. Actually, we were profitable the very first year. We've never lost money. But all that early profit was plowed back into expansion and equipment. We grew the label first. I knew early on I would love to buy some property in the Santa Lucia Highlands, for two reasons: It was clearly the best region for Chardonnay and Pinot Noir. Plus it was closest to the Salinas-Monterey Highway, and if I was going to build a winery, we realized most of the employees would live in Salinas, Monterey, and they'd be driving. So about the time the land was offered to us, we were actually in a good position to buy it.

Was it bare land?
Yes.

Who else was doing Pinot Noir in the Highlands?
Basically, just ourselves. Pisoni had some vineyards, but he had mostly home wine.

So Pinot Noir was really unproven here?
Yeah, it was. I think Pisoni was just coming to market, under the table. But yeah, that was about it.

What did you plant at Double L?
Two-thirds Pinot and one-third Chardonnay.

What Pinot clones?
We had a laundry list. We put in a good chunk of Dijon 115, 667, 777. Then we planted Wädenswil [UCD] 2A; [UCD] clone 12, which is pretty rare; a Spanish clone; [UCD] clone 23; and Pommard.

What was your first commercial vintage of Double L Pinot?
The first labeled vintage was 2000. Chardonnay, too.

Morgan Winery produces how many cases?
About 40,000. About half our Pinot comes from our ranch, and a third of the Chardonnay. The rest is purchased. The Pinot is all Santa Lucia Highlands. The Chardonnay, we still purchase some from Arroyo Seco, and that's labeled "Monterey."

What is Hat Trick Chardonnay?
A barrel selection off Double L. The first vintage was 2002. We had these barrels of Chardonnay that stuck out, and it became logical.

Do you have a barrel selection of Double L Pinot Noir?
Not right now. It's thought about, but it just hasn't come about. We haven't had the same situation on the Pinot Noir, where there's something that's like, "Wow!"

Could you hasten that by any interventions?
Well, perhaps. We're doing experiments where we're thinning down to very low crop levels. If it turns out well, that would be kind of a Hat Trick Pinot Noir. But we're not forcing it. If it happens, it happens.

What's production on these wines?
Double L Pinot's around 500 cases. Double L Chard is about 650. Hat Trick is only 75 cases. Most of the Pinot off the ranch goes into Twelve Clones, our appellation wine—a blend of our ranch, Paraiso, Garys', Rosella's [vineyards].

What is Metallico?
That was an idea our sales manager came up with. He said, "You know, I'm hearing people say they want an unoaked Chablis-style Chardonnay." So that's how Metallico was born.

Tell me about Tierra Mar Syrah.
We'd started making Syrah in '95, from Dry Creek [Vineyard], but then with Santa Lucia Highlands fruit in '96, very small amounts. Only three, four years ago it got up over 1,000 cases. But we did plant one acre of Syrah on Double L. We knew this was pushing the limits of Syrah to the very northern end. We knew it wouldn't ripen every year. So we picked very low-yielding clones, and dropped more fruit on the ground to harvest it at a reasonable sugar.

Is there a Tierra Mar Double L Syrah?
No. Double L Syrah is just coming into production. Tierra Mar came about when our assistant winemaker put together this six-barrel blend and said, "This is really killer Syrah, we've got to do it separately." It was a selection of best barrels, 1999. The fruit, I think, was Paraiso, Scheid/San Lucas, if I remember correctly. The appellation was Monterey.

But in 2000 the appellation on Tierra Mar changed to Santa Lucia Highlands.
Yeah. That year, it was a blend of Garys' and Paraiso.

What are your intentions with Tierra Mar?
Actually, this year it went back to Monterey County, because we have this vineyard on the east side, up in the Gavilans. So for Tierra Mar, we look for our eight best Syrah barrels, no matter where we get them, and we'll change the appellation depending on the vintage.

Isn't it risky to have an expensive wine whose origins change every year?
Yeah, perhaps. But I think, if we tell them that it's the eight best barrels of Syrah in our shop that year, hopefully our credibility as a Syrah producer will mean something. It's like a Reserve Syrah from Morgan.

What goes through your head when you think, "Really, all I've got is my credibility"?
Yeah. You can't release crap. You've got to make sure it's in the bottle. If I have a wine that I, personally, don't take home and drink in my house, to me it's not worth selling.

Have you ever released crap?
Yes. *[laughs]* I mean, *crap* is a relative word. I go back to the 1983 Chardonnay. I wasn't real proud of that wine. But it was an off vintage throughout California.

Are you still doing Cotes du Crow's?
Yeah.

A cash-flow thing?
Well, it's a fun wine. It's not very expensive, and we're introducing people to Grenache and Syrah. And that has been, actually, a big success.

Any plans for anything new?
We're starting up another label, Lee Family Farm, and we'll just do fun things under it. This year we're doing a Verdelho, from Lodi. It's a grape that a friend of mine grows, he's of Portuguese descent. We're paying eleven hundred dollars a ton, so it will probably retail for twelve, fourteen dollars.

Why not do it under the Morgan label?
We just feel like we have too many wines under the Morgan label. What happens in the marketplace is, a producer starts being known for doing one or two wines. We have four different wines, different permutations.

You're already at 40,000 cases. When does this start getting away from you?
We've got to build that sucker [the new winery] first!

Even at that point, when does it run away from your personal attention?
Oh, I think it has to get pretty darned big before it's out of the realm. It's kind of like if you make a recipe in the kitchen and you want to make more of it, you just put the same good-quality ingredients into it. You can't skimp on the ingredients.

What will production capacity be at the new winery?
About 50,000 cases.

So would that be your natural limit?
That's a good natural limit.

Of all your lineup, is there one wine that has captured your heart more than any other?
Well, I'd have to tell you that at our house, probably six out of ten bottles of wine are Pinot Noir.

At what point did you realize, "Hey, I'm a Pinot Noir specialist"?
You know, I'm surprised. I think back to when I got out of school. I liked Cabernet then, loved it, or at least I thought I did. Now I drink about two bottles of Cabernet a year, probably even less.

Times are good for you. You're getting all these accolades.
Oh, you know, I'm in a real sweet spot in life. I mean, family, what's happening in the winery, it's marvelous. What else could you ask for?

GENEVIEVE JANSSENS

ROBERT MONDAVI WINERY

She says it was destiny that brought her to Robert Mondavi Winery nearly thirty years ago, and Genevieve Janssens's story surely contains elements of the improbable. The longtime winemaker at Napa's, and California's, most famous estate recounted, in the French–North African accent that stays with her, her career from the winery's glory days to its unhappy collapse and eventual 2005 sale. We chatted in the summer of 2006; the winery grounds were mobbed with tourists and the only quiet place to talk was in the barrel room.

You were born where?
In Morocco. My parents had wineries and vineyards in Algeria. My dad was making wine at the bulk level, selling to *négociants*.

So you grew up around barrels.
No barrels! Concrete tanks. I learned to work with fine wine later, in Bordeaux and then in Napa Valley.

Did you always want to be a winemaker?
Absolutely not. I wanted to be a geologist. Then one day my dad said, "Why don't you learn winemaking and come and work with me?" Because after the Algerian War, the French government was giving to anybody who wanted to develop Corsica, as an agricultural region, a loan. So my dad developed a vineyard and winery, and ended up selling bulk wine to *négociants* in France.

You received a diploma of enology from the University of Bordeaux in 1974.
Yes. And then I worked two years in a consulting lab in Bordeaux.

Do most winemakers start off working in labs?
For a female at that time, absolutely yes.

Was it difficult being a female winemaker in France?
I would never be able to be a winemaker, I don't think, in France. At that time, women who had their diploma in enology knew they would end up working in a lab, not making wine at the château.

In 1978 you moved to the United States and came to Mondavi. How did that happen?
I consider it was my destiny. In '77, my father told me, "Why don't you go to California, because that's where is a new way of winemaking." And he said, "Don't forget Mondavi, it's one of the best."

So you came here as a tourist!
As a tourist is how I arrived here, yes. And I went everywhere, all the wineries, from Santa Barbara, to Paul Draper, Paul Masson, and up to Napa.

Did you have appointments?
No. I just walked in. Then I arrived here, at Mondavi. I had a wonderful tour, I was so impressed by everything. So I said, "I would like to talk to the winemaker." So they asked her to come talk to me.

Who was the winemaker?
Zelma Long. And she came, and we talked an hour together.

Were you surprised that the winemaker was a woman?

> Where I came from, Bordeaux, it was very strict, closed, difficult to meet people. Here, it was open.

Very surprised, and very surprised that she came on the call of a tourist! I couldn't believe it. Because in France, it was not like that. Where I came from, Bordeaux, it was very strict, closed, difficult to meet people. Here, it was open. If you want to talk to the head winemaker, we call her, she comes!

What happened from that meeting?
When I finished, I joked and said, "Hey, by the way, if you have a position for me, I'm coming right now! I quit everything in France, this is where I want to be!" And two or three months later, she called me.

You were back in France?
Back in France, yeah. It's a nice story, no?

What was your job when you came here?
Lab enologist. So I was stuck in the lab again. *[laughs]*

How long did you work in the lab?
Two years. But in the same time, I met my husband, Luc [a Belgian who was then teaching art in Merced]. And I decided it was very important to start a family, and being a winemaker was extremely demanding, and I didn't want to do that. So I quit that job; I was crazy to do that, but when you are in love, you are in love.

Where did you live?
In Merced. And getting two kids. I helped a winery in Mariposa to establish a vineyard, and I was the winemaker of the area, so people would call me when they needed something. And that was my contact with wine, for ten years.

When did you get back to winemaking?
When my son, Georges, was three years and a half, he could walk, talk, go to school. So I say, "Hmm, I'm ready to go back." And I called Tim [Mondavi], and he said, "Well, why don't you send me your résumé, because we might have something for you." And then the French, the Rothschilds, came, and they were looking for a director of production for Opus One [Winery, a joint venture of the Mondavis and the Baron de Rothschild]. They interviewed a lot of people, and when [Château Mouton-Rothschild winemaker] Patrick Léon saw my résumé, and Tim recommended me, I was hired, very quickly.

As the top winemaker at Opus One?
Yes, the only one.

That is amazing. You had not had much experience. For years you had been doing part-time consulting in the Central Valley, and before that you had worked only in the lab.
Well, I had my experience from my father's, at the winery.

Do you think the fact that you were French—
I'm sure it helps. Yes. Tim was ready to hire me anyway, because I work very well with him. But for the French, it was important for Opus One to get a portion of the French mentality and education, and I was there to offer that.

Between Patrick and Tim, did you have freedom?
Well, I would say I was inspired by them. I did not want freedom, because I accepted that my role was to blend two different visions. So the exercise, and I love that exercise, was more an interpretation of the two companies through Opus One. I was not the musician who invents a piece, I was more a performer, reading the music that they brought.

In the '80s and '90s, a lot of critics said Opus was too light. What kind of style were you looking for, and was it different from a Napa Valley Cabernet?
The style that both Tim Mondavi and Patrick Léon were looking for had elegance, finesse, complexity. And the wine was not treated in the same way as Napa Valley Cabernet Sauvignon, which was much more direct. Opus One was racked five to six times, to polish the tannins, adding a little bit of micro-oxygenation, but naturally.

Were you aware that critics said Opus was too light?
Yes, of course.

What was your reaction?
[laughs] Everybody has a test, and Opus One was doing very well! So somebody else might like it. So yes, I was very much aware, but it was great for the French not to change their vision.

And now, as we transition to Mondavi winery, that was a criticism for Tim, that the wines were too lean, at a time when everybody else was getting riper and fruitier.
I think Tim has been true to himself forever, and that's why he is a great winemaker. Because even if the criticism was strong, he didn't change his vision. He adapted his vision to modern winemaking, but he never wanted to change just because he was critiqued. The philosophy of Mr. Mondavi and Tim was to make wine which could be enjoyable at the table, and for the Cabernet Sauvignon Reserve to belong to the very recognizable wines of the world. And Tim has done a very good job to teach, to mentor me to go to that finesse and elegance, with structure.

You left Opus and returned to Mondavi when?
November '97, as director of winemaking.

I understand that the French were not happy.
You understand correctly.

Why?
Life was very easy, good at Opus One. I spent already nine years there; why not nine more? So by coming here, I perturbed a little bit the continuity of

the winemaking. This is true: when a winemaker leaves, the wine is suffering a little bit. So the Rothschilds complain, saying that it's a mess, why do we need a change?

But Tim wanted you.
Yeah. And I told him that I needed more challenges. I wanted to grow as a winemaker.

You couldn't grow at Opus?
No. I could grow in finesse, but I wanted to grow a little bit differently. I wanted to learn more about winemaking.

So when he offered you the position, there was no doubt you would take it?
Yes. Because it was gorgeous! I was exposed to Sauvignon Blanc, Pinot Noir, Chardonnay, Merlot, Zinfandel, Sauvignon Botrytis, Moscato d'Oro; there was no way I could have grown like that [elsewhere].

When you came here, you had associate winemakers.
Yes, four or five, but it did not last. That was Tim's vision, not completely my vision. Each variety was supposed to have a winemaker, and they were not called "winemaker," they were "variety sponsor." It was extremely difficult to manage, too complicated. Every variety sponsor acted like a winemaker in their territory, they wanted always the best for themselves, and not looking for the big picture. And my role was, let's say, the big picture. There was no compromise in their minds. I was spending my time managing, and I thought it wasn't my role to do that.

You said that the associate winemaker structure did not last. What happened?
I arrived end of '97. When you speak about the '90s, those were glorious years, where the sales were excellent. But '98 was the end of that era. We started to have too much wine on the market, and suddenly there was a big swing in the economy of the Mondavi corporation. The company asked a group of finance people to evaluate our system, and their recommendation was, if you want to survive, we need to lay off. And we did. My department had 20 percent [of its] people laid off.

Did those include the variety sponsors?
Yes. We replaced them.

When things started getting shaky, what was that like?
We had very direct recommendations from top management. You must maintain quality, but sorry, we cannot give you as much money as in the past.

And top management was who? Mr. Mondavi?
No. CEO, CFO.

Because it was a public company by then?
Yes. They went public in '92, I think.

And when was the sale to Constellation [Brands]?
A year ago. I think officially they took the lead in January [2005].

Did people here know that the winery was for sale?
Yes, because before the acquisition, the board of directors of the corporation of Robert Mondavi Winery announced to the world that this winery will be sold separately.

The Robert Mondavi Winery?
Yes, and they said the corporation will keep Woodbridge and Private Selection. So I think that's when the director and the executive announced, and Tim here, officially, in August [2004], that we will be sold, and much less tonnage, and hoping for the best. And then, in October, Constellation arrived.

And your attitude was, "I'll just go to work and do my job."
Yes. My attitude is, my role is to make the best wine. Mr. Mondavi is there, and I'm very in admiration, like so many other people, of Mr. Mondavi. He's a mentor, he inspires, he's a leader. So when I make the wine, I think of him: "We have to do the best."

There was a period when you knew the winery would be sold, but you didn't know who would buy it. There were all kinds of rumors.
You couldn't even listen to all of them, or count them, because it went spinning through the air.

Do you remember when you learned it was Constellation?
Yes. We had friends in each winery that was under the [Constellation] wing, like Franciscan [Oakville] Estate and Ravenswood, so they all told us, "Don't worry, they are not going to come and tell you what you are going to do, they are going to support you."

Did you go on the Web and research Constellation?
Everybody did, yes. The entire world did, to understand better what is their business.

Was it frightening?
Not for me, because I understood that in their huge business, beer, alcohol, fruit wines, whatever, they have a second name, *fine wine,* and Simi [Win-

ery] is under this, Franciscan, Ravenswood, they have like eleven wineries which are making very good wine. We're under their wing, but why not? So I changed a lot of things, but not really the principle.

Were you involved in the splintering of the Napa brand into District wines?
No. That's Tim Mondavi and his old crew. That was more in '92, '93. When I arrived, everything was in place already.

A lot of people, myself included, didn't understand why the winery had so many SKUs [stock keeping units]. It was so complicated. In Cabernet alone, you had Napa Valley, Napa Reserve, Stags Leap, Oakville, Carneros, Marjorie's, M-Bar, Equilibrium, To Kalon. It seemed crazy!
It was crazy. *[laughs]* But not impossible. It was a good challenge, and winemakers, they love challenges. But it was difficult to maintain, and it was a lot of work for the winemakers and the lab.

What was the actual number of SKUs?
I cannot say, but quite a bunch. Twenty-five, twenty-six.

What is it today?
I don't know. We dropped two from Merlot, one from Sauvignon Blanc, reduced quite a lot of Cabernet Sauvignon Stags Leap, and I'm cutting on small lots, too.

> Consumers are looking more for big, bright fruit and mature tannins. I cannot make a Cabernet Sauvignon of the '60s now.

Do you make all the Cabernets the same, so that the differences are strictly terroir?
No. The Reserve and Oakville Cabernet Sauvignon, and the best lots of Carneros and Stags Leap region, are done by small containers and oak tanks, all by gravity, and a special team, and that's the beauty of that cellar, we always have the same people in every year.

This is the new To Kalon cellar?
Yes. And our Cabernet Sauvignon Napa Valley, Merlot Napa Valley, it's done in the back of our [old] winery, which we have remodeled.

I want to talk about ripeness. Have you been picking riper?
I'm just like everyone else. But not by intention. Not because I wanted. I really believe we are under the gun of the weather, and the evolution of the style in general. Consumers are looking more for big, bright fruit and mature tannins. I cannot make a Cabernet Sauvignon of the '60s now, 13.5 alcohol,

lean and austere. I cannot. There is no way. Ten years ago, we could have very nice 13.5 wine. But now, we are at 14.5.

Is it the weather? Because as you were saying, the consumers want that, and the critics also.

I thought about it, because everybody's asking me the same question. But I think it's not just one way or the other. There's many explanations. With phylloxera, I arrived in 1989. We had St. George and AxR#1 [rootstock] and clone 7, and that was it for material, simple. But after phylloxera, we were much more complex, we had many different rootstocks, clones, an explosion of creativity in the vineyard, and I think we created something where maybe we have greater alcohol. It's possible. Then the weather reports show you we go through a cycle of more and more warm weather and heat spells during September. In 2002, we were shocked by the dry air; we had ten, twelve days below 20 percent [humidity], which was never seen in the past. And it's continued in every year. If you have dryness plus wind, we are in trouble.

What do you think of some of the cult Cabernets that are picked quite late?

I like them, because the vineyard is behind that; but definitely, it's a style, and I think the more different styles, the better, because the consumer is happier. And again, I'm going to endorse Mr. Mondavi's vision, the more the merrier. If all the winemakers embrace the different ways of dealing with great grapes, why not?

Are the critics also driving this tendency toward ripeness and extraction and—

—pleasure. And maybe it's because society changes, they need pleasure very quickly. It's more approachable. But it doesn't mean that the vineyard doesn't exist. When Helen Turley [of Marcassin] is working with her vineyard, it's a true great vineyard, but her interpretation of that piece of land is different from another winemaker.

RICK LONGORIA

RICHARD LONGORIA WINES

Rick Longoria is a wine industry veteran who came up the old-fashioned way, through the ranks. He worked as an employed winemaker for years before going out on his own. By then, there was little about wine he didn't understand. Although Longoria produces a range of wines, his Pinot Noirs have been the most compelling, at least for me, especially the single-vineyard bottlings from the Santa Rita Hills. We met at his little house in the ersatz-Danish town of Solvang, on a hot May day in 2005 that also saw Southern California's first wildfire of the season. Longoria reflected, in his soft-spoken way, on his long and peripatetic career; on Santa Barbara County; and, of course, on Pinot Noir.

When did you launch Longoria Wines?
In 1982. I had started in the wine business in '74, after graduating from UC Berkeley in sociology. During those days, I would go up to wine country, Napa-Sonoma, to tour and taste, and I really became fascinated with the process. It was a rural area, and I always gravitated to the country. I just fell in love with the whole wine scene, the tranquillity of it—at least from the outside. Now, many years later, I know it's anything but tranquil. I got my first job, at Buena Vista [Winery], as a cellar rat, in '74. I just loved it. There was no doubt that this was what I wanted to do for a lifetime. I studied viticulture and enology at Santa Rosa Junior College, although I never got a degree.

And that, plus reading textbooks from UC Davis, was my self-taught, quasi-formal education in enology.

After two harvests, I was befriended by André Tchelistcheff, who of course was consulting for Buena Vista. He told me he was consulting for a new winery in Santa Barbara County started by the Firestone family. He was very excited about it. Well, my dad, who was career Air Force, was stationed at Vandenberg [Air Force Base] in Lompoc, and I'd kind of grown up here, graduated from high school, gone to UC Santa Barbara. When I found out that a wine industry had started here, it was like, "Oh! This is meant for you." I expressed interest to André, and he said, "Well, you should go down there and interview." I don't know if he had anything to do with it, but I got the job. That was '76, when I came down to the [Santa Ynez] Valley.

I stayed at Firestone for two years, and then I just thought I'd accomplished what I could. I wanted to stay in the Valley, but unfortunately there were no job opportunities. I'd gotten married, and it seemed like it was time to move on. I found out about a cellarmaster position at Chappellet, up in St. Helena. Went up there, applied—Tony Soter was the winemaker, and he hired me. I worked for Chappellet for a year. And really, I just became homesick for Santa Ynez. And I think there were aspects to the wine scene in Napa that I didn't feel comfortable with, the more high-powered, money, glamour. So I put the word out to friends down here, if they heard of any opportunities, please let me know. And sure enough, [Santa Barbara winemaking pioneer] Fred Brander had helped a brand, J. Carey, that needed a winemaker. Fred told me about it, I came down, and was hired in the spring of '79. I also became the winemaker for Rancho Sisquoc, over in Santa Maria Valley.

What were the wines you made at Carey and Sisquoc?
There were only two grapes at Carey, Cabernet Sauvignon and Merlot. Sisquoc had Johannisberg Riesling, Franken Riesling or Sylvaner, Cabernet Sauvignon, and Merlot. I was at Sisquoc just one year. I stayed at Carey through the '84 harvest. But by about '82, the wines coming out of Santa Maria Valley—Chardonnay and Pinot Noir, and of course the Pinot Noir at Sanford & Benedict vineyard—started to really become the more written-about varietals from this area. Carey didn't have any plans to make those varietals. That's what inspired me to start making a little wine under my own label. I made my first vintage at J. Carey in 1982, Chardonnay and Pinot Noir. They both came from Santa Maria Valley, from the Sierra Madre vineyard.

When did you go entirely on your own?
Well, not until '97. After my stint at Carey, I was hired by the Gaineys to be their winemaker. I started there in '85 and stayed until '97.

What finally convinced you to go out on your own?
A combination of things. One, I'd been at Gainey for twelve years, which is a long time for a winemaker. The Gaineys were good people to work for, but you start to think, "Is this where I'm going to end up?" And secondly, the mid '90s was this wine boom we were enjoying. I'd been in the business long enough to know it's cyclical in nature. We get our booms and then a downturn, and then you go up again. And I felt like, "If you miss this upswing, then you'll have to wait until it goes back up again, and who knows how many years that will be? And I'll be that much older." So this is probably the right time to embark on a brand.

Where had you been making Longoria wines?
Oh, boy. A variety of places. I was one of those itinerant little brands.

Where is your production facility now?
In Lompoc, in an industrial park on the edge of the city. It's known as the Lompoc wine ghetto. Kathy Joseph [of Fiddlehead], Brewer-Clifton, Sea Smoke, Palmina, Longoria.

Do you own vineyards?
No. I have a lease on a small eight-acre Pinot Noir vineyard, Fe Ciega, that I planted in the Santa Rita Hills. I always had looked at it, and thought it would make a great vineyard site. When I met the owner, I blurted out my vision for it, and would he be interested. We went back and forth, and he finally agreed to do it.

Where had you been sourcing your earlier Pinot Noirs?
Santa Maria Valley was definitely the major source, not only for myself but everyone else, because there was very little development in what is now known as Santa Rita Hills.

What do you produce now at Longoria?
We do four vineyard-designated Pinots: three from Santa Rita Hills, Fe Ciega, Sanford & Benedict, and Mount Carmel Vineyard; and Bien Nacido, from Santa Maria Valley. I started working with that fruit in '93. From time to time, I have a Santa Rita Hills Pinot Noir.

What else do you make besides Pinot and Chardonnay?
We make Pinot Grigio, we do a Bordeaux blend called Blues Cuvee, and Syrah. And we recently started making two Spanish varietals, Albariño and Tempranillo, both from Santa Ynez.

Do you consider Pinot Noir your flagship wine?
Well, all the wine I try to make very good. But at the same time, I guess because I've been making Pinot Noir the longest, it's sort of the signature or flagship varietal for the brand.

What is total case production at Longoria?
Thirty-five hundred.

What's your largest?
Our estate Pinot, Fe Ciega, about 750 cases a year. Total production of Pinot is about 1,500, 1,700, so it's easily 40, 50 percent of my production.

Did you have an "Aha!" moment when you realized that Santa Rita Hills Pinot Noir and Longoria brand were inextricably tied together?
Well, it wasn't any one moment. When I first came to Santa Barbara and met Michael [Benedict] and Richard [Sanford], we used to hang out together. I'd go out there and taste. I liked the wines incredibly, but also there was a really neat quality to that vineyard site that was different from anywhere in Santa Ynez Valley. It was cooler, the soil was different, that clay with shale fragments in there. The classic old barn where they made the wines set the tone for this more authentic approach to making wine. It was the antithesis of Napa Valley. Here were two young, strong personalities, and they just conveyed a sense of purpose, of having done their homework. So that was my introduction to what is now Santa Rita Hills. And when Michael suggested I could buy some of the grapes, in '85, I clocked! I mean, I ran over there. I felt so lucky. I revered those grapes.

Do your three vineyard-designated Santa Rita Pinot Noirs differ, terroir-*wise?*
Yes. Mount Carmel, Fe Ciega, and Sanford & Benedict are all within sight of each other, so the climate isn't that different. They're all in the southern valley, what I call the Santa Rosa Road corridor. Mount Carmel's on the north side of the [Santa Ynez] river, and that's where Fe Ciega is as well. If you were standing at Sanford & Benedict and looked across the river, you'd see, immediately in front of, or to the north, up on top of the bench, the Sea Smoke property. And if you scan to the left, immediately adjacent is Mount Carmel. And if you look again west, there's a blank spot, and then there's Fe Ciega. And they're all definitely different.

How so?
Well, that's where you get into subtleties. You'd have to have glasses of each side by side. Now, if you actually went into the sites and kicked the dirt and looked at the slope and orientation and exposure and all that, there's differ-

ences. The clonal selections are different, the age of vines, depth of the root system, that all makes a difference.

Can you pick them out blind?
Yeah. Fe Ciega is quite unique. Mount Carmel is quite unique. Sanford & Benedict is harder to tell.

Do you make all your Pinots the same way?
Yes. The grapes are handpicked, then brought to Lompoc. We run them through a table where we have an opportunity to sort out anything we don't like—moldy clusters, underripe clusters. Then they go into our destemmer-crusher. We 100 percent destem all our clusters.

Some Pinot producers prefer whole or partial clusters.
It's my belief that, in our wine region here, stems are not lignified enough, not dried enough, so they impart a green, vegetative quality to the wine, a little astringency. The other thing, too, is, you need to ask yourself: "What is the point of stem inclusion anyway?"

People say it's for tannins and structure.
Exactly. But what if you don't have that problem? I mean, grapes from Santa Rita Hills already have a lot of structure and tannin.

After destemming, then what?
We use these little one-and-a-half-ton wooden fermenters. In the beginning we'll do a cold soak, where the grapes are soaking in their own juices for three or four days. We layer dry ice over the crushed grapes in the fermenter, and then we cover it with a tarp. The philosophy behind that is, you're able to extract tannins and phenolics without alcohol, which is superior to that which you get later on with alcohol, which breaks down phenolics. Then we add yeast. Fermentation starts off cool, then at its peak it's up to about 88 or 90 degrees, then it cools back down. This year I'm going to refrigerate two of my stainless fermenters, to throttle it down. I want to see, "How did that work out, not allowing it to get up to 90?" After fermentation, the wine goes into a variety of tanks, to let the gross sediment settle. Then they get transferred to barrel, all French, about 30 percent new. I don't like a lot of new oak influence on Pinot Noir—or any wine, for that matter.

What comprises your Santa Rita Hills bottling?
It's the barrels that may have developed an off character, for whatever reason, or a lot that is a little weaker. Really, it's a matter of practicality. If I have two barrels that I'm putting aside, well, that's not a whole lot of wine to deal with, so I'm compelled to find some other lot so it makes sense to bottle it. To give

you an example: in '03, my Mount Carmel did not turn out well. The own-ers, who were very understanding, said I wasn't the only one of their clients to tell them that, so they lowered the price. I had this Mount Carmel lot, but it wasn't enough. So I made a few calls, found out that Fess Parker had avail-able Pinot Noir from Ashley's vineyard, and bought six barrels. Brought it over to my winery, blended it with the Mount Carmel and one or two bar-rels of Fe Ciega, and that was my Santa Rita Hills Pinot Noir.

That's a pretty good pedigree for $25.
It's a very nice wine.

Do you feel that, with thirty years' experience, you've learned things that result in better wine—not necessarily technical things, but approach, style?
Well, you know, young winemakers are so excited about making wine, they want to manipulate, to do something, instead of back off. Because to them, it can't be that easy— "I know I got to do something." So they're con-stantly feeling like they need to intrude or im-pose something on the wine; and that, to them, is winemaking. And I think that it takes a number of years before you get over that and you realize, "You know, maybe less is more. Maybe I don't need to impose this or that."

> Young winemakers are so excited about making wine, they want to manipulate, to do something, instead of back off. Because to them, it can't be that easy.

What sorts of things do they impose?
Like manipulate with toast, wanting to have wood be an important part of the style. Adding tannin to the must. Wanting to extract as much as you can with the introduction of enzymes. Also extended maceration, where the wine will be on the skins for a month, two months, where they take given proce-dures and tweak them. It's like, "Oh, I heard so-and-so gives it two weeks. What if I go a month? Maybe it will be better." That's their thinking. They feel that they've inherited the status quo, and it's their job, as a young per-son, as an innovator, to take it off in some other direction.

Are you letting your fruit get riper than you did fifteen years ago?
Yeah.

How much riper?
With Pinot, I would have been quite content, fifteen years ago, at 23½ [Brix]. And now it's more, up to 25.

What accounts for that change?

In my early days of winemaking, I had an eye towards what I considered a European model, which was higher acid, lower pH, and lower alcohol. That was my take. But something's changed. Maybe I've just become more pragmatic about that ideal. I still have it, but realizing it's hard to replicate Burgundy when you're obviously [in] a whole different area. I think subconsciously I have—I don't know what the word is—succumbed to the general trend that's developed in California to have bigger, riper wines. I still believe that I'm balancing my earlier ideals and concepts with the developments of today. You said yourself you found my wines to be balanced and harmonious. Nonetheless, all these years have taught me that it probably is better to pick a little riper. Overall, you get a better wine. But only up to a point. There's a real limit to that. You can graph the expression of *terroir*. Underripe grapes have less of it, then as you ripen you get more, but then, if you get too ripe, it's like a ripe red wine from who-knows-what vineyard.

MERRY EDWARDS

MERRY EDWARDS WINES

Outspoken, with strong views, and enjoying the fruits of her labors over a long and checkered career, Merry Edwards is comfortable in her skin. Her winery has become a staple of upscale restaurant wine lists; her Pinot Noirs, particularly the vineyard designates, are eagerly sought by collectors. We chatted in 2005 at the rented facility, in the little town of Windsor in the Russian River Valley, where she currently makes her wines. She's finally building her own winery after making wine for more than thirty years.

When did you start in the business?
Seventy-four. But the Merry Edwards brand, in '97. We've gone from a disjointed presence in the marketplace to a real brand. People don't ask what year they're buying, which vineyard designate, they just want Merry Edwards.

So there's been a real breakthrough for you.
Yeah. It's been building for thirty years. You could say I finally found the right niche.

It must be gratifying.
Well, I mean, it's just best to move forward. With 2003 being my thirtieth vintage, I was like, "Oh, my God, I'm getting so old!" Now, finally, I have the brand that is the culmination of those years, that I wanted but didn't have the connections, or getting the business part together. My husband [Ken

Coopersmith] keeps asking, "Are you going to retire?" Well, winemakers don't retire! They just keep going until they drop by the side of the road.

Tell me about your vineyard, Meredith Estate.
We planted in '98, running down the side of a hill, in an area called Sebastopol Hills. We also planted a new vineyard, Coopersmith, in 2001. I have a small blend for '04 and I'll be evaluating it next week. Coopersmith is where our new winery is going.

And you buy grapes for individual Pinot bottlings from where?
Klopp Ranch, on Laguna [Road], near Dehlinger and Kistler, in the area I call the Golden Triangle. And Olivet Lane, north of De Loach. Windsor Gardens, we lost. It was a year-to-year lease, so we've been waiting for when we wouldn't have it anymore. It was clear the owners were going to develop it. It's going to be a *huge* housing subdivision. The frightening part is, if you look at the new [Sonoma County] general plan, it's very anti-agriculture.

> There's no experience like owning your own vineyard.... Now I *really* understand viticulture.

How much did you yearn to own your own grapes, so what happened to Windsor Gardens can never happen again?
Well, there's no experience like owning your own vineyard. Before, I thought I understood viticulture, and I worked with my growers. But now I *really* understand viticulture.

Why make different Pinots? Most people would not make four single-vineyard Cabernet Sauvignons, they'd make a blend.
That's because Cabernet doesn't have the finesse or complexity that Pinot has.

A Bordeauxphile might disagree.
Maybe they would. I think Cabernet and Merlot are very unsophisticated wines. If you try to do an aroma profile, there isn't one. Pinot is more like white wine, in that it has a substantial and very complex aroma.

What's the first Pinot you made?
At Mount Eden [Vineyards, in the Santa Cruz Mountains]. I have some of that very clone at Meredith.

How did you learn how to make Pinot?
I had Dick Graff that first year at Mount Eden. I just lucked out.

Graff had cofounded Chalone [Vineyard], and was consulting at Mount Eden?
Uh-huh. Then he and the company had a falling out, so he went back to Chalone.

You were at Mount Eden for three years?
Right. And then I went to Matanzas Creek.

And you'd met [Russian River Pinot pioneer] Joe Swan in the interim?
That's what brought me to Sonoma. Joe and I became good friends. I also really liked the wine character from Sonoma. I could pick it out in tastings, more fruit-forward than Napa—not just Pinot, but any varietal. Then Gerry [Gerard] Lambert asked me to make his first Chardonnay, at Lambert Bridge. This was, like, 1975.

How many female winemakers were around then?
Zelma [Long] was here, and Mary Ann [Graf]. I met them when I moved here. Zelma was at Mondavi, and Mary Ann was finishing her term at Simi. And then, of course, Zelma went to Simi.

So was that it, you, Mary Ann, and Zelma?
Yeah. There were some women winery owners around, but—

—and women worked in labs.
Right. I pointedly ignored that option, because it was someplace you got stuck. Like, Zelma got stuck in the lab at Mondavi. I didn't want that. I wanted outdoors, I wanted to work in the winery. I didn't want to get pigeonholed in a big company.

Was it more difficult for you as a woman to get a winemaker job?
From day one! I had been totally unconscious of my sex. Here I was, trying to get a job in this conservative community. Farming, for chrissake! I was so naive. See, my given name was Meredith, which is really a man's name. Merry is a nickname. People would read my résumé and they'd say, "Great!" And then somebody would make the interview call to come in, and I'd get there, and they'd go, "My God, she's a woman!"

Wow.
A very famous winemaker in Napa practically lost his teeth when I walked in. All they wanted was to get me out. He didn't want to interview me, but since I was there he had no choice. I said, "You didn't know I was a woman, did you?" He said, "No." I said, "You never would have interviewed me if you'd known?" He goes, "No."

Who was he?
Jack Davies [of Schramsberg Vineyards].

He's deceased.
Right. So it's okay to—but, you know, I also experienced that when I interviewed at Almaden.

Do you think the only reason you got the job at Mount Eden was because of Dick Graff?
Well, the partner who was responsible for interviewing was a friend of [UC Davis professor Maynard] Amerine's, and he was also gay, which I think was helpful to me.

For the record, Dick Graff was gay.
And so was Dr. Amerine. If I hadn't had this little group of guys who understood that I was in the same position they were . . . they were my moral support team.

When do you think the industry became neutral on gender?
It's not neutral now.

You don't think? There are a lot of female winemakers.
There's a lot more wineries. If you look at the proportions, it's still very light. It's also very hard for a young woman to have children.

Do you have children?
Yes, two. You know, you can't take a few years off. You lose momentum. This is a job where it's a constant learning experience, and to be out of it and then try and go back, it's really difficult.

Your husband, Ken, works here too.
He does the vineyard management side. He speaks fluent Spanish; he graduated in citrus production and ran a huge orchard.

How many employees do you have?
Including Ken and me, we're up to ten now.

When do you stop growing the winery?
When I can't maintain the quality I want. This winery we're building, we're taking a use permit for 25,000 cases, but I don't expect to fill it. We're growing at a pace that is comfortable, and [will do so] only as long as I have the grapes I want.

Do people approach you to buy grapes?
They do now. I get tons of calls. People know who you are and what you can do for their vineyard. They understand the value to their vineyard name to have good people.

Let's talk about your Tobias Glen Pinot. You've made three vintages but didn't release the first two. Why not?

First year, it made too big of a Pinot. You know how big my Klopp is, but these tannins were too much, and hard. The aroma was gorgeous, blueberries and rose petals. But in the mouth, the tannins didn't develop properly. The problem was, the owners have gone back and forth on how to farm, sometimes doing it themselves, sometimes hiring people. When they thinned, they didn't understand you're supposed to take off the *green* fruit and leave the *red* fruit! So the crop became vegetative. I started working with them, and supplied them with compost. The second year it was better, but not where I wanted it. This year it's pretty darned good. I'm looking for something with a different personality than anything else I have.

Are there any vineyards you'd kill for?

Olivet Lane.

Well, you have access to it.

I know, but it's not a long-term contract. The owner just tells me every year if I can have it again. It's a blessing.

Any vineyards you'll never get that you wish you had?

[thinks] I mean, everybody asks why I don't buy from Pisoni. Pisoni asks why I don't buy from them. They offered me grapes. Because I can't farm it from here. I am averse to going out of county. This is my home. I'm not into running around the country. I've been there, done that. Been to Oregon, made wine up there.

How about Carneros?

I've made wine out of Carneros. Carneros is not the place. *This* is the place. Why would I go to Central Coast? People think because Pisoni's a famous vineyard, I should be making something from it. I would rather take something like Tobias Glen and develop it.

Why don't you make Chardonnay?

Well, I OD'd on Chardonnay.

At Matanzas?

It's like when you're an actor and you're typecast. It's Chardonnay, Chardonnay, Chardonnay. I got bored with it.

What do people want in Merry Edwards Pinot Noir?

Consistent quality. They don't want to be surprised. That was our problem in the past, it was very hit-and-miss. Twenty years ago, the Pinots were terrible. No consistency. I was talking with somebody yesterday about Yellow Tail [an inexpensive Australian import]. It's not that great a wine, but you know what you're getting. And for the money, it's okay. For us, from day one, our wines are not expensive. We're a bargain for the quality.

Do you ever declassify?
I do. My declassified wines are Russian River and Sonoma Coast. They're all the same vineyards.

Is it harder to make a vineyard-designated wine or a regional wine?
It's always harder to make a vineyard designate.

Why? You just choose your best barrels.
But are they the best? And how are they going to taste a year from now?

How different are vintages here?
In general, pretty similar. They may seem different on the outside, but the resulting wines are not that different. The range is much less than you would find in Oregon or Burgundy.

How have you dealt with the September heat waves of the past several years?
It's scary, those heat waves. We started picking at night, because picking the fruit in that heat, you automatically raise alcohol because you picked when it's dehydrated. Last year, we picked almost all of Meredith under [artificial] light.

There's been a lot of commentary on darker, higher-alcohol, later-picked, riper wines. Are your Pinots getting more alcoholic?
See, what you said right there is the problem. People confuse bigness with alcohol. Dark color is not necessarily connected with alcohol. Actually, when a wine's too alcoholic, it makes it weaker, because alcohol is thinner than water, and you can go over the edge the other way, where the wine becomes thinner.

What I'm driving at is, have you changed your style over the years?
Well, we do make wines now that are more alcoholic. When I was at Mount Eden, I was picking at 25-plus [Brix], and I was making wines under 14 [percent alcohol]. So how is it that, thirty years later, we struggle to keep to 14.4? My theory is that the yeasts are stronger now, and fermentations are so efficient that we're getting all this alcohol. The other problem here in Russian River is that we have so much Pinot planted. It all gets ripe at the same time. We can't handle it!

You run out of fermenters?
No. We run out of people to pick it.

So the grapes hang longer?
And with Pinot, even a day can be *huge!* There's nothing you can do to slow it down. You could water the vines day and night, it wouldn't make a damned bit of difference. Excuse me, a bit of difference.

Would you ever dealcoholize a wine?
That's something I wouldn't go into on tape.

Are you becoming more protective of your image?
No. I just understand what the public and most wine writers want. See, in California, we don't have the same latitude winemakers have in Europe. In Europe, it's okay to add sugar to your wine, to take water out. It's not okay here to take alcohol out, although that seems stupid, because isn't that better for everybody, to have wines that are healthier, lower-alcohol?

It's controversial.
Because—I don't mean to pick on you—but certain wine writers have said, things like filtration are bad. People joke about how when Robert [M.] Parker [Jr.] comes to their winery, they hide their filter!

When I first went to work for Mount Eden, it just wasn't Pinot's time yet. But I thought, "Someday, it's going to be." And that time is now.

That's like hiding the wood chips under a tarp out on the back loading dock.
Not everybody really wants to know how wine is made. Not everybody wants to know how babies are made, either. They still like the end result! *[laughs]*

How do you see the role of wine writers?
I appreciate the support I have in the press. But the people I'm concerned about are my sommeliers, my wine buyers and floor staff. They're the ones who are out there going, "You have to have Merry Edwards Pinot."

Do you enjoy going out and selling?
I enjoy it, but it's very hard work. The travel's hard, and eating too much is hard, and making one presentation right after another is hard. Making sure that you're genuine and you can really meet the needs of those people. I'm a comfortable speaker, and I can kind of, when I walk in, sense what the group needs.

What more do you have to learn about Pinot Noir?
How do I know until I've learned it? I didn't know, thirty years ago, that viti-culture was what we would come down to. But I've never become bored with it. There's always something new. So how can I say, ten years down the line, what I'll think is important, or what will be open to me? Maybe there's something subtle I'm not seeing now.

Are you doing anything biodynamically?
I do a lot of things that are considered "organic." I like sustainable farming. We've always used mulch. We transplanted the big oak trees off our property, live. The bird stuff, the ponds. But I don't want to be in a box where I can't make a decision about what to do. And the thing I don't like is that people will say to the press, "We're doing this biodynamic thing," and then when I talk to them, I go, "What about the animal part, you're supposed to have animals?" and they go, "Oh, we're not doing that part." You know? It's something people say because it sounds good.

Following Sideways, *do you think America is becoming a Pinot Noir–drinking country?*
They're starting to. The numbers are increasing. The only thing that competes with Pinot is people's reticence to try it. It's like, "I'm drinking Cabernet and I'm afraid to drink Pinot because" whatever. When I first went to work for Mount Eden, it just wasn't Pinot's time yet. But I thought, "Someday, it's going to be." And that time is now. People ask, "After *Sideways* dies down, do you think it will go away?" Well, no. It's been building for ten years at least. The base is solid now. People can count on Pinot. There's good quality, a lot of names to choose from, and that's what we're building on now.

TONY SOTER

ETUDE WINES

Concerning Tony Soter, the following adjectives come to mind: *gentlemanly, scholarly, precise, diplomatic, self-effacing, soft-spoken*. He has been a wildly successful consulting winemaker, assisting some of Napa Valley's most prestigious Cabernet Sauvignon houses and mentor to a generation of winemakers. These days, however, he has ceased consulting to focus on his two brands, Etude in California and Soter Vineyards, which is mostly Oregon. Ironically, he now specializes in Pinot Noir. We chatted one Indian summer November day in 2005 at Etude, on the Napa side of Los Carneros.

Did you study winemaking?
No. I have a degree in philosophy. I got through college without ever taking a science class. But I did have a taste for wine. After college I worked in a wine shop, then moved to Napa and started dragging hoses.

So the wine bug bit you.
It wasn't a career intention, just an inclination to learn about a subject I would always be interested in, even if I didn't know how I was going to make a living.

What was your first wine job?
In 1975 I moved to Napa with a duffel bag and looked in the Yellow Pages. There were only thirty wineries listed. I sent a letter to every one, and found

an opening at Stag's Leap Wine Cellars. I'd see André [Tchelistcheff] whisper with [Stag's Leap winemaker] Warren [Winiarski]. Then I took a position at Stonegate, the do-anything guy, but I got a chance to work in the vineyards and prune. I was convinced, as soon as I got my hands on some grapes, that this fascinating challenge would be something that would keep me busy and entirely occupied and happy for the rest of my life. And it has. Within two years I worked at four wineries: Stag's Leap, Stonegate, Spring Mountain under Chuck Ortman, and then Chappellet.

All mainly Cabernet houses.
Right. I managed to last a full year at Chappellet, and then applied at [Robert] Keenan. Got the job and gave my notice, when out of a sudden quirk of fate, my boss at Chappellet quit, and that left Donn Chappellet holding the empty bag. Donn made me an offer to stay, so I did.

Were you thinking of yourself as a Cabernet specialist?
I don't think so. Even today I don't think of myself as a Cabernet specialist.

I know today you don't, but this was before you had made Pinot Noir.
Yeah. Well, clearly I was exposed to the possibility of making Cabernet, but I made my first Pinot Noir in 1980.

Who was that for?
Myself. It was ultimately sold as Etude.

You were still at Chappellet?
I'd given notice: "I'm going off to start a career as a consultant."

Why did you want to be a consultant?
Accident and opportunity. I had ambition and ants in my pants. After five years at a great job, I needed to broaden my horizons. There was much about the wine business I wanted to get my hands on, and one property wasn't going to satisfy my curiosity. Consulting often is a euphemism for being unemployed. I happily was gainfully employed for twenty-something years. But when I started, it was jumping into the woods and hoping you can find some work.

Why did you start Etude in 1980, and why Pinot Noir?
Well, I didn't want to start my own brand, I just wanted to make Pinot. That came out of being in love with the wine. When I'd worked in the wine shop, I was exposed to terrific Burgundy. At Chappellet, a grower came by to deliver some grapes, and he said, "I have this Pinot Noir from Oakville." Not exactly the place you'd grow Pinot Noir, but . . . "Will you do me a favor and

take a few tons?" I said, "Sure." The wine was not an incredible success. I did it only so I could expose myself to the challenge of making this elusive and difficult wine.

How come it wasn't a very good wine?
It wasn't a bad wine, actually, but it wasn't going to light the world on fire. Donn had a personal relationship with [Burgundian winemaker] Lalou Bize-Leroy. She was visiting one day, and I had her taste it. She was very kind and complimentary, in a polite way, but the gesture was important. She saw something that was Pinot-like, and I didn't need much in the way of encouragement. I went a year thinking, "What am I going to do with this stuff?" I didn't want to be in business. I left Chappellet in 1980, '81. Meanwhile, I was consulting. By '82, I made the decision to bottle it, came up with the name and concept. *Etude* means "study" in classical music; it's a focus on the craftsmanship.

Now we enter this high period when you're a hot commodity as a consultant. Was there one winery that made your reputation?
It came organically. The first person who took a chance on me was Mary Novak, at Spottswoode. I started with her in 1982 and worked there for fifteen years. In 1990 I went to Araujo. Dalla Valle was 1989, Viader '88, Shafer '86, I think. Niebaum-Coppola, 1991.

You must have been very happy that you'd reached the pinnacle of success.
Well, I was just delighted to have graduated from worrying about where the next check was going to come from.

Do you think you gave a Soter style to those wines?
You undoubtedly do [impart a style], because you are who you are. Anybody who makes wine with any kind of consistency will create a style. Some people say they can tell my wines from others. On the other hand, I did not want to make a "Soterized" wine. This raises the next question, which is how you "get" a vineyard. What Cabernet tastes like at Coppola's is different from Spottswoode or Araujo. I say, "If this is the character at this place, then let's work with this." So, for example, an Araujo Cabernet is never acidic but has rich tannins, and that gives it a compensating structure that doesn't tire your palate. At Spottswoode, you have to be careful about not getting too much tannin, because the high acidity would have a negative synergy; high acid and high tannin could turn

> Anybody who makes wine with any kind of consistency will create a style.... On the other hand, I did not want to make a "Soterized" wine.

the wine into some shrill, brittle thing. The real standard is to do estate-bottled wines for clients with a great property and the means to extract the best out of it.

Do you think a single-vineyard wine is better than a blended wine?
No. I've said heretical things in Burgundy. I would think that a blend of La Tâche and Richebourg would be killer. It defies logic that it couldn't.

Why do people think Pinot Noir has to be a single-vineyard wine, even more than Cabernet?
There is a value placed in the marketplace on single-vineyard wines. The producers want you to believe there's something inherently superior about them. I would argue there's something inherently distinct about them. The myth is they're superior.

What does Etude produce?
About 20,000 cases a year, predominantly Pinot Noir and Cabernet Sauvignon. Little bits of Pinot Gris, Merlot.

Did you build this production facility?
No, we bought it, in 2003. It had been RMS [brandy] Distillery.

When did you develop your estate vineyard?
In 2000. You couldn't be any further west or north in Carneros before you'd trip into Sonoma Coast. We planted it primarily to Pinot Noir. There are twenty clones. Ten are heirloom clones. The others are really good, state-of-the-art commercial selections.

What is an heirloom clone? Swan? Martini?
Something like that. Rarer than Martini. True heirloom selections are things you cannot buy commercially. You take them by cuttings.

Have you produced any wine from the new estate?
There were a few grapes in 2003, just to tantalize us, but 2004 is the first. It will be released next spring [2006].

Where had you been sourcing Pinot?
From good growers in the Carneros. Lee Hudson and Larry Hyde are two prominent examples.

Do you expect your Pinot, and particularly Heirloom, to change significantly once the estate is up and running?
We do. Some people might think, "Don't mess with a good thing," but I'm so convinced of the superiority of this site, and so stimulated by the oppor-

tunity to make Pinot on rocky ground instead of clay ground, that I'm willing to lay it out there and let people taste the difference.

Is there a character to Carneros Pinot you can differentiate from Russian River or Sonoma Coast?
You know, it's funny, because average Pinots taste more like each other, no matter where they come from, than not. At the high end, guys more eloquent than me would say Carneros Pinot has a suppleness, a red fruit tone going on, cherries but never blackberries. The black fruits are the venue of Oregon and some Sonoma Coast wines. Sometimes you'll get tea or cinnamon spice in a Carneros wine. There's a brighter edge to the Russian River wines, a juicy acidity that makes a distinctive quality, vis-à-vis Carneros.

Do you own any Cabernet vineyards?
Never have. The anchor of Etude Cabernet is the Vine Hill Ranch in Oakville. Great vineyard, with esteemed neighbors: Heitz [Wine Cellars'] Martha's, Dominus, Harlan up the hill.

What is Soter brand?
In 1996 I got married to a lovely woman, Michelle, who was raised in Portland, and I was born there. So we had that in common. Came to a notion that Oregon might be a better place to raise kids than Napa, and to afford property and a wine company that a family might inherit. We bought a vineyard in the Willamette Valley, twenty-five planted acres, mainly Pinot Noir, and three acres of Chardonnay as a base for a sparkling wine.

In 2001 you sold Etude to Beringer Blass. Why?
Well, what I wouldn't want you to conclude is, I sold it so I could move to Oregon. I sold it because I could do things with Etude that I couldn't afford myself.

Like what?
Have a permanent winery and an estate vineyard.

Did you have that understanding with them when you made the deal?
That was the nature of the deal.

So this was a vote of confidence in you by Beringer Blass.
Yeah. And a reciprocal one, because I had confidence they were a partner I could do business with. Walt Klenz, who was the chairman of Beringer, was a great man. He had a vision that his company wasn't into Pinot Noir, and they wanted to get there. And here I'm one of those quasi-pioneers with

enough arrows in my back to know that I paid my dues learning how to deal with Pinot Noir, and I had a successful brand. I didn't have any grapes of my own. I didn't have a winery of my own. What they had was a vineyard they committed to for state-of-the-art Pinot Noir and yet hardly any brands to take those grapes to market. So they put two and two together.

Was it difficult to sell Etude and yield control?
That's a great question. You've seen other companies drive perfectly good brands into the dust. I could see what was in it for both of us. I get control of my own vineyard and a facility and have the backing from, let's call it, "a banker." They got somebody with expertise in Pinot Noir and other wines, and a brand vehicle for Pinot Noir grapes they had in the ground. I told them, "I don't want your winemakers or production people involved in anything we do here. I want to run that. I want to control the marketing and PR and everything about Etude Wines." And that's what Walt said, too.

But now Beringer Blass has been bought by Foster's, right?
Right. In four years I've worked with four presidents. It's a revolving door.

What's that like?
Well, a little frustrating, because every year you have to get to know somebody else who presumably has your fate in his hands. But frankly, he's too busy getting his hands around this mega-wine company, so they just leave Etude alone. We're in the corner there, and we just keep doing what we're doing. So I feel very supported.

Is your heart as into Etude as it is into Soter?
Yeah, equally, for sure. I've been with this brand for a long time. I would like to eventually evolve, maybe over ten years, to have a consulting status with Etude.

I want to ask about changing Pinot Noir styles. Have you seen an evolution to higher alcohol?
Quite topical. It's lamentable that wines that are so out of balance are so positively reinforced in the critics' minds.

What do you mean, "out of balance"?
They're undrinkable at the dinner table. They're not undrinkable when you have them in a competition with wines lined up, but if we're talking about table wines, I'm finding some even that *I* made are up there in alcohol, difficult to drink.

So you're 'fessing up.

Sure I'm 'fessing up. Look, there are wines out there that are 15½ percent alcohol that are abominations as table wines. They are enological curiosities and perhaps even enological triumphs, but lousy table wine.

How did we get there?

One sociological reason is, there's something wrong with the way we evaluate wines, in this beauty-contest sweepstakes. When you realize what happens to a fatigued palate, in a context that has no food involved, where you select wines that have more oomph because it's all you can taste the difference in. I mean no disrespect, but I can give you, after a series of those, a perfectly balanced, 13½ percent alcohol Napa Valley red, and you'll like the 15 percent one because it's got more "more" there. But take that wine home and have dinner with it, and you'll have a buzz before you're halfway through.

> There's something wrong with the way we evaluate wines, in this beauty-contest sweepstakes.

Is higher alcohol a deliberate choice on the part of winemakers?

There's plenty of winemakers who realize that they're being rewarded by critics for these wines, where they're doing it on purpose. To make these 15 or 16 percent alcohol wines does not take any rocket science or art. Just wait for the grapes to shrivel. Now, that is a bogus approach to making wine. I don't even know what a Santa Rita Hills Pinot Noir tastes like anymore. I used to know it when it was Sanford & Benedict, long ago. But these wines are overblown.

What are you doing about it?

Getting an awareness is the first thing. I like to say that grapes are getting better until they're getting worse. When a grape gets over a potential alcohol of 15, it's getting worse because I have to dilute it to make it balanced. That is defeating the purpose. So I try to find ways to get the grapes to be physiologically mature at a reasonable sugar.

How?

Choosing our vineyard, to begin with. It's in the coolest corner of Carneros, on rocky ground that dramatically limits the vigor of the vine. A vigorous vine makes sugar more readily than a stressed vine. A vine that has excess canopy will just be a sugar machine.

Do you have a sense that the ripeness pendulum is swinging back toward balance? You see any evidence of that? You talk to anyone who's lamenting that? And it's not just Pinot Noir. I'll give you an example. In the *[Wine] Spectator,* the Merlot issue had the top ten. Our Etude was one of them, great. So I collected the other wines and sent them to the laboratory to see what the alcohols were. Of those ten, only one was under 14 percent. Only two were under 15. Seven of them were over 15. And the top two were 16! So two powerful critics, at least, are reinforcing the success of these wines that are essentially made from shriveled, raisined grapes.

ANDY BECKSTOFFER

BECKSTOFFER VINEYARDS

William Andrew (Andy) Beckstoffer is not a winemaker, but since there are so many issues concerning grape growing in these interviews, I thought it appropriate for one interview to be with "the grand old man of Napa Valley grapegrowers" (in *Forbes* magazine's words). Beckstoffer is, simply, the largest private vineyard owner in the North Coast, and owner of a good chunk of the famed To Kalon vineyard. We met in his office at Beckstoffer Vineyards, in Rutherford, on a cool June morning. After commenting on the 2006 vintage ("Looks good so far"), he answered my questions, looking ultracool in cowboy boots and tight jeans.

Did you have an agricultural background?
No. I was a finance guy. I did the negotiation to buy Allied Grape Growers for Heublein, so I had to learn to talk to farmers. And I found that I liked them. And then, when Heublein bought Inglenook and Beaulieu, I had to convince people of the financial aspects of growing prime varietal grapes in Napa Valley. Nobody was investing in new vineyards back then. They said, "Who's going to farm it?" So I was forced to set up a farming company.

I read that you knew it was controversial when you came to the Valley as a big corporation, buying these veteran wineries.
Yes. I was an outsider. I didn't know much, so I asked a lot of what some-

body might call stupid questions. Why can't we do this? Why can't we close up vine spacing? Why can't we develop bigger trellises? Why can't we plant great grapes in Carneros? I was trying to find out. And we were this corporate thing, and nobody liked the idea of us buying Beaulieu. I was a young man from an eastern corporation who didn't know his place. It was sort of, "Who *is* this guy?" And when you do that, people get their hackles up.

How did Beckstoffer Vineyards develop?
Well, Heublein assigned me André Tchelistcheff for my viticulture, and Bob Steinhauer and I went out and hired a staff. And they hired mostly Fresno State–trained viticulturalists, and we put together a highly trained team. And we gave them benefits and paid them more.

It must have been an exciting time.
Oh, it was extremely exciting. We planted close vine spacing in 1970 before anybody, six by ten when eight by twelve was the rule. I went to see Dr. [Albert] Winkler [at UC Davis] and said, "Dr. Winkler, I'd like to do this," and he said, "You can't." I said, "Why?" He said, "You can't get the vines." I said I could. He said, "Well, you can't get the equipment." I said, "If I can get the equipment, do you think it's okay for me to close up the vines and get more efficiency out of the vineyards?" He said, "I think you ought to try it." So we did close vine spacing.

All these little guys, the Chappellets and Heitzes, did you run into them, or were you operating in a whole different dimension?
No, no, I ran into them all. Bob Travers [of Mayacamas Vineyards] was a good friend; Donn Chappellet. But they didn't want to expand, and they weren't in the high technology and vineyards business. They were in the boutique business.

Why did Inglenook die while Beaulieu eventually thrived?
Inglenook died because—and this is important, because people did it again and are doing it again—I remember the day, somebody said, "We need to expand this thing, we can't get enough grapes in Napa, so we'll take the Inglenook name and put it on California grapes," Navalle [an inexpensive brand] and these other things. So they took that name and expanded it, and they killed the boutique.

But the same people were running Beaulieu.
The thing was, the big investment was in Inglenook. Now, Beaulieu they saw as a boutique. They couldn't build both Inglenook and Beaulieu, so they left Beaulieu alone.

So you built a team. Then what?
We started farming grapes and implementing new technologies. By 1972, we projected out the grape supply and Heublein thought they had enough to build Inglenook and Beaulieu as they wanted. But none of their motivation systems, incentive systems, worked for farmers. A little farming company as a subsidiary of a big eastern marketing company was not going to work. So they said to me, "Go sell the company." They wanted to divest. And I said, "Find me a job."

What made them think that by selling they would get a better outcome?
All they wanted was to make sure they had a good farmer that gave them quality. They wanted to set somebody up in business outside their corporation to farm for them.

Who might that have been?
Well, we went to lots of people. I initially wanted to sell the company and go back into the corporation. But there was nobody here who was interested. So I decided I wanted the entrepreneurial experience. I wanted to do my own thing. I convinced them, if they would lend me the money, I would take over the company and assure them of a quality supply of grapes.

Was that scary? Suddenly you're in debt.
Nothing scared me in those days. Someone asked me, "What was your toughest day in business?" Well, it was the first day, because the day before I bought the company, my wife had our fifth child. I was thirty-three and president of the Vinifera Development Corporation. We hired good vineyard managers. We were big and aggressive and we wanted to know about all the new stuff. For instance, this guy came to me in '71 and said, "I'd like to introduce you to this very successful irrigation system from Israel, it's called drip irrigation." I knew we had a big problem with water in Carneros. I didn't need anybody telling me I ought to look at that. In Napa Valley, they were sprinkler-irrigating, very inefficient. So we did right on drip irrigation, and that's what allowed us really to get Carneros going.

When did VDC morph to Beckstoffer Vineyards?
In 1973, when I bought the company.

How many acres did you own on day one?
All the property in Mendocino, 600 acres, and in Napa, probably 350 acres.

What does Beckstoffer own today?
Well, let me tell you, first of all: 1978, I lost most of the Napa vineyards. Couldn't pay my debts, and Heublein took them back.

What was that like?
Oh, Jesus. And the thing was, I personally guaranteed everything!

Did you suddenly have to ratchet down your lifestyle?
Oh, sure. Everything. It's a shock. They had the right to the house, my car, my wedding ring.

What happened?
Well, we negotiated. They took back most of the Napa land, and they made me sign a personal servitude contract that said I'd farm for them as long as they wanted, I would do everything they told me to do.

Personal servitude. Sounds like slavery!
Well, I've been there. Unbelievable.

Did you think, "To hell with this, I'm getting out"?
No. I was going to make it work. I guess the world turned for us a bit after '78. Things got better. The debt was cut down. Mendocino grape prices went up.

So today, how many acres?
A thousand in Napa, a thousand in Lake, and a thousand in Mendocino. But, see, people look at successful people and think there's a straight line to success. Well, we lost everything in '78, and it was devastating. But it's not a different story than other people.

You have branded the Beckstoffer name in such a way that it's almost a guarantor of quality. Was branding intentional?
Oh, sure. Just look at *terroir*. I believe *terroir* is the total of all the physical aspects, and is more than the sum of the parts. But I also believe it's those things as manipulated by the farmer. So it's important who the farmer is. We wanted to communicate that, to let people know that that was your assurance of quality. But we couldn't do this without good land. I could be the best farmer in the world, but with poor land it wouldn't work. Part of the Beckstoffer program is, we farm only the best land. We're willing to pay more than anybody. Somebody asked me last night, could I afford to buy more land in Napa Valley? I said, "Yes, but only the highest-priced land, only the best." We never looked for financial deals for land. People should know that. Then we farmed it with the highest technology, and we hired very good people. That needs to be communicated as a form of security for the consumer, and it also builds my business.

> People look at successful people and think there's a straight line to success. Well, we lost everything in '78 and it was devastating.

Tell me about this "bottle price formula."
Another very important thing, because it puts us on the same page as the winemaker. Traditionally, the grape grower wanted to overcrop, and the vintner wanted to underpay. That was a historic clash. Now, since the bottle price formula, the winemaker pays us a percentage of his retail price.

Does that change every year?
Every time he changes the bottle price.

So I couldn't sign a multiyear contract with you?
Yes, you can. We just price the grapes every year, depending on what your retail bottle price is.

So if I charge $150 for my wine, what am I paying for grapes?
Fifteen thousand per ton. A hundred times the retail bottle price.

How did you come up with that?
Well, I went back to the '70s and found out what percentage the grapes' cost was of your wholesale bottle price. And I found it was roughly 26 percent. So if you take the 26 percent times the cases per ton times that wholesale price, and then assume the price is half of retail, the number at about sixty cases per ton is like ninety-seven times the retail price. So when the price of the bottle was $7, the price was roughly $700. We did some surveys—the average price of Napa Cabernet was about $40, and lo and behold the average price of Cabernet [grapes] was about $4,000.

I read that Paul Hobbs paid you $25,000 per ton in 2002.
He had a $250 bottle of wine on the market.

If I'm selling steel to Toyota and Porsche, it's the same steel, but you don't see the steel company charging Porsche ten times more.
The difference is that the steel doesn't make a difference. The grapes make a difference. If you didn't have Porsche grapes, you're not going to have a Porsche. If you had Chevrolet grapes, you'd make a Chevrolet.

If I want to buy grapes from you and sell a forty-dollar Heimoff Beckstoffer Tokalon wine, could I?
We can't accept four thousand dollars a ton. And I don't want to charge you so much that I drive you out of business. So it doesn't happen.

What are you doing in Lake County?
Trying to grow great Cabernet. There's very little land left in Napa, Sonoma, Mendocino. So we said, "Where are we going to go?" We began to look in Lake County, and most of the things with red grapes prior to us going up

there were wrong. Wrong soils. We did a study and found, if you could get elevation—we grow grapes up to two thousand feet—and on these volcanic soils and you had water, that everything we saw, the diurnals [daily temperature swings], said you could grow great Cabernet.

Are you selling to anyone yet?
A bunch of people. Sutter Home, Schrader [Cellars], Jed Steele, a couple other little guys. But at this point, we're producing more grapes than people [are] making wine. So we're making bulk wine, we're selling to a lot of people where it disappears.

Actually, you used to make a Fremont Creek brand. Is that gone now?
That was for less than four years. It was another way to sell grapes, and mainly Mendocino fruit. But we never organized for it, never put together a marketing department. Never really had an interest in making wine.

So your hope for those Lake County grapes is what?
Our first hope is that they're an eighteen-, twenty-dollar bottle of great North Coast Cabernet. Then we can begin to find the sweet spots and do some higher-priced vineyard designations.

When you sell grapes, do you have a concern with winemaking issues, like high alcohol and high pH, or do you say, "That's none of my business"?
Both. For an individual winery, it's their business. For Napa Valley wines, it's my business. In other words, I don't think a wine region can be great unless the wines can stand the test of time. If you want to create a great region, the wines need ageability.

For how long?
Well, I don't know. Depends on the vintage. But a long time. If someone says, "Why are European wines great?" [it's] because they last a long time. So for an individual brand, that's their business. But it's *my* business when you begin to play with the family jewels, which is the overall sense of place and reputation of Napa Valley. And when you go to high-pH wines, you probably aren't getting ageability. And that worries me. It's just like the high-alcohol wines. I get comments from all over the world that tell me, "Your wines are so high in alcohol, I don't want to drink them anymore." That bothers me. Now, talk to the guys, they say, "Well, I've got to do this to get a rating from Parker." I un-

> If Napa Valley gets to be known for wines that are so high-alcohol you can't drink two glasses, and they don't age, that's bad.

derstand that for an individual winery. But my concern is long-term. If Napa Valley gets to be known for wines that are so high-alcohol you can't drink two glasses, and they don't age, that's bad.

The seminars you sponsored on long hang time really got people talking about high alcohol.
Right. The conversation was all over the coffee shops. And we said, "Let's raise it to a professional plane." Because the wineries were saying, "I need all this ripeness, but I hate this alcohol." Everybody said, "You're going to have this big fight," but what happened is, the growers' concern with yields was matched by the winemakers' concern with high alcohol. We found out we both had a problem. So we have got to be very interested in finding ways to resolve it.

What are those ways?
Those ways are first in the vineyards. Here's the situation, in a nutshell. The winery says, "I want you to cut yields." But we know that when you cut yields, the vines get out of balance, and you get veggie flavors in the wines.

I thought if you cut yields, you get more concentration.
Stay with me. You cannot taste wine flavors by tasting grapes. You can't taste the beneficial flavors of wine. All you can taste is the defects, the veggie flavors. So winemakers are letting the grapes hang to get rid of the veggie flavors that they created by putting the vines out of balance in the first place! What we need to do is increase the yields to get the vegginess out; that solves it.

Help me out here. How does increasing yields get vegginess out?
By putting the vines in balance.

Why are they out of balance at low yields?
Too many leaves. Too much canopy and too little fruit. The [kitchen] sink that is the fruit gets too much veggie flavors in it. And that's how you get the veggie flavors. That's just one piece of it. Irrigation is another. And we're finding things we can do in the vineyard that can get you greater ripeness at less sugar.

The Holy Grail. Where are you in that process now?
We're experimenting. But I think it's great that the growers and vintners are finally working together, rather than fighting each other. We've got to do something to solve our common problem. And I think the seminars, as they developed, helped to define things better as a joint problem.

TED SEGHESIO

Seghesio is on everyone's short list for some of the best Zinfandels and Sangioveses in California, but it wasn't always so. Beginning in 1902, four generations of Seghesios churned out oceans of bulk wine until, by fits and starts, they belatedly figured out how to play the boutique game. Nowadays, Pete Jr. does the business side, while cousin Ted makes the wines. Ted is an engaging, high-energy guy whose tales evoke visions of the old-time Italian American immigrants who founded California's wine industry—little wonder, since his great-grandfather Edoardo was winemaker at Italian Swiss Colony in the 1890s.

How did you get started in the winery?
I've been making wine since 1979. I've seen a huge transition. We had redwood storage tanks. No one around here knew what stainless steel or oak was. That was my task.

How was it your task?
We never had an official winemaker. We had a chemist who would come up from UC Berkeley and run analysis on bulk wines we were going to sell. In '79, our family was not unified. Few Italian families are. Part of the family wanted to go forward with bottling our own wines, and part didn't.

Who didn't?

That was essentially my cousin Peter's father, Eugene, who had grown up in the Depression and didn't want to spend money. His famous quote to me was, "There's no future in spending money." So my father, Ed, and I just decided to go forward. That was a monumental task, given that the family was not unified, but we'd seen enough. The grapes we were selling were not in favor. We had Zinfandel, but we didn't have much else that was worthy. The world had turned to Pinot, Cab, and Chardonnay. So the handwriting was on the wall. It wasn't until 1983 that we finally put out a wine with our name on it.

> After eighty-odd years in business, we had to get a label on the bottle. The bulk wine business had died, and we were dying as a family company.

What was that?

Our first wine we bottled was eight-year-old Zinfandel we aged in redwood. It was a 1975 vintage we bottled in 1983.

What were you thinking? Why did you hold the wine that long?

Well, we were thinking as clear as we could, but there was nobody—there was just myself and Dad. We didn't have outside consultants. We didn't bring in experts. We just figured, after eighty-odd years in business, we had to get a label on the bottle. The bulk wine business had died, and we were dying as a family company.

Whom had you been selling bulk wine to?

Gallo and Paul Masson. Back then, it was a handshake. Then the dynamics in the industry changed, and handshakes were no longer guaranteed. In '79, '80, '81 we couldn't sell a drop of wine, because Gallo walked away from us. We just weren't forward-thinking, didn't have any intuitive thoughts at all. The owners were aging, getting older, and they'd spent a lifetime of hard work, Peter's father and my father, just working hard.

I'm struck by how—

—backwards we were? Yeah. Totally backwards. We just didn't know. Then we hired a brokerage firm to sell our wines—that was our first encounter with wine professionals that could actually give us sound advice. By the late '80s, we were selling '84 Zinfandel.

When did Pete Jr. come on board?

In '87, I believe. We needed someone to sell wine. He was twenty-three years old, and we put him on the road. He had this little Mazda, and he'd go around the country, meeting with distributors. You know how distributors are: pretty hard-core. There's little Peter, twenty-three looking like twelve; he still looks young. But he was sincere and he learned on the job. He has really grown a lot in this business.

What finally made Seghesio's fortunes? You were so backwards, and now you're coveted.
Well, we always had Zinfandel in the ground, and of the four hundred acres we own, over a hundred are old-vine Zin from Dry Creek Valley and upper Alexander Valley. We just had to manifest them in the bottle. We were sitting on a treasure of vineyards we didn't know we had. In 1986, I'll never forget, I bought some Zin from Dry Creek Valley from a buddy of mine. He couldn't sell it, five tons. It was, quote, "overripe." Well, overripe back then was not even close to what overripe is today. So I fermented it, let it dry, had a tasting, and realized this was Zin we'd never made before. And it could only have been the ripeness level that gave these flavors. So from that point, I kind of adjusted our parameters for ripeness. And then, '90 and '91 were exceptional years for Zinfandel, back-to-back, and I think those two years put Zinfandel on the map. Permanently.

How come, for eighty-two years, your family didn't know about ripeness in Zinfandel?
Because Gallo liked the acidity. Its Hearty Burgundy was one of the best wines Gallo made, and they could blend our Sonoma County with their nonexistent-acid red wine in the [Central] Valley and come up with a decent wine. So there was never a real push for riper levels of fruit, until by accident in '86.

Let's talk about the winery. What's current case production?
Well, I have to back up a little. Finally got a label with our name [in] '83. Started making Zin, Mary's Reserve, which was a proprietary blend of Petite Sirah, Carignan, and Zin, the old dago red. Then we started making Chardonnay, Sauvignon Blanc, Merlot, Cabernet, Table Red, Table White. White Zin was a big deal for years.

Why did you make all those things?
The market wanted Cabernet and Chardonnay, so we had to have it. Or thought we had to have it. We didn't grow French varietals, so we bought them from all over California. We got to 120,000 cases by 1990, and you know what? It was ridiculous. We're competing with Gallo and Beringer, K-J [Kendall-Jackson], and we just couldn't. So we met with our accountant in '93, what do we do? One of the scenarios he came up with was, discontinue all the varietals you make from grapes you purchase, and rededicate your

efforts on what your vineyards produce. So in one year, we went from 120,000 cases down to 35,000 cases. We got rid of everyone that worked here, and started over.

What was that like?
Emotionally, I was excited as hell. Every distributor we talked to was excited. They all embraced it proudly. The last thing they wanted was another Cab or Chardonnay at ten dollars a bottle. So from '94, we started growing [the] Zinfandel category. We stopped making white Zin, just kept on inching towards quality, and taking price increases when we could. At the same time, we hired Phil Frieze as vineyard consultant. He was Mondavi's vineyard manager twenty years, planted Opus One. It's always less is more. We started dropping fruit, and used drip irrigation, even the hundred-year-old vineyards. It was an incredible transformation, from six tons the acre Zinfandel down to three and two. We just started eliminating crop on the vine—because in the past, my dad had never dropped a cluster in seventy years. Never. And Peter's father dropped even less. First time we dropped fruit, Peter's father was up there in Reno on vacation, and my dad was fishing. We wanted to do it when nobody was around. So we got down to 35,000 cases. Gradually, we're back up to about 90[,000]. We'll do 100,000 in 2005.

> I've seen people with ten-year-old vines call them old vines… our old vines are truly old vines.

What varieties?
Oh, 80 percent Zin. We have the San Lorenzo Zin, planted in the 1890s, in Alexander Valley, in a cooler part. It used to be Russian River Valley appellation, but they changed it. That's interplanted with Petite Sirah, so much so that we're actually able to mark the vines and make an old-vine Petite Sirah and still have enough Petite Sirah left for the Zin blend. Then the next tier is the Old Vine Zin, Cortina Zin, and Home Ranch Zin. Old Vine Zin, we grow about half and we source about half.

What does "old-vine" mean?
Ahh. Good question. There is no legislation. We always thought it was forty years old or older.

So if "Old Vine" is on a Seghesio bottle, the vines are more than forty years old?
Oh, for sure. I've seen "mature vines," I've seen people with ten-year-old vines call them old vines. It's kind of like, whatever. But, no, our old vines are truly old vines. And then, Cortina is our Dry Creek Valley single-vineyard Zin. We planted it in 1970.

Why did you go to Dry Creek to plant Zinfandel?
We used to have an old prune orchard there. We did a lot of prunes in the '50s and '60s.

And the prune market was collapsing?
I don't know how there ever was a prune market to begin with. It wasn't collapsing, there just wasn't any money in it.

What makes old-vine Zin better?
The beauty of these old vines is, the root system is devigorized, so it's not producing a lot of foliage or fruit. They're kind of at equilibrium with the environment. The other great thing about old-vine Zin is the acidity. That's one of the things about Zinfandel a lot of people don't realize. You have high alcohol, occasionally some sugar, but it's the acid that gives you the structure and carries the flavors through the finish. Home Ranch acid's always about 7½ grams per liter, which is fairly high.

Are these old vines head-trained?
All head-trained, in the old style. A lot of the modern viticulturalists contend that the configuration of an old vine can never give even ripening, because it's a goblet shape, and the center's kind of open, so sunlight just bowls in through the vine and fries everything inside. Well, we know that, so we leave a kicker cane, or one of the spurs, that kind of umbrellas over the interior of the canopy so it has more shade.

When you planted Cortina, what was the canopy?
Half trellised and half head-trained. We were just curious to see if it would make a difference.

Does it?
No. *[laughs]* We do a side-by-side every year, and I can't tell a difference. I like them both.

Home Ranch is sort of right on the Russian River.
Yeah. Across the freeway, but close.

It's basically flatland.
Peter would call it "benchland," but he's trying to sell it.

Most people say the floor of the valley is not the best place for complex red wines.
Cabernet, I'll agree with that.

What is Chianti Station?
It was a train station on the road going north. The old station was on our property. We moved it across the freeway up to where the house is now, but by the station was a little vineyard, planted in 1910 by my great-grandfather and my grandfather, and for sure they got that wood from ISC [Italian Swiss Colony]. So we make a Chianti Station old-vine Sangiovese.

Was that the first Sangiovese in California?
Well, ISC had their Tipo Chianti, so they would be first. But since, I guess, post-Prohibition, we'd be the first Sangiovese producer.

When was the first Seghesio Sangiovese bottling?
That was 1980, but it was a nonvintage. The first vintage Sangiovese would have been '84.

Was that the first varietal Sangiovese in California?
I'm certain of that. The next one was Atlas Peak, in '89.

Do you remember the Sangiovese frenzy in the late '80s, early '90s? "The next big red"?
Oh, yeah. There were over a hundred producers.

What did you think of that?
Well, they were all horrible. I could drink Swanson's, Pepi's on occasion. And then there was a small producer in the foothills, [Vino] Noceto. The rest of 'em . . .

But the whole marketing frenzy, were you part of that?
Yeah. We joined the Consorzio Cal-Italia, we attended all the tastings. It brought awareness to this tiny varietal. But Sangiovese's not easy. It's like Pinot. Sometimes it comes out pink.

When did you develop Rattlesnake Hill Venom Sangiovese?
Rattlesnake Hill we didn't plant until the early '90s, mid '90s. It's expensive, and we didn't have water up there. Then my dad's good buddy is a witch. Stuck a wand down, and [found water].

How would you contrast Chianti Station and Rattlesnake Hill Sangiovese?
Totally different. The Chianti Station vineyard, that's four clones of Sangiovese. One of them in particular has real small berries, cluster formations. We made two barrels of that, and realized that was the quality. So that's our Rattlesnake Hill. It has tannin like Sangiovese never had. Sangiovese's difficult. There's a big old bullet hole right down the middle of the wine. Sangiovese can grow like a weed; there are issues of overcropping. But Venom,

nobody else has that ancient clone. Even on the valley floor, vigor is not a problem. Somebody actually stole our clones at nighttime.

Let's talk a little about Brix. You were saying at some point you started picking Zinfandel riper. Fast-forward to today: Is there a typical Brix you like?
We target 26 to 26½, a narrow window.

What do the alcohols run?
Fifteen, 15½.

That's riper than your father ever—
Oh, definitely, by probably three points Brix.

What are the factors driving that?
Well, a lot of experience. I've been making Zinfandel for twenty-seven years. I've picked at 21, 22, 23, 24, '5, '6, '7, '8, '9, 30.

You picked at 30?
Not by choice. That was in '97.

Do your Zinfandels ever have residual sugar?
Not by the time they get in the bottle. We fine it like the plague. I still have a couple lots that are a little sweet, but fortunately I can blend it out. Red wine that has residual sugar in it is not real wine to me.

A lot of Petite Sirah and Zin does.
Yeah. I can empathize with winemakers that do that, because when you have a lot of alcohol, a lot of heat, the sugar's going to coat it, mask it. So it's a solution that works, to allow your wine to have a certain balance. But it's not the solution I seek.

What do you think is the winery's value, if you sold it?
Oh, we almost sold it two years ago. I don't know. Who knows? It's worth more today than it was yesterday.

I mean, look at Ravenswood. What did [Ravenswood founder] Joel Peterson get? [Ed.: $148 million, from Constellation Brands.] You could probably sell for at least that.
You know, we came very close. But I don't see it ever happening. I just went through that exercise to open our eyes to what we have here. We have a little treasure. Generations of Seghesios have worked together with these ancient vineyards. We have a product people seem to want, and while it took us over a century to figure out where we needed to be, we finally settled on the right mix.

KENT ROSENBLUM

ROSENBLUM CELLARS

The island city of Alameda—blue-collar, hard by Oakland—isn't exactly wine country, but it's where Kent Rosenblum (at left with his wife, Kathy) makes wine, in an old shipyard building across a weed-choked parking lot from an abandoned naval base. In May 2006 we sat outside on the wooden deck he'd built, with flowers in planter boxes, and chatted. Rosenblum explained the winemaking style he's famed for: big, dark, rich, fruity red wines, high in alcohol, yet more often than not balanced. Rosenblum makes an astounding fifty-odd wines each year, probably more vineyard designates than anyone else in California, and they're eagerly snapped up by fans who've been on his mailing list for years.

How did the winery end up in a shipyard building?
We started out here with one room in 1987 after moving from Emeryville, and Oakland before that, to what we thought was more space than we'd ever need. But pretty soon we filled that up and took on another room, then a third, a fourth, a fifth, so we now go end-to-end on the whole building.

You'd been a veterinarian?
Yes. I lived in Minnesota, which is why we have the Norwegian stories. Ya, sure, y'know? Got married the year after I graduated from vet school, and realized making six hundred dollars a month and working eighteen hours a

day was not going to pay school loans, so I came to California to make money. As I got into wine with my wife, Kathy, and friends, [I] finally got curious enough to buy enough grapes to make five gallons of Riesling in 1972 from this little store up in Berkeley. They'd sell you grapes for a dollar a pound. I was part of a vet practice in Alameda, and I had the scientific background, I'd done the chemistry. Did a lot of reading on home winemaking, pretty much went from not knowing anything to making something drinkable. So we made a very dry Riesling. Didn't kill anybody! We also tried reds at that point, Zin, Cabernet.

And you did this where?
We had a house in Alameda, a basement, and I bought two tanks to fit in there, and barrels. We were all set to go when some neighbors protested, kind of old, stodgy Alamedeans. We got reversed on a vote of the city council. They had all these rules and regulations, no grapes on the street, no trucks, no this. People were passing petitions around saying the house would blow up, César Chávez was going to be picketing, we would be making amphetamines with our lab! All sorts of crazy stuff. So we had to abandon our plans. Went to Oakland, found a place called the Dead End Bar, which was actually a barbershop-speakeasy during the '30s. Stayed there five years. We were bonded in '77, but '78 was our official year open.

What was your wife, Kathy's, attitude to all this?
We jumped into this winemaking thing together. I think most wives would've blown their tops after a couple years of not making any money, working until five in the morning, getting up, doing your day job, but she pitched right in, helped pump grapes, and when the babies were born, she was down there riding the forklift with them. It would have been pretty hard to do without her support.

So you were still a vet during that period?
Oh, absolutely. You don't want to quit your day job too soon. I still do it today.

Does Rosenblum Cellars not provide you with a comfortable enough income?
Being a vet right now hardly provides anything compared to the winery. I only do it a day every other month, sort of when they need something nobody else can do, or they have certain clients they want you to see.

So moving right along, what's case production?
About 160,000.

Is that bigger than you had thought?
You know, it always gets bigger than you think.

Why?
Well, the opportunity is there, the grapes are there, and unfortunately, it's like a kid in a candy shop. A great hundred-year-old Petite Sirah vineyard becomes available, how could I refuse that? Or a mountaintop Zin vineyard with 120-year-old vines, can't refuse that! We don't know if that will make good wine, but the odds are it will. So we'll do a one-year contract, and if it turns out good, we'll do a longer curve.

> A great hundred-year-old Petite Sirah vineyard becomes available, how could I refuse that?

Do you own any grapes?
No. Our model is to let growers grow, and let the winemakers make the wine.

How many different products do you have?
About forty-eight. Eleven Syrahs. Five Petite Sirahs. Zinfandels are eighteen, down from twenty-two. Then we have Viognier, Marsanne, Roussanne, Chardonnay, Côte du Bone Roan, Côte du Bone Blanc, Mourvèdre, two Pinot Noirs, Cab Franc, Merlot, Holbrook Mitchell Trio, and I'm sure there's some we've forgotten. Ports, late-harvest Viognier, Sémillons, all that stuff. Kind of adds up.

How do you keep it from getting away from you?
Well, we're organized like twenty little wineries all under one roof. We have a good computer system that works it out. The key is really to be in the cellar, with Jeff Cohn, who works with me, tasting through those barrels, identifying the problems, what needs to be done, and translating that into work orders and blending and making the whole thing come together. [Cohn left Rosenblum in February 2006.]

Is there any kind of wine you wouldn't do?
[laughs] I like the challenge, and I like good wine, so it really doesn't matter if it's Riesling or Verdelho or Grüner Veltliner. Those grapes aren't readily available, but I would be open. The only problem is, I now have a professional sales and marketing crew, and they've said, "Give us more single-vineyard Zins and get out of Cabernet! Forget Merlot!" They want to focus on Zins and Rhônes, and that's the way we're headed.

There's a school of thought that says you can get good at making only one or two types of wine. If you're a Pinot Noir guy, you don't want to be messing with Zin, or Viognier, or whatever. I take it you don't subscribe to that view.

You know, I think you become maybe a stylistic winemaker, and if anything described our style, it would be probably large, fruit-driven, somewhat extracted Zinfandels. So when I make a Pinot Noir, it comes out somewhat large and extracted.

Which came first, that fruit-driven style because that's what you like, or did the fruit sourcing come first, from these warm-climate old vines that dictate a riper style?

A little of both. To be a winemaker, you have to have a picture in your mind of what you want the wine to be, even before you pick the grapes. And we'd always enjoyed the old Mayacamas, the Ridge [Vineyards] wines, the bigger styles, so that's what we were shooting for. If we can't sell it, we have to drink it, so we might as well do it as we like it, right? So that's what we do. We have our growers grow for that, sun on the fruit.

> If we can't sell it, we have to drink it, so we might as well do it as we like it.

That's a trellising or canopy issue?

It is, or leaf-pulling, whatever you have to do. You can't do too much or you're raisins, but you need to have some to build the phenolic content of the grapes. Then you have to get them ripe enough to be able to extract that. If you pick at 21 or 22 [Brix], you have a hard time getting that color because it isn't developed yet. But if you let them sit until 25, 26 and a little shriveling happens, then you're apt, without even a lot of effort, to get some great structure.

Do people approach you to buy their fruit?
Oh, yeah.

Was it always like that, or was it hard in the beginning?
You know, because we were dealing with Zinfandel, which nobody wanted, the opportunity to get those relationships and work with the growers early on was there. Could we have bought Cabernet in 1978? No. You couldn't get it.

So people call you and say, "Kent, I've got this vineyard."
Yes, and at this point there's some I'll say, "That's interesting, I'll come and take a look." Like we looked at one last week, out in the Anderson Valley, up on a steep mountaintop, Zinfandel. It's the sort of thing we'll try, and if it isn't quite what we're looking for, it'll go in the North Coast program.

Is there anything you would say no to?

Oh, absolutely. Bottomland stuff. Production is too big per vine, the water table is too close, the berries will be big and swollen.

Let's talk about two things that arise in some of these big wines, especially from warmer climates: alcohol levels and residual sugar. Your Rominger [vineyard] Syrah, from Yolo County, has an alcohol level of 16.5 percent. Do you have a problem with that?

No, as long as the wine is balanced and tasting the way I think it should. Could we run it through a spinning cone or reverse osmosis? We could. But that beats up the wine.

You've never done that?

The only wine we've done that on is our Viognier. For some reason, we're getting 17.5 percent alcohol on Viogniers, and that sort of tastes like firewater. So we bring that down to low 14s.

But back to the reds. Pickett Road Petite [Sirah] is 16 percent.

Again, I think it's a wine writer issue, I don't think it's a consumer issue.

Well, I hear blowback from consumers.

Sure. I see that, too. However, the people that come here to taste wine, that's where they go. The bigger, the badder, the better, the quicker it sells. So how can we honestly say we're making these horrible things for the public when that's what they want? That's where you get the fruit, the phenolics, the extract. And that's what we like.

I also want to talk about residual sugar. Do you always ferment your table wines to dryness?

Well, let me say, we would like to, but there are often times the bigger reds don't get there. It isn't an easy process.

On the '04 Heritage Clones Petite Sirah, even at 15.4 alcohol, it seems like there's residual sugar in there. I don't know if there actually is, but it tastes like it.

Yeah. We're looking [at], with a number of our Zins, anywhere from 0.5 up to even 1.0 percent residual sugar, and again, with the wine being the structure it is, it just kind of adds a fatness, as opposed to a sweetness to it.

Well, you said you aim for dryness, but you can't always get there. So in a table wine, if residual sugar is not intentional, then it seems to me it's a fault.

We're aiming for a flavor and a structure, and if that does in fact have 0.25 or 0.50 residual sugar, that's fine. We live with it. We'd rather have the bigness. Would it taste better dry? Maybe. We don't know. We've done everything we can to get it as far as it's gonna go. So yes, there are some. Heritage Clones is one. Paso Robles [Zinfandel] Appellation Series, a little over 1.0, for me, [is] a little too sweet. But it all goes back to, Does the wine smell and taste good? If it does, and we can't improve on it, then that's where we go.

Are there ways to remove residual sugar the way you can with alcohol?
The only way to get rid of residual sugar is to ferment it.

So the reason wines retain residual sugar is because they stop fermenting?
Yeah. The alcohol goes up to the point where they just slow down.

Can you rejuvenate the fermentation?
Well, we actually have some yeasts now in tea bags you can put in that work out. We've done that in barrels and tanks. We've got the Roussanne right now, has about three-quarters of a percent residual, it's been slowly working along, but it's at the point where it needs to get together, so we're gonna put it in the tank and tea-bag it.

Could you have tea-bagged the Heritage Clones to dryness?
Oh, I think we could've, but it's such a huge lot, it would've been a major effort. We have six different lots going in there, and some of 'em are dry, some of 'em are not quite, some of 'em have some VA [volatile acidity]. Now, when we put it all together, it tasted good, so rather than fiddle with it, we wanted to get it in the bottle.

You said your marketing and sales people are trying to get you away from Cab, Chardonnay. Where do they want you to go?
Well, Zin, obviously. There just isn't enough for [Richard] Sauret, Rockpile [vineyards], all this stuff that gets 90-plus reviews. They also want us to do a reserve combination Zin. Take the best barrels of the best vineyards and try and create something that would be seventy-five dollars.

A seventy-five-dollar Zinfandel from Rosenblum!
Yeah. And they think it would be a no-brainer to sell. But what it does, it kind of makes your fifty-dollar bottle look inexpensive.

So what will you do?
I'll probably do it from the '05 vintage, which we still are evaluating which barrels, which lots—and of course if it fits, because you can take two great wines, put them together, and get nothing. So it's important to set up the bench trials and see what we're doing.

This seventy-five-dollar Zin would be a blend as opposed to a single-vineyard?
That's what our sales and marketing people want. Let's take the crème de la crème of the best barrels, St. Peter's [Church], Rockpile, maybe Cullinane [vineyards]—and see how it all fits together, 300 cases that you could never duplicate again.

How would we know you're not just taking advantage of the Rosenblum name by suddenly coming out with a seventy-five-dollar Zin because you can?
Well, it would really have to be a small production lot that we believed in and when people tasted it, they believed in, too. And of course, if it got some nice score somewhere, that would validate it to some degree. Obviously it wouldn't be in our interests to create something that wasn't as good as the best we've ever done.

What is the role of scores and critics?
Oh, depending on which critics—I mean, Mr. Parker and the *[Wine] Spectator,* obviously, have tremendous influence. Unfortunately, a lot of guys live or die by the critics. I think we're a little different. We've got a tremendous mailing list, we've got a lot of support out there, and we've been doing it for so long that we're known. But if you're a new kid on the block, a nice score is helpful.

Any thoughts of retirement?
You've got to remember, this is my hobby! This *is* retirement.

MARGO VAN STAAVEREN

CHATEAU ST. JEAN

Compared to many of the winemakers in this book, Margo van Staaveren, winemaker and director of winemaking operations, has had the most stable of careers, having worked at Chateau St. Jean for twenty-eight years as I write these words. Through ups and downs in the wine industry, through multiple changes in ownership, St. Jean has remained remarkably consistent, and much of the credit for that must go to van Staaveren. We met up in her office at the Sonoma Valley winery in June 2005.

Did you go to UC Davis?
Yes. I'd wanted to be a special ed teacher. But I was aware of the wine industry because I had a boyfriend who took glider lessons in Calistoga, and we used to come up. When I went over to the enology department, I was intimidated by the chemistry, so I went to plant science. But then I realized that to get a job I'd have to get a master's degree, so I went back to enology. I started working in the lab at Beringer in '79, for Ed Sbragia.

How did the St. Jean job come about?
A friend had come to St. Jean, and she called Beringer and said, "I need a lab technician; do you have anyone who's looking for a move?" So I came here. I remember one rainy night, walking across boards because there weren't pathways yet, and got the job.

Was Dick Arrowood the winemaker?
Yes. The owners had hired him, and he helped develop the property. The '75 was the first actual crush here, with purchased grapes.

The winery got known quickly for single-vineyard Chardonnays, didn't it?
Right. Robert Young [vineyard], Belle Terre [Ranch]. In '80, '81, we had nine vineyard-designated Chardonnays. Dick had such a great eye for vineyards— Les Pierres, McCrea Ranch. I really have to hand it to him.

What was Dick's philosophy on these single-vineyard Chards?
Part of that came from the owners' desire to follow a Burgundian model of single-vineyard wines. It wasn't done in California, and Dick was up for the challenge. All the wines were made with the same techniques. The theory was, whatever you tasted in the bottle only represented that vineyard differ-ence. It was a good premise. As we evolved, we realized that some winemaking style wasn't necessarily the best for each vineyard. For example, Robert Young we make in a nonmalolactic style, because it's big and dense and doesn't need that. Belle Terre evolved into a malolactic style. It needed that flesh.

In order to follow your career, we must now bring your husband, Don, into this.
We should probably bring Don in!

When did you meet him?
My first day here. He was assistant cellarmaster. We got married in 1983. Even-tually I became an enologist here, which was a raise; it was considered a higher position. Dick always tasted by himself, but he would involve you in what he was doing. [Dick Arrowood remained at St. Jean until the spring of 1990, when Don became winemaker.]

So your evolution in titles was . . . ?
Enologist, lab manager, and then assistant winemaker.

Meanwhile, ownership changed?
Yes. The owners sold in 1984 to Suntory, the Japanese beverage company.

What effect did that have on employees?
Well, it was a difficult time because everyone was very sorry to see the fam-ily not own the winery. It was a huge cultural and environmental change, to be corporately owned and foreign-owned. Nobody knew what to expect. On the flip side, it felt very stable because Suntory was a big company, so there was a lot of stability for all of us.

Did you consider leaving?
No. When they came in, there was nothing bad. Really, the criticism was on the outside. We were hopeful there would be some momentum behind the brand. It was the early 1980s, not a good time in the industry, things were lagging. We had this big popularity and then, as happens, popularity wanes after a while. So it wasn't the most "up" time, I don't think. What we thought was going to happen, but didn't, was buying vineyards, and that's what we wanted to do—to secure our own sources. But we found out that wasn't exactly

> It was a huge cultural and environmental change, to be corporately owned and foreign-owned.

what Suntory was going to do. They had just spent a fortune on this place, and they weren't going to buy more property. That was a downside. I understand it from their perspective; they weren't ready to invest a lot of capital.

Does Suntory still own St. Jean?
No. Suntory sold to the Texas Pacific Group, a venture capital group. They kept it for a few years, and purchased what was then Wine World Estates in January 1996. They purchased us in the spring of 1996 and put us together into Beringer Wine Estates. And then Beringer was bought by Foster's in 2000. And then we became Beringer Blass Wine Estates, because we merged with the Mildara Blass division of Foster's. And now, after the acquisition of Southcorp in the spring, we're Foster's Wine Estates.

Whew.
But you know, the net of the whole thing, from my perspective, has been minimal. I have to say that's one really wonderful thing. This site has maintained its identity, its history. And being part of another group does bring advantages, especially when we joined Beringer. What happened was, Suntory *wasn't* investing in this. Beringer was a wine company; they knew what it took to have fine wines, with things like more new barrels. They opened doors for us. So that was a really positive change.

So you never felt pressure to increase production and profits at the expense of quality?
It's a business. At the expense of quality? No. Honestly, this has been a fairly sheltered brand. The image of this brand is important. That's what they paid for.

What does St. Jean own now in vineyards?
This property is about 250 acres.

You were promoted to winemaker when?
Two thousand three. Don had left in 1996, to go to Artesa, and Steve Reeder came from Kendall-Jackson to take his place.

Were you considered for the job in '96?
Yes. They asked me. But I had a two-year-old and a six-year-old. Don and I had always agreed there would not be two full-time winemakers in the family. It's a demanding schedule—not only harvest, but travel, PR, and all the other responsibilities. And we always said, "That's insane." When he left, it was like, "No." I enjoyed being associate winemaker.

Why was it you, the woman, who had to make the sacrifice?
Well, I don't know if it's the woman who *has* to. I think it's the woman who *wants* to. You're somebody's mother, and that has different feelings to it than being somebody's father. But right now, in my family, it is topsy-turvy. My husband left Artesa for a small winery project, and he's the one driving the kids around.

So why did you take the full-time job?
Well, Steve decided to go to Simi, and I can't put it more bluntly than to say: "Oh, no. *[laughs]* Don't do this to me again!" I had a really good setup where I was leaving at three to get my kids. Now I'm director of operations, so the plant is my responsibility, and that brings with it all kinds of other things.

Let's talk about St. Jean today. Total case production is what?
About 400,000 cases.

That's a lot for one person to keep track of.
It is! And it's over about thirty different products.

What are the tiers?
Technically there's four: California, which is Cabernet and Merlot; Sonoma County, which is the mainstay of our production; our vineyard-designated wine, so you have the Chardonnays, and we include Cinq Cépages in that; and then a small Reserve line.

Do you make everything yourself?
[laughs] People wonder, do you only do some wines? Yeah. Not every wine is made on-site here. We don't have the space to do that, so the California reds are made at [Chateau] Souverain and Meridian at the moment, because it's Central Coast sourcing on half of it.

The company just sold Souverain to Francis Ford Coppola.
Right, so we'll move up to Asti.

What are the single-vineyard Chards?
Robert Young, Belle Terre, Durell, and Robert Young Reserve.

Has the formula for those changed much over the years?
I'm sure you'd see riper fruit now. Why? To get more stone fruit, more lemon drop [flavors], depending on the region you're coming from, to get those less-green flavors and more of that sweet melon, tropical—the only way to get it is to pick it riper.

Where did the impulse for that come from?
I think the style of wines has changed, whether it's come from the press or the consumer. Who's leading whom? It's hard to tell. But St. Jean isn't into the megaripe stuff, the 27, 28 Brix thing. I really think that's more of a Napa Valley phenomenon. At least, that's what I hear people talk.

> I think the style of wines has changed, whether it's come from the press or the consumer. Who's leading whom? It's hard to tell.

For Chardonnay?
No, really more for Cabernet.

Which brings us to Cinq Cépages.
The first time we put it in the bottle and called it Cinq Cépages was 1990. That evolution was interesting, because that was one thing Suntory did bring back to St. Jean. We had stopped making red wines in the early 1980s. We'd made a little McCrea Pinot Noir for the tasting room, because Don and I lived on the ranch.

Was not making reds a corporate decision?
Well, that was when the Merzoians [St. Jean cofounders Robert and Edward Merzoian] owned us, and that had to do with cash flow, really. But Suntory owned Château Lagrange, in Bordeaux, and when they purchased us, they asked, "Where's the red wine?" *[laughs]* So the whole thing was to get back into red-wine making. But we didn't have the sourcing for it. At the same time, we started seeing phylloxera everywhere, and certainly on-site here. So it was, "How are we going to go about this?" Well, Don's drive was to make a blended Cabernet. That's what he wanted to do. If you go back to the Cabernets we made in the late 1970s, those were pretty tough wines, very high-extract, very tannic. And so how are we going to get around that, not repeat that same thing where you have to keep them for ten years before you can drink it? Don was interested in working with the other varieties, too. He was very excited about that. He wanted a new challenge. So when we had to re-

plant here, we decided to put in some other varieties. This place, it's a nice site for white wines, but it's great for red wines.

So is Cinq Cépages totally off this property?
No. It's based on this property. It comes from various appellations in Sonoma County—Carneros, Russian River Valley, Knights [Valley], Alexander Valley, Sonoma Valley, so we've got cool regions, warm regions.

How did the name, Cinq Cépages, come about?
We wanted to do a fancy name, because other people were starting to do that. But sales was saying, "There's no way anybody's going to buy something called Cinq Cépages from Chateau St. Jean when we're not known for red wines at all." So they said, "You've got to label this thing 'Cabernet Sauvignon' as well." So if you look at a bottle of CC, it also says "Cabernet Sauvignon."

So did that tie Don's hands, because he needed the wine to be at least 75 percent Cabernet?
No. Because it's a Cabernet, a blended Cabernet, and that's important, because there have been times where there's only so much good Cabernet in Sonoma County, and the idea was, originally, to drop the Cinq Cépages. There was a moment in time when there was a push-back: "Let's just drop it, we can make more cases, we can have more Merlot." Certainly sales and marketing were in favor of that. And we came back and said, "No. The signature of this wine was that it's a Sonoma County Cabernet Sauvignon."

So it's usually about what percent Cabernet?
Seventy-five, 76 percent Cabernet.

Do you feel locked into using all five varieties every year?
It's an interesting thing, because I thought Cain Five [from Cain Vineyard & Winery] was all five varietals, and it's not!

So you're not handcuffing yourself?
I never thought of it that way. I think it's exciting to put them together.

Has it ever been less than the five varietals?
No.

What does each variety bring?
Cabernet is the foundation. It's the structure, the real signature, by far. It's bringing in blackberry fruit, and using the different appellations is important, too, because you get the different expressions of the different appellations.

What does warm-climate Cabernet bring, and cool-climate Cabernet?
This is true for all varieties, with the exception of Malbec and Petit Verdot, which only come from warm regions. But Merlot, Cabernet Franc, and Cabernet all come from warm and cool regions. That's important because just as a clone or variety will express itself differently on-site, the climate has a lot to do with it. I tend to find rounder, softer—not "soft," it's never soft-soft, softness isn't a problem, we don't have Cabernets that are too soft, it's trying to make them softer through tannin management. I think we get more blackberry, black cherry fruit from warmer areas, and we get these dark, maybe more linear wines, but very full of extract, black raspberry, more exotic aromas and flavors, from the cooler regions. I don't think I'd like those cool regions alone all the time.

What does Merlot bring to the blend?
Merlot adds that fleshiness, that softness that does help the Cabernet. Cabernet tends to be more closed generally than I want it to be. I think Cinq Cépages is very tight upon release.

And Cab Franc?
Brings in floral, spice, in good years blueberry, and more texture. And its tannins tend to come in at the finish, so it sort of stretches out that length. You get that early hit from the Merlot, and then you finish out with the Cab Franc.

And the Petit Verdot and Malbec?
Malbec can go anywhere, as far as I'm concerned. I'd put it in everything! *[laughs]* Overstated, but I love working with Malbec because it's juicy, grapy, all those things, you can't believe it's wine. It's so, like, candy. And it's big, fleshy, I love that juice. Petit Verdot brings in the coffee, the dusty character, pomegranate. We never have a color problem. People think, "Oh, Petit Verdot's for color." That's not so. Malbec's actually darker than Petit Verdot.

What's case production on CC?
About 15,000 cases.

Is there room to grow production?
To some degree. We're always looking for Cabernet. It's always about the Cabernet. In Sonoma County five years ago, you couldn't touch a Cabernet grape because the sources were so locked down. Now the market's opened up, so we've been going out to see what we could possibly add.

There must be some pressure to increase production on a seventy-five-dollar wine.
Not huge. I mean, they ask for more, and then we do the harvest and come back with the same amount. With a wine like Cinq Cépages, which is the flagship of our winery, I don't understand why you would increase production at the expense of quality.

Cinq Cépages was discovered by Wine Spectator, *right?*
Uh-huh, in the 1996 vintage that occurred in 1999, the year it was named.

Did that surprise you?
Oh, yeah, sure.

Did the price go up after that?
Sort of, in a couple little jumps. In that vintage ['99] we were going to charge $35. We had been at $28. What happened was, it was published with a price of $28, and we said, "Okay," and when it became wine of the year, *[laughs]* "Ehhh," so we kept it at $28, we didn't raise that price. What are you going to do? But the next vintage, we raised the price.

But seventy-five dollars, these days, isn't really high for great Cabernet.
When you look at the Cabernets that people are looking for, I'm choking over here. I can't defend these prices. I mean, what are you going to say?

How would you compare CC with, say, an Oakville Cabernet?
I think then you get into appellation differences. When I taste Napa Cabs, it's a tighter structure. With Sonoma, they seem big and bold: "Come drink me." To me, Napa tends to be tighter upon its youth, not as juicy. Not as showy, maybe. Over here, I think the fruit tends to be very forward.

Do you think of Cinq Cépages as an aging wine? What do you suggest to people?
Well, the 1990 is still drinking very nicely. But it all depends on what they like. I taste so many young wines, so for me, I'm looking for the fruit. I think we tend to have this idea that we have to keep things forever. But most people don't store it properly, so what's the point? Sometimes it's just time to move on—drink it up and enjoy it.

What do you think of critics' wine descriptions?
I think I rarely get what I see written. I've pulled out wines, especially ours. What do they see? I want to see what the critic got, and sometimes my impressions are so different.

Is that a problem, this inconsistency?
I don't know that it's a problem. I think for the wine-buying public, they're so mystified by the process anyway that whatever they can grab on to is helpful. For professionals, I don't know that you could ever standardize it.

Do you taste a lot of other people's wines?
Not as much as I would like to. Just dealing with our own inventory is a considerable take. When you consider Robert Young Chardonnay, for example, there are twenty blocks.

1980s

The California wine industry was undergoing something similar to a bull market by the time the twentieth century's penultimate decade began, and certainly by the time it ended. The Paris tasting, already enshrined in myth, had seemingly proved that at least some California wines could be as great as nearly any in the world. Wine critics, who were beginning to have real influence in America, praised the Cabernets of Napa, the Chardonnays of Sonoma, and the odd wine from almost anyplace else. Consumers began to take note. Dry wines had finally over-taken sweet wines in sales, and the various food revolutions, from Julia Child's to nouvelle cuisine, were inspiring many Americans not only to eat better, but to drink better, too. Restaurateurs now could put California wine on their wine lists, right next to bottles from France, without embarrassment—with, in fact, a sense of pride.

The number of wineries across the state began to explode. About this time, a famous wine writer said that keeping track of wineries in California was like trying to take a census in a rabbit hutch. Everybody seemed to want to start a winery, and not just in the North Coast; new winegrowing areas (especially the Central-South Coast) were discovered—or rediscovered, after having lost their earlier plantings to Prohibition. Established wineries increased their production, or started second labels, as per capita consumption in America rose. The viti-culture and enology departments at schools—mainly the University of Califor-nia's, at Davis—saw steadily increasing enrollments. To growing numbers of young people, winemaking seemed to be a fun, healthy way to make a living (although you can almost hear a parent saying to her child, "You want to be a *what?*").

But wine was also becoming big business. After all, once you produced it you had to sell it, and the greater the number of brands, the more intense became the competition. Wineries now had to be launched not merely with great dreams, but with game plans. University degrees were called for; investors were needed; grapes had to be secured by contracts, not just handshakes; distributors were required, and sales staffs, too (often the extended family); the expertise of public relations and marketing experts, and sometimes lawyers, was called in; and expensive equipment had to be bought and paid for. The romance remained, only now leavened with reality.

Enter the winemakers in this section of the book. They not only had to learn to be great vintners, they also had to be better than their colleagues, to scramble to the top of the heap and figure out how to stay there. It was not predetermined that just because a winery was launched during this hopeful, expansive period it would be successful. You need look no further than any standard reference book on the wineries of California during the 1980s to see how many have fallen by the wayside.

In this heady environment, whenever a new wine, winery, or winemaker came along with something special, it generated huge buzz among the cognoscenti of the time, who constituted a sort of underground. Word of mouth has always been a powerful factor in making (or breaking) any given wine. The winemakers who started their careers in the '80s all began to get their first serious taste of buzz during this period. They've come a long way since, presiding over some of the most prestigious wineries in America and making wines that, in many cases, are sold out even before they're bottled (and are priced accordingly). Some have chosen to work for themselves, others prefer to work as hired winemakers, but all are at the height of their creative powers right now. Their most formidable years are ahead.

BOB LEVY

HARLAN ESTATE

In an industry known for the fickleness of its consumers, Harlan Estate has accomplished the ultimate: staying power. Almost from the moment of its first release, in 1991, the Napa Valley Bordeaux-style wine has been a legend, a status accompanied by legendary prices. At the 2000 Napa Valley Wine Auction, ten magnums went for seven hundred thousand dollars.

Harlan Estate's founder, Bill Harlan, a Southern California real estate developer, has shown an unerring eye for developing upscale niches in which to produce and sell Cabernet Sauvignon–based wine. It was his selection of a relatively unknown winemaker, Bob Levy, that proved crucial in realizing the vision of what the two men dub "a generational mission"—to build a brand that, like the great châteaus of Bordeaux, will last for a hundred years and longer.

Levy and I met on a rainy May day in 2005 at the Oakville winery. A new road was being (noisily) built right outside his office, and there were private tours scheduled, which invariably involve a meet-and-greet with the winemaker. For privacy, we hopped into Bob's truck and drove up to the vineyard's highest point. As the rain poured down, we chatted about all manner of things.

When did you meet Bill Harlan?
In 1982, when he was starting Merryvale Vineyards. I was winemaker at Rombauer, and he came to me to make wine. We were doing custom crushing,

and they didn't have a facility. I eventually left Rombauer in '88 and became Merryvale's winemaker.

How did you become Harlan Estate's winemaker?
In 1984, Bill purchased forty acres up here. I was involved with him clearing the land, laying out vineyards, choosing rootstock and varieties. I think we saw in each other—I certainly saw in Bill—a like mind, in wanting to do things at the highest level. He had the commitment, not only philosophically but financially, to accomplish that. I didn't, so it was a good relationship.

Why couldn't you do all that at Merryvale?
Well, Bill had partners. Merryvale was a way to get into the business, learn about it, to help formulate the ideas and directions for Harlan Estate.

How was this site selected?
Bill had looked at vineyards around the world. And my experience was, if you take Burgundy, the best vineyards were not on the top of the hill, not on the valley floor, they were in the middle, a tenderloin. Historically, the land between north of Yountville and south of St. Helena was best for Cabernet Sauvignon. So if you combine these two ideas, it's a pretty good idea that we'd have success in these foothills.

Would this be Oakville bench?
Well, "bench" is more where the hill meets the valley floor. This is foothills. The elevation of our property is from 225 to about 1,200 feet. The vineyards are planted from about 325 to 625 feet.

Why are foothills better than valley floors, benches, or mountains?
We wanted to be influenced by the fog pattern during the growing season. In the mountains the daytime temperature tends to be cooler, nighttime temperature warmer, than in the valley, and they're almost always above the fog. We like the qualities from the fog, the warmer days and cooler nights and cool, wet mornings. Now, the valley floor and benchland have that same quality; but the difference, certainly in the valley floor, is more vigorous, deeper soils that produce bigger plants, greater crop levels. In the foothills, you have more rock, less-vigorous soils, so the plants are smaller.

Driving up here, I noticed red soil. Is that volcanic?
It is. Most of the soils in the hills around Napa Valley are of volcanic origin. On the western hills, starting about where we are, there's a series of fault lines, so we have a combination of both volcanic soils and what's called Great Valley [Sequence], which is ocean-derived rocks and soils. Great Valley is frac-

tured, almost shale-like, but it has some clay material between the fractures, a very unique combination of both water-holding capacity and drainage.

Do you plant different varieties in the different soils?
Absolutely. In the Great Valley we favor Merlot, with low-vigor rootstocks. And Cabernet in the volcanic soils, because it doesn't mind struggling.

Struggling because of lack of water?
Because of the water-holding capacities there, yes. Of course, we can put as much water on as we want, because we have irrigation.

What is the vineyard's yield?
About two tons per acre. We're about 65 percent Cabernet, 25 percent Merlot, 8 percent Cab Franc, and 2 percent Petit Verdot.

The vineyard seems to be set in a bowl.
Well, about half is in a bowl. The other half is on the other side of the ridge that forms the bowl. So we have all four exposures. I don't know that that's necessary, but it does contribute to a complex phenomenon we're looking for.

Does everything from this vineyard go into Harlan Estate?
Everything aspires to go into Harlan Estate. We have a second wine, The Maiden, and between those two, and whatever we don't use, that's the entire deal of what's grown here.

What is the price difference between Harlan and The Maiden?
The current [2002] Harlan Estate is $245 a bottle. The [2001] Maiden was offered at $95.

Is the difference between Harlan Estate and The Maiden a subjective evaluation on your part?
That's a fair question. Certainly, it's subjective. The Maiden tends to be Harlanesque, aromatically. If someone were to have Harlan Estate next to The Maiden, there will be a recognition of the ranch, the *terroir*. The difference tends to be that The Maiden may not have as full a mid-palate, and the tannins tend to be not as supple.

Where does the wine go that doesn't make it into Harlan or The Maiden?
We sell it off, under confidentiality agreements.

What's case production?
We average between 1,500 and 1,800 cases of Harlan, 800 cases of The Maiden. We have younger vineyards just coming into their own. We hope to have 2,500 cases of Harlan and maybe 1,000 cases of The Maiden.

What's the blend on Harlan Estate?
It's different every year. Some years, Merlot might not do well, or certain blocks of Cabernet. If you asked me what percentage any particular vintage was, I couldn't tell you, because I concentrate on making the best wine we can, without focusing on variety. A lot of times, we coferment varieties, based on the optimum maturity level.

How do you determine optimum maturity?
By tasting the skin. There's been a lot of [aspersions] as to how effective that is in a human's ability, but that's how I do it literally here.

Who makes the decision of what's Harlan and what's Maiden?
We have four of us who sit down. Myself, Bill Harlan, Don Weaver [director of marketing and sales], and [international winemaking consultant] Michel Rolland.

Rolland's the famous French flying winemaker?
Yes. We have wine samples, and we sit down at a big table and taste them all, talk about them, and start putting things together. We'll typically spend one day on Harlan and The Maiden, and one day on Bond [another Harlan project]. And then there's lots of follow-up.

Rolland leaves after the two days?
Yeah. He's just here for the blending. Then there's a reassessment. Before I feel comfortable finalizing anything, I review it and try to improve it.

You can overrule Rolland?
I mean, Michel is a consultant. We pay him to come and offer his advice. It's like anything, you can take that advice or not take it.

Is the mailing list the only way to buy Harlan or The Maiden?

> We feel strongly that great red wines evolve better in new oak than in used oak.

Yes. We take everybody's name, and send them what we call our "welcome and wait" letter. Usually the first offer will be for Maiden, and it can be anywhere between twelve and eighteen months after their first inquiry. Having said that, there are sightings of The Maiden and Harlan on restaurant lists and in wine shops.

Both wines receive 100 percent new oak. Isn't that a lot?
It is. We feel strongly that great red wines evolve better in new oak than in used oak. The tannins and wine flavors both evolve better. So for those who

feel that's too much oak, the solution lies, in our opinion, in the length of time in oak, not the amount of new oak.

How long does Harlan stay in oak?
I would say in November we're in barrels. We come out in January two years later, so it's about twenty-five, twenty-six months.

Are the wines fermented in stainless steel?
Some. About one-third stainless and two-thirds oak upright tanks.

Why ferment in both stainless and oak?
We started working with oak fermentation in the late '90s. We liked two properties it contributes. One is a symbiotic relationship between very fine-quality tannins and fermentation in oak. The other is the consistency of temperature. We've designed steel tanks to mimic the insulative properties of oak, but they don't have the oak quality. We also want to make sure the yeast has every chance it can to start and finish the fermentation. We use native yeast. They're finicky cultures, and their degree of tolerance to temperature fluctuations can be significantly impaired.

Why not ferment everything in oak?
Okay. So why we don't use all oak is because sometimes, if we haven't had success in achieving tannin maturity in certain blocks, we feel we get a better result in stainless steel than in oak.

Tell me more about how you taste tannins in the skins.
It took me a long time to recognize, in tasting skins, what's happening, and project if there's a chance to achieve what we want, or if we have to cut our losses and pick a specific block because there's a feeling it won't turn the corner before the sugar's higher than we can tolerate.

Describe what your mouth is telling you as you're chewing on a skin.
Well, I plop the grape in my mouth, I sort of extract the skin away from the pulp and spit the pulp out, and then chew on the skin. I'm looking for this fuzzy quality on the cheeks, whether the tannin's more or less developed.

You can't tell that by a laboratory result?
Apparently not! *[laughs]* Nobody's doing it. Nobody's been able to do it.

Do you ever taste a grape and think, "The flavor's there, but the tannins aren't ready"?
It's always the tannins that aren't ready. My goal in life is to figure out how we can get tannin maturity to coincide with the flavor maturity at a low sugar.

Has your approach to that changed over the years?

In viticulture, I've gone down this pathway of striving for low yields. You get better mouth texture and earlier-ripening tannins. The downside—and this is the argument growers make—is, sugars are going to get too high, because when you have a lower crop load, sugar elevates very quickly, so your time of ripening is moved up. Let's say [you get] five tons to the acre [yield] and 25 Brix at the end of September. If you drop that down to two tons per acre, you're going to move that 25 Brix date up to the first of September. You won't have tannin maturity at that time, but you'll probably have a chance to wait it out, whereas one month later, you won't. Those tannins aren't mature, you have too big a crop load for that vine to accomplish that task, and you're losing calendar days and sun activity because the days are getting shorter. In the early years, I had recognition that we had better results with lower crop yields, but the missing element was to try and figure out what in the vine's health status is going to coax it to maintain its balanced growth at the right nutrient base, so that vine will focus on tannin maturity, which is not something that it needs primordially for self-preservation.

What Brix do you pick at?

Every year it's different. To say that we're always going to pick at 25 Brix and have tannin maturity is simplistic. But probably 24 to 27.

Winemakers thirty years ago would have been shocked at picking at 27. What changed?

I don't know. We were looking at things so different back then. And there's a movement back to that, because this business is cyclical. I'm seeing instances of picking at lower sugars. But personally, I feel that the riper we have fruit, the more exemplified is, not the *terroir,* but the site-specific characteristics.

What's the difference between terroir *and site-specificity?*

Well, *terroir* encompasses the person making the wine, the climate, the cellar it ages in. But whatever soil and site contribute to a wine, irrespective of an individual, I feel that [grape] maturity has the ability to show more of that site-specificity than picking before that maturity. You will end up with a better result.

Why didn't vintners know that thirty years ago?

I'll tell you exactly why. They all went to the same school I went to [UC Davis], which spent its entire time, from the '40s well into the '80s, trying to fix winemaking bad habits, and so they developed a pro forma of practices to make "correct" wines.

Why would a 22 Brix wine be more "correct" than a 27 Brix wine?
Because at 22 Brix you're not going to have excessive alcohol or a problem fermenting to dryness. But you also won't have a wine of as much character, in my opinion, or as much pleasure, as one that's harvested later.

> At 22 Brix you're not going to have excessive alcohol or a problem fermenting to dryness. But you also won't have a wine of as much character... or as much pleasure.

Some critics suggest that this later-ripening phenomenon is leading to an internationalization of wine, where everything tastes alike.
I don't agree. It seems to me if there's a way to extract the best of what you have in a site, vis-à-vis viticulture and vinification, that's not going to make sameness of wine, it's going to make greater exemplification of site-specificity.

What's the typical alcohol on Harlan?
From 15 to 16 [percent].

You don't feel that's getting too high for balance, not to mention ageability?
I don't think it has an impact on ageworthiness. I think as it pushes 16, the only risk is serving the wine too warm, in having it be out of balance and noticeable.

Have you ever reduced alcohol?
No. The wines I've tasted that have been alcohol-reduced have suffered over what their starting material was. There's something less than what was there to begin with.

Why do you think people are willing to pay so much for Harlan Estate?
Maybe I should ask you! *[laughs]* In any product, there's perceived quality and demonstrable quality that are reflected in what one's willing to pay. I like to believe that both are at a level that's commensurate with what we're charging. There are also supply issues that come into play.

What do you think of the cult-wine thing?
It's not a word that really sits well, because cults are something that come and go, and we built this thing as a generational mission. And secondly, *cult* has a negative connotation, with Jim Jones. If the demonstrable quality is not there, then clearly those will fall by the wayside. A first bottle of wine is just a point; it has no traceability. Many times, these are not people who have any track record. But you know, we put in the time that proves what we can do, and here's what you can expect from us in the future.

Do you follow the critics?
Yeah. Some—not all, I guess. I'll file it away. It interests me more to read about how they describe the wines than what the scores are.

What's it like to be the winemaker of what is arguably America's greatest red wine?
Boy, I don't know what the right word is. Constantly challenged. It's also like [being] the kid who might be knocked off the platform all the time.

Do you feel insecure?
I'm not. *[laughs]* But at the same time, I don't feel smug. I don't want to feel like we can't always make improvements.

What sorts of improvements?
I could list fifty things we could be doing, that we've looked at and talked about, and for one reason or another, we recognized are not appropriate, or not significant, or not affordable. And if something's not affordable at our level, then it's probably not affordable.

BRIAN TALLEY

TALLEY VINEYARDS

Born into a farming family in California's Central Coast, Brian Talley might have spent his life growing row crops had his father not decided twenty-five years ago to make use of a hillside that was unsuitable for vegetables by planting wine grapes. Today Talley Vineyards produces some of California's most sophisticated Pinot Noirs and Chardonnays, and as general manager, Brian Talley is involved in every step of the process. We talked at the winery in San Luis Obispo County, one sunny day in late August 2005, as the early-ripening grapes were nearing harvest.

Locate us geographically.
We're in the Arroyo Grande Valley, about eight miles from the Pacific. The strong marine influence we get ends about two miles east of us.

How did the Talley family get here?
My grandfather Oliver Talley was born in Bradley, in southern Monterey County. He was raised in Santa Maria and got involved in agriculture. The gentleman he worked for decided to relocate his farming operation to Arroyo Grande in the early 1940s. My grandfather became his partner, and then in 1948 bought him out and formed Talley Farms.

What were his crops?
Beans, cauliflower, broccoli. My father was raised a few miles from here and went to school in a two-room schoolhouse that my daughters now go to.

Where were you born?
In Santa Maria, because they didn't have a hospital in Arroyo Grande.

Did you always know you'd work here?
I always knew I'd come back to the family business. I think my mom wanted me to go to law school, but I figured out early on I didn't want to push paper.

Whose idea was it to start the vineyard?
My father's. He's always tried to figure out what's the best thing we could do with every piece of land. We bought this particular ranch in 1974, and it included the hill that goes up behind me. Right away my dad started thinking, "Gee, we can't grow vegetables on those hillsides, what should we be doing there?" So in '81, '82, he started planting grapevines—Chardonnay, Sauvignon Blanc, Riesling, Pinot Noir, and Cabernet Sauvignon. And only one of those five got the ax!

Cabernet! How long did it take to figure out it wouldn't ripen?
Two vintages.

> I had an obnoxious punk-rock band... and my parents became concerned that the vibration from this music would adversely affect the wine in barrels.

What was your involvement at that time?
I was still in high school. I had an obnoxious punk-rock band, and we used to rehearse in the winery, and my parents became concerned that the vibration from this music would adversely affect the wine in barrels. By the time Steve Rasmussen, who has been our winemaker since 1986, got involved, I was at UC Berkeley. Steve said, "You ought to get a job in a wine shop." At the time I had a miserable job, and I thought it would be more fun to work in a wine shop.

Did you like wine?
You know, I was more of a beer drinker. After I went to work at the wine shop, I became totally obsessed with wine.

You never studied winemaking?
No, I never did. I learned everything—well, not everything, but a lot—from two people. From Steve, more of hands-on, technical winemaking. And from

Jim Clendenen, at Au Bon Climat, an appreciation of French wines, old-world wines.

What, specifically, about old-world wines?
How good they were, and also the concepts of *terroir*, typicity, complexity, subtlety. When I started here in 1991, California winemaking was much more technical, this UC Davis model, where everything you did was dictated by numbers. Everybody was obsessed with Brix, pH, acidity; everything had to fit into a little box. Now, I consider myself a winegrower. My thing is focused more on stylistically what we want to do, whereas Steve is focused more on the technical issues.

How do you define terroir?
Terroir to me means a unique place. And by *place* I mean everything: soil, aspect, climate. It's not just wine, it's any crop, even bell peppers. We grow some in the Central Valley, and the very first time we brought some of those peppers here to Arroyo Grande, my grandfather said, "Something's wrong. These bell peppers don't have any smell." You know, the bell peppers that come in from Arroyo Grande, there's just such a pungent pepper smell. The peppers that come from the Valley, just as the wines that come from the Valley, don't have the intensity of flavor.

What's case production at Talley?
About 15,000 cases.

The main grapes are Pinot Noir and Chardonnay?
Yes. Sauvignon Blanc, about 600 cases. We make a very small amount of Riesling. It was my grandfather's favorite wine. He thought this whole grape-growing thing was not the wisest move, but we should plant Riesling because at least then we'd have some good wine!

All the grandpas thought grape growing was crazy.
Well, he didn't like the cash flow. He liked growing a crop, getting it out of the field in sixty days, getting paid in thirty days, and put the money in the bank.

How many planted acres of Pinot Noir do you have?
About seventy. There are four different Pinot vineyards: East Rincon, West Rincon, Rosemary's, and Stone Corral, which is brand-new, planted in 2001.

Is all your wine estate-bottled?
Talley is. We buy fruit for [our second label,] Bishop's Peak. Most boutique wineries are buying at least some, if not the majority, of their grapes. We have

> If it says "Talley," it means... we have planted every single one of these vineyards, we control all the farming. And I never want to stray from that.

positioned Talley, because of my family's history of farming, as 100 percent estate grown, and if it says "Talley," it means we grow the grapes, we own the vineyards, we have planted every single one of these vineyards, we control all the farming. And I never want to stray from that.

You've had a Rincon vineyard bottling. Will you now have an East and West Rincon bottling?
We've produced two vintages of a West Rincon bottling, in 2000 and 2001, but that was more of an experimental bottling. Starting in 2002, we incorporated that portion into the Rincon vineyard bottling.

So you have how many Pinots now?
In 2004 we had four: Rincon; Rosemary's; the Estate, which is a blend of Rincon and Rosemary's; and then we declassified Stone Corral to Edna Valley.

Was Stone Corral your first move into Edna Valley?
Oliver's vineyard [all Chardonnay] is in Edna Valley.

Why did you plant Pinot there?
It was another case where we were leasing pastureland and we thought we'd do better there with grapes than letting cows run around on it. But the reason we declassified was, this was the first production year, and it didn't merit the quality of a single-vineyard bottling.

What was it that you didn't feel lived up to single-vineyard?
It just wasn't quite as concentrated, didn't have the attributes. To me, our single-vineyard wines have good concentration of flavor, yet they also have nice elegance, persistence on the palate. The Edna Valley bottling was awkward.

Do you know if you'll ever have a Stone Corral bottling?
Well, I don't know for sure. But there are two other bottlings of Stone Corral, from Stephen Ross [Wine Cellars] and Kynsi, and they both chose to release Stone Corral bottlings in 2003.

Did you taste them?
Yes, we all get together and taste our wines and discuss what we're going to do.

So were their vineyard designations from Stone Corral more deserved than yours?
Steve's is, for sure. I haven't tasted the Kynsi since they bottled it. Each winery has different blocks they control.

And his blocks are better?
Well, I have a strong suspicion. For one thing, he used more new wood than we did.

New oak can't improve a wine. It just makes an average wine oakier.
That's true. I think the really significant thing he did was select the very best he got from Stone Corral and made a bottling, then he declassified the balance to his Edna Valley bottling.

So you didn't have enough good barrels to do the same thing?
Well, eventually we might do that, but we're in a different position than Steve or Kynsi, in that we already had two single-vineyard bottlings ourselves, and— I think we should shut off your tape recorder for a second.

Nope. Against the rules.
Uh, well, so, I think my own standards and expectations—what I expect to produce here as a single-vineyard bottling—the wine didn't meet those standards.

If it does meet that standard, what will you charge for it?
Forty dollars.

What are the prices on Rincon, Rosemary's, and Estate?
Estate is thirty-two dollars, Rincon is fifty, and Rosemary's is sixty-five.

Why is there that spread?
The market! When we started the single-vineyard bottlings back in '93, we set them at the same price. Over time, it was the demand for Rosemary's.

Do you feel there's a limit to how much you can get for a San Luis Obispo Pinot Noir?
I think one of the things that holds us back a little is that our appellation is not nearly as established or well known as the Russian River Valley.

Do you need the appellation name to push the price, or can the winery be so famous on its own that it drives prices?
I think the winery can, but being in a highly regarded, well-promoted appellation with a number of other wineries that are also doing good work, I think, enhances the ability of the winery to sell the wines for more money.

What is the difference between Rincon and Rosemary's Pinot Noirs?
The wines or the places?

Both.
Well, Rosemary's vineyard is cooler. It's a mile closer to the ocean and has a stronger marine influence. I think Rosemary's tends to be more elegant, a little bit more purity of fruit. Rincon tends to be more masculine, has a more mineral and iron component, and more tannin.

What about clones and selections?
We're learning about clones later than some people because our predominant clone, the one that has made most of the wine over the years, was [UCD] 2A, or Wädenswil. We're certainly seeing differences as we start with the Dijon clones—like 667 tends to produce darker, more tannic wines, while 777 tends to produce very dark but softer wines, 115 seems to be a little softer, and certainly all three are lower in acidity than Wädenswil. They also have smaller clusters and smaller berries. But all of these vines are significantly younger than our older, original plantings, which are about twenty years old.

What is the impact of vine age on Pinot Noir?
I think the impact of vine age on everything, assuming you're growing grapes the way we are, in a good place, is really significant. But you have to take care of them, and farm with moderate yields, and make sure they're happy and healthy.

What percentage of Rincon and Rosemary's fruit goes into the named wines?
On average, we're producing somewhere between 400, 500 cases of each in a vintage. It ends up being maybe 25 percent.

Does it tend to be the same blocks or rows?
Very much so.

Why?
I think it's mostly site, but what's happening in both vineyards—in West Rincon and Rosemary's, actually—is, we've got all these new plantings that are getting really good really quick, and I think it's because of the way they're planted, at higher densities. So I think they're better cared for and better farmed.

Is there equivalent progress in the winery?
This year, actually, is going to be a very important year in the winery. Steve Rasmussen, who has been with us since 1986, went back to a consulting role.

Why?
Well, Steve's always been interested in new projects, and he's actually setting up a new winemaking operation up in Templeton, working with a grower

on a custom-crush operation. It's his own deal, and that's something that's very appealing to him.

There was no falling-out between you two?
There was a mutual decision. . . .

Is losing Steve a matter of concern? When a winery loses its longtime winemaker, the style almost invariably changes.
Well, once we made the initial decision that Steve was going to leave, my initial thought was, "Okay, gee, I guess I'm going to hire another winemaker. But I want to be very careful, because I don't want to change the style." I mean, a winemaker who comes in here is going to have to understand that their role is not a stylistic thing. It's about continuing what has been established.

What is your role? Do you get involved in the winemaking process?
Extremely. I'm very hands-on. I'm not a winemaker, but I certainly have opinions about things like how much sulfur dioxide we're going to use at the crusher and how much new wood to use.

What is the Talley Pinot Noir style that you don't want tinkered with?
I don't want a huge, high-alcohol, low-acid, low-tannin, tutti-frutti—I don't know how to describe it. There are a lot of wines from California that I consider undrinkable.

From where?
All over. I'm not going to say, "Gee, I had this wine the other night, and I hated it." I taste wines all the time that I just consider undrinkable. I mean, they have these wonderful aromas and initial flavor that I really enjoy, but after that, I can't drink any more. It's palate fatigue. It's too much.

Do you think this problem is getting worse?
Well, there's certainly been an evolution toward the bigger style throughout California premium wine. Everything's getting bigger and richer, and our wines have, too. But as this whole thing goes up, if Talley Vineyards is here in this continuum, we're just all kind of rising like that.

To what do you attribute this phenomenon?
Better viticulture and picking riper grapes.

How much riper are you picking than ten years ago?
Oh, I would say, 20 to 30 percent riper.

Why? Are the critics pushing you?
Well, I've never tried to, like, "Okay, let's make a wine for Robert Parker."

That's never been my MO. But I think we're in a business where critics play a very important role, just as they do with film and other art forms. I tend to pay more attention to the general consensus of what people are saying, as opposed to what one particular person says. If the general consensus is good, that's good. If the consensus is bad, you probably ought to look at what you're doing. And we have been blessed over the years that the general consensus has been positive.

Is there, aside from a Talley style, a San Luis Obispo style to Pinot Noir and Chardonnay?
Well, I think that there is something distinct about this little area. I've felt this way for a long time, ever since John Alban got started right around the corner, and extending up to where Domaine Alfred is, and out to Laetitia [Vineyard & Winery]. The wines from this area have this elegance and this acid profile that makes the kind of wine that I enjoy. I've had wines over the years from Laetitia, from Alban [Vineyards]—I just had a bottle from Domaine Alfred, the Califa, and that's a big wine, but it still has this elegance that I find really appealing. John has done the same thing for a number of years. They're these big, powerful wines, but they still have this elegance.

HEIDI PETERSON BARRETT

LA SIRENA, SHOWKET, PARADIGM, OTHER WINERIES

If there were a court of Napa Valley royalty, its reigning queen would be Heidi Peterson Barrett. Her dad is Richard Peterson, Beaulieu Vineyards' former winemaster. Her husband is James P. "Bo" Barrett, winemaker at Chateau Montelena Winery. Her sister, Holly, was married to Tim Mondavi. And Peterson Barrett is a superstar in her own right, the "wine diva of Napa" in *Time* magazine's words. After leaving Buehler Vineyards as winemaker in 1988, she surprised even herself by becoming a celebrity, famous as the maker of Screaming Eagle, Dalla Valle's Maya, Showket, and others. Peterson Barrett's name behind a bottle of Napa Valley Cabernet Sauvignon or Bordeaux blend is a virtual guarantee that it will be coveted. Yet for all that, it took Peterson Barrett years to establish her own brand, La Sirena Wines, and she has struggled to obtain for it the same prominence as her client wines. We met one fine spring day in 2005 in Napa Valley and chatted about her remarkable career.

Where are we?
Revana winery, in St. Helena. Dr. [Madaiah] Revana, a cardiologist, hired me to make wine from this vineyard. In 2004, after the winery building was constructed, I moved in my own wine, La Sirena.

Where do you make your other wines?
Screaming Eagle and Paradigm have their own wineries. Showket, Lamborn, and Jones Family are custom-crushed at Napa Wine Company.

Those are your current brands?
Yes. On occasion I'll do outside consulting work, but it's not my keep-it-in-your-brain winemaking, where I'm "it."

Let's jump into the cult thing.
Why not?

How does a wine become a cult wine?
I don't know that I'm the expert, but I've sort of gotten to be known for that. A couple things. One is limited production; it has to be hard to get. People like to have something not everyone else has. And it has to be not only high-quality once, but consistently. And then there's what I think of as the magic factor. It happened with Screaming Eagle, word of mouth, this wildfire undercurrent, person to person: "Have you tried this?" You can't make that happen.

How did your reputation as the cult queen of Napa come about?
I think with the 1992 Dalla Valle Maya, which I helped create. Also the '92 Screaming Eagle. So I had back-to-back [Robert] Parker 100s. I also had Grace Family [Vineyards]—three of the biggies. I got a lot of attention.

What was your reaction?
It put a smile on my face. You work hard, you hope people notice, and when they do, you feel pretty good about it.

Was the phone ringing off the hook with offers?
Somewhat. I'd been offered a lot of jobs over time, but early on, I switched from being a full-time winemaker to this more independent status because I had two kids, and I needed to be home.

What's your personal take on the wine diva thing?
It's kind of entertaining. *[laughs]* Why I've gotten so much attention, I think, is because I don't just work for one winery. My name keeps popping up. It's like, "Oh, her again," and they think, "Maybe it's not the vineyard, maybe the winemaker has something to do with it."

Is there a Barrett style across your wines?
There is, very much. I didn't really know what it was until I lined them all up at a couple of tastings. One they did with, actually, Parker, was kind of a Heidi wine seminar. A few hundred people came, and I'd never tasted all the wines together. And it dawned on me that they're all really distinct. They all show the variety, the vineyard, but my part is they're all really elegant and balanced. The style is unmistakable, and yet they're very different.

Are the differences exclusively due to terroir?
Vineyard. Yes, yes. My job is not to show off what I do, but "What's the best use, how can I help this block of grapes reach its maximum potential?"

How do you establish a style for a start-up wine that doesn't exist?
Okay. I look at the vineyard, and sometimes I get the hang of it right away, and sometimes it takes years. I'll give it my best guess, based on other wines I've made, how they've reacted to oak, cap management, fermentation temperature, type of yeast, all that. Or say it's a hillside vineyard, and I think it's going to be concentrated, versus valley floor, which is a whole different thing.

Do you feel there are differences between hillside and floor? Some people argue that with modern viticulture there no longer is.
I don't buy it. You could fool some of the people some of the time, but generally, hillside wines are more dense and concentrated, because they have better drainage, less soil, the vines have to struggle more, smaller crop. Versus valley floor, richer soil, bigger crop, more lush, broader flavors. There are exceptions. But I'm doing similar winemaking with both, and I see differences in the way they ripen and handle in the winery. I have everything from Jones Family and Showket [Vineyards] along the hills, to more valley floor or slopes, Screaming Eagle, Paradigm [Winery], and, going across Oakville, I used to make Oakford [Vineyards wine], which was very tannic. I mean, just in that Oakville strip, really different.

How do you decide what clients to take on?
The first thing is if I like the people. If they want to do something special. If they're passionate about wine, and it would be a fun project. Number two is location from my house. We live north of Calistoga, at the foot of Mount St. Helena, so anything within a half hour is my range.

Do you have a waiting list for clients?
I get a lot of calls, but I haven't taken anything new in years. If something exciting came along, I would have to drop something.

What do you charge?
I'd rather not say, because it varies. Some of my clients that I've had for a long time, we started with an agreement that, by today's standards, was not very expensive, and we've become friends, and it's hard to go back now. So I think it's pretty modest, compared to what some winemakers charge.

Would you consider Sonoma?
No. Not because I don't think they make some terrific wines "across the border," as we say. But realistically, when things are fermenting I must taste every

tank, every day, and so I'm going to four locations, and that maxes me out. Some days I barely get everywhere. But I thrive on it, in a weird way. It's like, "Yeah! Let's go, go, go." You run off that adrenaline rush for that six-week period, or whatever.

> Oakville is my territory.... It's just a magic little part of our planet that's best for Cabernet.

Do you see a difference between Oakville and Rutherford Cabernet?
Yes. Oakville is my territory. I know it pretty well. It's distinct, lots of cherry-berry flavors. In Rutherford, sometimes you get the classic Rutherford dust. But the fruit is different. I don't know how to describe it—not vegetative, that's too strong—but herbaceous? Maybe more like a dried herb character.

And Yountville is too cool?
It's starting to get too cool, yeah.

That would indict, say, Dominus [Estate].
They're right on the border. That's probably still okay. I just think the best wines are in this little pocket. It's just a magic little part of our planet that's best for Cabernet.

How do you make the decision of when to harvest?
Just keeping up on "How's ripening going, are the flavors developing, do we have tank space, what's the weather doing, do we have pickers that day?" And I have people sampling for me.

What do you mean by "sampling for you"?
Go out and grape-sample, fax me the sugar level. When we get close, I need to go out and start tasting and walking the vineyard.

What is that range that brings you into the vineyard?
Pretty much anything over 22, 23, 24 [Brix].

When you're in the vineyard, what do you do? Plop grapes in your mouth?
Yup.

What are you looking for?
Flavor, ripeness, softness, color change, condition of the vine, any number of things.

Was La Sirena your first personal brand?
Yeah.

What was the first La Sirena wine?
Nineteen ninety-four Sangiovese.

Why did it take you twenty years to create your own brand? Did you always want to?
No. I finally did because an opportunity came along.

What?
That particular Sangiovese started as a custom crush that Dennis and Sara Cakebread hired me to make. I'd worked for Atlas Peak on Sangiovese. This was in the Sangiovese boom of the early 1990s, when everybody thought it was the next big thing. The Cakebreads were going to bulk the Sangiovese out, and I thought, "Why can't I buy it? This could be my chance." Within a month I got a bank loan, designed the label, and *boom,* I was in the wine business.

What wines do you make now?
The Cab, which I started in '96; Syrah from Napa and also from Santa Ynez Valley; and a dry Muscat Canelli called Moscato Azul, from Napa.

Why Santa Ynez? You're such a Napaphile.
Because I love Syrah from that area, Qupé, Andrew Murray, a couple others. Just delicious.

Is the Sirena Cabernet a single-vineyard wine?
No. It's from three vineyards. Most is one vineyard from Calistoga, and then a small vineyard right above my house, named Pearl. I've debated keeping it separate, but it's easier to have just one wine. And then a little Cab Franc from the Showkets, Oakville hills.

Do you own any vineyards?
Yeah, I own Pearl, and also Bo and I have fourteen acres planted in Calistoga, mostly Cabernet, and two acres of Syrah, which I keep for La Sirena. The Cab is contracted to Chateau Montelena.

How much does the 2001 La Sirena Cabernet cost?
One hundred twenty-five dollars.

That's a lot of money for an unproved wine.
Well, it started off at seventy-five, and everyone told me it was too cheap. Everybody else was charging one hundred–plus. I was hesitant, but I did raise it. But it's been the same price for five years. I sell most of it through wholesale, though, so it's not like I actually get a hundred and twenty-five!

What's the alcohol on the '01 Sirena Cab?
Mid 14s, something like that.

Have you been picking riper over the years?
The answer is yes. Absolutely.

Why?
More fruit character. But you can get carried away with it, and I try not to.
We had wines last year [2004] where it got so hot, so fast, that we had de-
hydration and sugars were too high. But I've always been more of that high-
middle-range thing, not over the top. I know people who are picking at 30
[Brix], you know? That's crazy. But I think people are going to smarten up,
I mean, that's the buzz I hear. It's like, "Whoa, we've got to get a grip on this
thing."

Long hang time seems to be an issue lately.
It's a pendulum. First, remember, there were these wimpy "food wines." Now
people are way over here, with what used to be called "late-harvest" wines.
But it will come back in this middle range of balance.

Do you think of the critics when you make wine?
Not much. You can't. If you focus on that, it's really distracting.

*There has to be a part of you that thinks, "Parker's going to love this. I know how
to make a 100-point Parker wine."*
But he doesn't always see it the way I hope. Of course, you hope you'll get
100 every time, but it can't happen.

*Have you ever reduced alcohol through spinning cones, adding water, or some-
thing else?*
Sure. Not frequently.

A lot of winemakers wouldn't admit that.
It's not something you want to advertise. As are other things we do in the
winery, like filtration, which has a bad rap. And it shouldn't. It's a valuable
tool. We filter most of the time.

*People think that the less a wine is manipulated, the better it is. I take it you don't
agree.*
No, because I've seen what technology can do. Even acidification, some purists
think that's a no-no. But have you tasted the difference between a wine you
didn't acidify versus one you did, if it needed it? Or the opposite is true. If
it's so tart it makes you cry, you just take out a little acid and use potassium
carbonate. What a difference that makes!

How come you're not at Dalla Valle anymore?
Before Gustav Dalla Valle died, in 1995, he asked me to continue the winery in the same fashion, which I agreed to do. A few months later, Naoko, his wife, fired me.

How important is marketing for selling wine, especially your own brand?
My deal with everybody I make wine for is, I don't do marketing, because I don't have time. If I did, say, one winemaker dinner a month for eight clients, I would never be home! But for La Sirena, I'm seeing the value of that now. This is my thing, I'm going to have to do this. It dawned on me last year: I've had this brand for ten years, and no one knows! So I've been going to tastings lately.

Do you like it? Because you seem—not shy, but . . .
I'm actually decent at it, once I get down and start talking to people.

What do you think your image is? A lot of people have heard of you.
Apparently they have. That's new for me. I'm just sort of holed up in my own little world, working and raising my family and growing my garden, painting and doing my life, and I get out, and some of them are, like, star status with me, they get all "Oh, my God."

Do they ask for autographs?
Oh, yeah. I sign a lot of bottles, which I'm happy to do!

Do you ever think of yourself as Napa royalty?
I don't think of myself that way. But I do think of myself as kind of an authentic part of the Valley.

How has the Valley changed over the years?
It's just exploded with wineries, and how expensive things have become, and the face of our towns has changed. St. Helena is all chichi. When my sister and I grew up, there weren't fences between vineyards. We used to ride our horses all the way to Ehlers Lane. Now you can't do that.

When my sister and I grew up, there weren't fences between vineyards. We used to ride our horses all the way to Ehlers Lane.

Do you drink a lot of expensive wines?
Things like [Guigal Côte Rotie] La Mouline, which I love, I'll have at a seminar where they're pouring. But I don't buy them.

Why not?
Well, I only started making decent money in the last five years. It's so funny, people think Bo and I—they have misconceptions. We're doing fine, but we're not what people think. I still drive a beat-up crummy old Subaru.

Do you think Cabernet Sauvignon will maintain its hold on consumers as the number one red wine?
Yes, followed by, I think, Syrah. It will really surpass what happened to Sangiovese, because Syrah likes to grow, and does well, in many different climates and soil types.

Do you think Napa Valley will always be in the lead in California on Cabernet Sauvignon?
Personally, I do. I put my whole career into Napa Valley because I've always believed that Cabernet is king and Napa Valley is the lead in that. You know, the climate in Sonoma is a little different. They're a little closer to the ocean, a little cooler. Even among Napa Valley, the way it's situated, you see a lot of differences, from Calistoga all the way down to Carneros. But probably the main area for Cabernet being Oakville north to Calistoga.

————————

In the summer of 2006, following the sale of the brand and winery, Peterson Barrett left Screaming Eagle Winery and Vineyards.

GREG LA FOLLETTE

DE LOACH VINEYARDS, TANDEM WINERY

It has been said of Greg La Follette that he could bring a church to tears about Pinot Noir. A winemaker's winemaker, La Follette worked for others for years (and still does) before garnering the resources to establish his own Tandem Winery along with his longtime friend, viticulturalist Greg Bjornstad. (The two split up late in 2005.) Tandem produces single-vineyard Pinot Noirs and Chardonnays that carry exploration of Sonoma County's varied *terroirs* to a fascinated extreme. La Follette, a youthful-looking forty-seven, and I chatted in 2005 in his office at De Loach Vineyards, his "day job" since 2004, when he was hired as chief winemaker by its new owners, the Boissets (Jean-Claude and Jean-Charles), one of France's most powerful winemaking families.

How did you get into winemaking?
I had a career doing AIDS research at UCSF. But I'd wanted to be a winemaker since I was seventeen, so in my late twenties I went back to school, at UC Davis, graduating in '90 with a degree in food science and technology with an emphasis on winemaking. I also took all the viticulture classes.

Where are you from?
I was born in Iceland, but my elementary years were spent in Germany. My dad was in the Air Force, but he believed in living "on the economy," not on

a military base, so he imbibed heavily in the local culture. My parents hauled me through wineries across Europe.

What was your first winery job?
At Simi, in 1984, working with Zelma Long. I knew I'd be going back to school, to Davis, and I wanted experience. I'd ride my bike up from San Francisco and stay at Zelma's house.

You'd ride from San Francisco to Healdsburg [about sixty miles]?
Yeah. I was a competitive cyclist.

How long did you stay at Simi?
Two years. Then, in 1988, I took a year and a half off for bike racing.

Did you have a sense of what variety you wanted to specialize in?
Well, I sure as hell didn't want to work with Pinot Noir!

Had you made Pinot?
No. But I was investigating Burgundian winemaking techniques and was quite interested in them. And I had come to love Pinot Noir.

Then why didn't you want to make it?
Because I wasn't crazy. I knew it was a difficult varietal.

When you talk about "Burgundian techniques," you mean sur lie *[aging wine on its lees], malolactic, barrel fermentation?*
All that. My thesis title was "Chemical and Sensory Influences of *Sur Lies* on Chardonnay Wines." At the time, you could count on one hand the people using *sur lie*. Dick Graff, with whom I did some research in '90, at Edna Valley Vineyard; Zelma; and Steve Kistler [of Kistler Vineyards in Russian River]. I tore his wines apart chemically to look at them.

Would you say you're more lab-oriented than many winemakers?
I probably have a greater technical background, from a chemical standpoint.

Do you think that's a help?
Yeah, I think so.

One thinks of sur lie *for white wines. Could you do a red wine* sur lie?
Oh, yeah. In my early days at Flowers, I was making these massive, angry Pinots that can only be made by angry young men. What I'd do was take a gallon of Chardonnay lees and dump it into the young Pinot, and stir it *bâtonnage*. Now that I'm older, I'm looking for grace and gentility, not just in my life but in my wines, too. But being out on the Sonoma Coast, the tannins were huge.

And the Chardonnay lees helped that?
Well, the yeast, being little bags of protein, grabbed on to those tannins and took them down. And the other thing the lees did was plump up that mid-palate and give more richness.

Around this time [early 1990s], you started working at Beaulieu with Joel Aiken and André Tchelistcheff. How did that come about?
I think Joel was interested in what I was doing. André was winemaker emeritus for three days a week. He was becoming infirm, but really passionate about Pinot Noir. They hired me to work on the Pinot Noir and Chardonnay programs.

> In my early days at Flowers, I was making these massive, angry Pinots that can only be made by angry young men.

Why did BV hire you for Pinot Noir when you hadn't had much experience with it?
Well, I had more than most. When I was cellarman for the Davis student winery, I'd investigated cold soak technique. Very few people had done that.

What was it like working with André?
Anything you could possibly read about André doesn't come close to as good of a man as he was. He himself was like a really great Pinot, so powerful yet so gentle. But he could be very demanding. Our early days were rough, because he thought I was a technical asshole. He'd say, "You should go back to Davis and be a researcher, because you're not thinking about the heart and the soul of wine."

That's why I asked earlier if you thought your technical orientation was a help, and I almost added "or a hindrance."
Yes. But, like Vladimir Nabokov, who said, "There is no art without science or fact without fancy," I'm a believer that the language of wine is actually the language of yeast biology, of vine physiology, of chemistry.

How long did you stay at BV?
Until '94. Eventually, André was so sick he couldn't come to the winery, so I brought samples to him. But he could raise a glass of Pinot to his nose, that's how intense this guy was. I was at his house, and a good friend, Michael Silacci, who's now winemaker at Opus One, was there. I'd been approached by Kendall-Jackson to fire up Hartford Court, and I was on the fence about it. Michael and André both said, "Look, this is your future, to start up this label, whereas at BV you're buttonholed as this research guy." That Sunday night is when André went into the hospital, never to

come out again. I followed his and Michael's advice and went with K-J and stayed into early '97.

Hartford Court [now Hartford Family Winery] was a Pinot house?
Yes, and Chardonnay, and a little Zin. I was excited about Chardonnay; but André loved Pinot, that was his favorite grape, and I caught the bug. So by '94 I'd said, "Okay, Pinot, I'm yours, take me."

What was it like working at Hartford Court?
It was fun, but what happened was, I got approached by Delicato to start up high-end brands and the San Bernabe vineyard. So I went to Charles Thomas, who was head of production at K-J, and said, "I'm going over to this other project and do all this stuff." And Charles said, "Why don't you write down what you think would be the coolest job in the wine industry?" I did, and he said, "Okay, that's your job."

What was it?
I just went around the K-J empire and looked at vine and wine quality.

But you weren't making wine?
Well, that was the problem. After a couple years, I came back to Charles and said, "I'm tired of babysitting everybody else's wines, I want my own." We talked about me getting my own brand somewhere in the empire. But he said, "You're doing too good of a job, we need you." Two weeks later, I was leading a vine-by-vine pick at the Martinelli ranch on the Gualala River, running ahead of the picking crew and flagging vines for the Grand Reserve Chardonnay. And I looked on the other side of the river, and Joan and Walt Flowers were picking Pinot.

Did you know them?
No. I thought, "That's strange, having another vineyard way out here." So I drove around the river to the other side and introduced myself.

You just walked up and said—?
"Hi, I'm Greg La Follette, what's going on?" And Joan, the night before, had read an article I had written about how to build a winery for minimum cash input and maximum quality. She said, "We've been looking for a winemaker."

This is in the Fort Ross hills, on the far Sonoma Coast.
Yeah, just two miles as the crow flies, or the seagull, from the ocean. High altitude, above the fog; people thought it was nutty being out there. Ten days and five meetings later, they hired me.

What was the challenge of growing Pinot Noir out there?
Oh, boy. Very challenging. The disease pressures are much higher, and your potential for harsh tannins is much higher. But it was a beautiful place. The grapes were fantastic. I loved living there, totally immersed in myself and the start-up of a new brand.

Flowers became a famous, culty winery fairly quickly.
Oh, yeah, right off the bat.

How did that affect you?
Well, it was good for my reputation. Until that point, I had been known as an intense, wine-focused guy who lived in his own little wine world and was feeding other people information. Now I had a chance to apply this to my own vision of what the wine should be.

Of course, it wasn't your winery.
Well, there was a promise of equity at the time.

How long did you stay at Flowers?
I was there over a span of six years. I stayed on as a consultant until harvest of 2001. I really wanted to do my own label. I'd gone through a divorce, I was a single dad, and it was tough for my kids to be up there, so far from civilization.

Where did you transition after Flowers?
I consulted all over the world. It was interesting to work with different people and make friends, but the downside was too much time away from my kids.

How did Tandem start?
In 2000, I was consulting for another winery and the owner gave me a bunch of Pisoni wine to finish for my own, in part as thank-you, in part as payment. Greg Bjornstad, whom I'd been working with for years, and I said, "Let's do what we've been talking about, start our own brand." Now we had fruit, barrels, things we couldn't afford before. Tandem made a couple hundred cases.

You weren't a rich guy?
Heavens, no. The depth of my pockets consisted of the hole in the bottom where you could wiggle your finger. There was this old apple processing plant north of Sebastopol. We signed a lease and I put out the call to all my original crew and growers who had been at Flowers, and we literally, in two weeks, had a barn-raising party, welding copper pipes, sweating, laying out conduit.

They did this for free?
No, I paid them.

Where did you get the money?
Selling shares of the new company. And my kids' college fund. Second mortgage on the house. My 401(k). I maxed out every credit card I had. It was scary. I had nine months of no hot water at my house because I chose to pay my crew rather than refill my propane tank. It was like the *Apollo* 13 mission. Failure was not an option.

You had the Pisoni wine. Where did you think you'd source your future fruit?
Oh, all these growers said, "Hell, we're going to work with you!" I'm not sure why they were willing to take a risk. Some of them, particularly the Sangiacomos, extended us two years of payback terms.

What do you make now at Tandem? Start with the Pinot Noirs.
Okay, we're making Sangiacomo—not Carneros, from the Sonoma Coast, where the Petaluma Gap coldness piles up against Sonoma Mountain, on the western side.

What else?
Van der Kamp and Silver Pines, which are also Sonoma Mountain; Keefer, in the Green Valley. Pisoni is in the past. We're working with Hellenthal, near Hirsch [on Creighton Ridge]. We're doing Hawk's Roost, which is here on Olivet Bench. And Kent Ritchie, in the heart of the Russian River [Valley], where the old Mark West Winery is.

Do you like making vineyard-designated lots of different Pinots?
I do, because each one has their own personality, and you can enter into this dialogue with these wines and listen to them and watch them grow. I love being a dad of six kids, because each is really different, and it's fun. I mean, it's challenging and frustrating, but you're making a difference in someone's life. And with Pinot, the winemaker can make a difference.

Did you ever have a bad vineyard?
I've been disappointed in my own interaction with the vineyard. I don't think there's such a thing as a "bad vineyard." André Tchelistcheff once told me, "Your job as a winemaker is to make each wine absolutely as good as it can be."

I understand that, but you couldn't make a great Pinot Noir in Lodi.
No, but I've worked with Lodi Pinot, and it has a place. I like seeing Pinot Noir on everybody's dinner table, and you have to have different price points.

Does Tandem own any vineyards?
We will, when we start making money.

When will that be?
I don't know. Right now, that large sucking sound you hear is money still going into the brand.

How will you make a profit? By increasing production?
Well, we're only going to get up to 10,000 cases. This year we'll stay about 6,600, because I can't afford to buy grapes or barrels. Once our debt gets paid down, that money can go into our pockets.

> Pinot Noir can love your tongue like no other varietal. It has weight and texture but can levitate.

I was in Healdsburg and saw your fancy tasting kiosk in that new little marketplace.
Yeah, it's a cooperative where we all share in the costs and help each other out.

You had Tandem T-shirts and some nice printed materials.
Yeah. Well, we didn't go to a printer for that. That's all off our laser-jet printers. We're not market whizzes; we've never laid out a dime for paying a marketing consultant. Quite frankly, I don't do a lot of marketing on Tandem. We sell out all our wine, so we haven't felt the need to hype it.

What's Tandem's most expensive Pinot?
Our auction block, fifty-four dollars, which is the only blended Pinot we do. It's the wine we give away to charity.

If you give it away, how do you get a price for it?
Well, we sell some off.

Do you think a vineyard-designated Pinot Noir is better than a blend?
No. It's only different, not better or worse. When you have a single-vineyard wine, you're always looking at the high points, the voice, and you don't care so much about the valleys. I mean, you work on those, but you want the purity of the voice of the vineyard to speak. But when you have a blend, you can work on front-to-back pull-through. If you have little potholes or divots, you can push those up. Either way, Pinot Noir can love your tongue like no other varietal. It has weight and texture but can levitate off the ground.

Was it last year you got hired by De Loach?
Yes, sir, 2004.

How's it going?

Good. What I've done is replace a lot of little clients for one large client, and I'm traveling less. The year before [new owner Jean-Charles] Boisset hired me, I was out of the country for three months. Now I'll be out maybe six weeks.

Can you make great Pinot Noir at De Loach?

You want to taste them? There's some crackerjack wines here!

That you made?

Yeah, in '04. But I have to say, the people here are veterans. They've been through hardship, bankruptcy, they have a lot of guts and a lot of heart. I'm really honored to be working with them.

RANDY ULLOM

Randy Ullom doesn't preside over California's largest wine company—that would be Gallo. But Kendall-Jackson's five-million-case annual production is entirely under his supervision. It's a job that might be daunting to most winemakers, but Ullom thrives in the controlled chaos of Jess Jackson's empire. A few weeks before this interview, Ullom had tasted me through his new line of limited-production Highland Estates wines, of which he was very proud. We talked at K-J's baroque-style visitors center, outside Santa Rosa, on a raw, cold December morning in 2005.

How did you get into winemaking?
The seed was planted in high school. I shouldn't have been drinking, but I liked wine better than beer. I studied mining engineering at the University of Utah, but skiing was more important to me. When the snow ran out, I decided to live the Endless Summer, only it was the Endless Winter. Went down to Chile to ski. While I was there I fell in love with a gal, and her father took me under his wing. He was a connoisseur of fine wine. So I went to the next level, ended up renting a farm in the south of Chile, and the neighbors taught me about grape growing and countrified winemaking. Came back to the states and decided I had to get my career aligned with my passion, so I made a beeline to Ohio and studied grape growing and winemaking.

Why Ohio?
My family had moved there, and I was on my own dime, and I utilized their status as residents to get me through school [at Ohio State]. I did my practical training in New York State. I knew *Vitis vinifera* was the way to go, but it was very cold there, so you had to work with these hybrids that had this funky, foxy aroma and flavor. I spent five years constantly trying to get Chardonnay to grow, and Merlot. But every year or two, with the cold climate, they'd get wiped out. Then in '81, seeing there was no future in New York, I needed to get to where the action was, California. Came out, got a job at De Loach.

Where you were promoted to winemaker and vice president. How long were you there?
Thirteen years.

You went straight from De Loach to K-J?
Yeah, in 1993. I was brought on board to start up a new brand, Camelot, in Santa Barbara, and also to reopen the Edmeades winery, in Mendocino, and thirdly to start a winery in Chile.

Let's get this straight, because the Jackson empire is complex. In the beginning, Jess had Kendall-Jackson.
Right, the main winery.

And he bought Edmeades?
Right. It had been mothballed.

And he started Camelot from scratch?
Yes. He wanted a brand that would be what's called a "flanker" to K-J.

And what was the operation in Chile?
Well, it had no name. It didn't exist. My task was to reconnoiter the country and ascertain where we could buy land and set up a winery. Today it's called [Viña] Calina.

How did you become aware of the opening at K-J?
I had been recruited by them before, when Jed Steele was leaving. Jess was looking for someone to replace him, and I was on his hit list. But I was in heaven at De Loach. Our roads met up again in '93, and he offered me this position.

If you were so happy at De Loach, why did you leave?
The carrot was that De Loach did not have the capacity for me to go down to Chile, which was my dream.

So here you're going from a little winery to a big, big winery. Was that intimidating?
Not at the beginning, because it was just a larger family winery, and I was just a portion of that. I think the awe came in 1997, when Jess asked me to take over all of Kendall-Jackson. Now, there you're looking at a fair amount of wine! But once you figure it all out, it's no big deal.

What does "all of Kendall-Jackson" mean?
It pushes five million cases. Winewise, Kendall-Jackson, including Vintner's Reserve and Grand Reserve, Stature, and inclusive of that is Edmeades, Pepi, Camelot, Collage, and, today, Dog House and Wine Block.

What part of Jackson's brands are you not connected with?
Well, we're all interconnected, but on the Artisans & Estates side, it's Stonestreet, Avalon, Hartford, Cambria, Vérité, Lokoya, Cardinale, and Matanzas Creek.

Is there a hard-and-fast rule for what goes to K-J and what goes to Artisans & Estates?
Absolutely. If it has a winery and its own property and its own brand, it will be on the Artisans & Estates side.

Let me read you this quote from [Robert] Benson's book [Great Winemakers of California]. He's interviewing Warren Winiarski, from Stag's Leap [Wine Cellars]. Question: "Do you think larger wineries can produce wines as good as those from the small wineries like your own?" Answer: "I think they can, but it's more difficult in principle. If you have to watch over a hundred children, you can't spend the time with them you could if you had three children. You can't watch their development, nuances and small things going on. It's just not possible for the human organism to exceed its limitations." Reply, please.
Well *[smiles]*, that's an interesting answer. We can be on an equal par, if not a better par, than some of the smaller wineries because we have a tremendous team of people. Myself, I oversee the whole enchilada. We have a multitude of wineries up and down the coast, and we have, in each, a winemaker with at least two assistant winemakers and an enologist. They're my eyes and ears. And there's only one person who tastes every single wine there is—myself. It's a lot of tasting, but you are tracking and following what's going on.

It must have taken a while to get this working smoothly. What were some of the speed bumps?
I think one, believe it or not, was just information. When I started, being able to figure out what you had in your inventory, all the different lots, at all

the different wineries, being able to grasp what you had in wine and grapes. As we've gotten bigger, we've not done what a lot of people would think, which is, Well, you're getting bigger, so just get bigger tanks. Ironically, we do the opposite. We have more lots now than ever, and it's harder! It's ludicrous. But the way we do it is what affords us the opportunity to come up with all these tremendous quality levels of wine, to keep every single lot separate. I go back to the problem of information, to be able to get, at any time, "What have we got and where is it and how much? What's the detail?" It was impossible, and I couldn't believe that anybody could work like that. So we tried to come up with a plan, and in those days, the IT system, the manner of moving information around was really Neanderthalic.

This was as the Internet—
—was starting, and you'd have to do these fancy dial-up connections, and hook up all the wineries, and you'd lose someone—it was ridiculous. So one of the neat things, and this is where K-J is such a fine company, you get the green light. We designed our own in-house system for keeping track of the database. We call it BIMS, bulk inventory management something or other, and it was designed by winemakers, the dream of all dreams.

You have your own software people?
We do, and they are worth their weight in gold. We thought it would take a year. Well, it took four years, and it's so good, it's the envy of the world. We can see right down—because we have so many lots, when you look at just Chardonnay, a thousand-plus lots—we can subdivide each lot, know every barrel, how many new and old oak, or two-year-old oak, what's the grain tightness, the wood source, and we can go in and cherry-pick out within each lot.

What's the relationship between the winemakers on the spot and you?
I give them guidelines. We have a game plan, we get together a lot, we go to tastings. There's a window. If they stay within the window, we're all good. If someone wants to deviate off course, we talk about it. It's really an incredibly well-oiled Swiss watch.

How many different varieties do you make?
Labeled? Fourteen or so.

What's your case run on the Vintner's Reserve Chardonnay?
Several million.

What's your lowest case run?
Highland Estates. Hawkeye [Mountain Cabernet] was 185 cases last year.

Didn't I hear that 100 percent of K-J grapes are now estate?
Yes.

What does that mean?
We either grow the grapes ourselves, or we have an evergreen contract from a third party, meaning we control their farming for a minimum of three years.

What had been the situation before?
Before, we would buy grapes on the spot market under a one-year contract, a two-year contract, and we didn't necessarily have the right to dictate what should be done in the vineyard.

Why did it take so long to reach this 100 percent estate status?
Well, the idea just came about a year ago. We got a special dispensation from the BATF [the former Bureau of Alcohol, Tobacco, and Firearms, now TTB] to be able to use this on our label, because historically, "estate-grown" meant you're limited to one appellation. We're multiappellation, so we had to get permission from the federal government to blend across appellations.

> The most versatile of all grapes, that you can grow pretty much anywhere, is Syrah. And it's soft and smooth and silky and sexy.

How many acres does K-J own?
Well, we have twelve thousand acres of vineyards owned. And farmed, I think, twenty-five or thirty thousand total.

Are all those coastal?
Oh, yes. Every single acre we have is coastal and only coastal.

Tell me about Highland Estates. This is a commitment to individual vineyards, correct?
Yes. The ultimate expression of *terroir.* It's showcasing one block, or not even one block but one portion of a block. Because we're very proud of the vineyards we have. For Bordeaux reds, everything is North Coast mountains or hills. It's the hardest area to farm, gives you the lowest yields, but the best quality.

How many wines are there in the Highland Estates tier?
Five are distributed nationally, and a total of twelve or fourteen that are sold through our wine club, or online, or through the tasting room.

What are case productions?
Oh, 250 to 500 and change.

How does an individual vineyard get included in Highland Estates?
It has to have shown stellarly year in and year out.

Who makes the final decision? Jess?
On what part?

That we're going to label this property.
Well, he'll come up with the theme, the desire, the direction, and then we come up with, where are the best spots?

The nominees.
Yeah. Then we work with marketing. Then we present the list to him. In the end, he's signing off on what he believes in.

> I think K-J can give most other wineries a good run for their money. We are on an equal footing, vineyardwise. We've got the resources, the barrels, the people, the wineries.

Is there any one wine you feel personally closest to?
Well, you like them all. It's like asking which child is your favorite. They all have great attributes. I love the Chardonnay for the complexity and the logistical challenge. Pinots of course are so much fun because they're so challenging in the vineyard and during fermentation. North Coast Bordeaux, because you're climbing all over the best scenery and best mountains, Napa and Sonoma, the most intense grapes. They all have their neat parts.

Have you ever done your own wine thing?
Umm, not really. I've done the garage stuff, but after a while, you do it all day, then you come home, do it some more, and say, "Oh, wait a minute here." As for a parallel brand, I don't think it's fair to whomever it is you're working for if you can't give them 110 percent. If you're trying to do something else, there's always a conflict, and if there was a role reversal, I don't think I would really appreciate that.

Are you doing a Pinot Gris or Grigio?
Not at K-J, but on the Pepi line.

Pinot Grigio has become the hot new—
—hottest thing going.

So are you working on something now?
Not at K-J. We've thought about it, but basically, we wouldn't be a leader in the market because it's already established. We could join the market, but all of our indicators say we're too late, so why bother?

Is there a variety you're taking the lead on?
Oh, definitely Syrah. It's the next variety of choice, especially coming off Merlot and the limitation there is to good Pinot Noir, and the fact that Cabernet tends to be a little tough and rough for the masses, so to speak. So we're thinking, "Well, what's the next [red] wine?" Pinot we've been banking on, and that movie *[Sideways]* was a catalyst, but there's a limitation for Pinot, you can only grow it in so many areas. But the most versatile of all grapes, that you can grow pretty much anywhere, is Syrah. And it's soft and smooth and silky and sexy and easy to say, so that is the next stepping stone. And from there, you go to Cab, which we're prepped for also.

Anything exotic? Tempranillo, Dolcetto, Nebbiolo?
No. They're ultra-minisculey-niche-market, there's no future.

Is K-J still growing, casewise?
Yeah. Not as radically as we were, but that's because we've pared things down to become estate, so that limits our growth rate, and we've also been raising our prices. We made a strategic decision to not get too used to this volumetric growth we had in the 1990s, to slow down and focus on the good side of life and not chase cases, which means lower prices and getting into ditch warfare.

You have no plans on leaving anytime soon?
I'm very happy here. I'm incredibly fortunate to have the position I have, because it's one of the few in the state—there's probably five guys that have something similar—and it's a tremendous honor, and a hell of a lot of fun.

A lot of people wouldn't take your job if it was offered to them.
Yeah, that's true.

Do you still think of yourself as an artisanal winemaker?
Yeah, basically, just with a lot of barrels, and lots and lots of blocks!

Do you think you can make a wine, in any variety, as well as any other winery in California?
Oh, that would be presumptive. But I think K-J can give most other wineries a good run for their money. We are on an equal footing, vineyardwise. We've got the resources, the barrels, the people, the wineries. I'm not going to say we can guarantee unequivocally equal—I mean, that's not our style. But we'll give them a good run!

DOUG SHAFER AND ELIAS FERNANDEZ

SHAFER VINEYARDS

Shafer Vineyards is one of those can't-do-anything-wrong wineries, and one of the few in this book with a double interview—because winery president Doug Shafer (at right in the photo opposite) and winemaker Elias Fernandez are joined at the hip. The interplay between the two reminded me of an old married couple. They complete each other's sentences, they laugh at the same shared memories, and even though Shafer is Fernandez's boss, their connection is of the best-friend type. As we sat in a little room at the winery, nestled below the rocky Stags Leap palisades, in July 2005, they reviewed their long relationship, plans for the future, and the intricacies of Shafer's astounding Hillside Select Cabernet Sauvignon.

Where are we?
DS: Stags Leap District, the southeast portion of Napa Valley. It's cooler than Oakville and Rutherford because we get those breezes from San Francisco Bay.

What is the orientation of the vineyard?
EF: We have a mixture of exposures, so in any year, one will do better. The southwest exposure right here, behind us, has always been in Hillside Select.

Are all Shafer wines 100 percent from the estate?
DS: We source about 10 to 15 percent from other growers.

EF: But Hillside Select, obviously, is all our fruit.

DS: Here at the winery, we have fifty-five acres, all Cabernet Sauvignon. And Hillside Select's 100 percent Cabernet.

When was the vineyard planted?

DS: We moved here in '73 from Chicago, and my dad, John, put in Chardonnay, Zinfandel, and Cabernet. In '78 he made his first wine, the '78 Cab— a famous wine, still holding up. Over the years, we wanted grapes growing in the best places, and it was silly to have Chardonnay here, too warm. So we went to Carneros and turned this ranch into Cabernet. Hillside Select has evolved into a feeling that this is a wine of a place, this is what Cabernet Sauvignon on the hillsides of Stags Leap District does.

Your dad had been doing what?

DS: Publishing textbooks.

He came out here as a second career?

DS: He was supposed to be semiretired, a gentleman farmer, if you will. Ended up in Napa because people said that's the place to go. He was aware that the wine boom was happening, that it was going to be the next big thing.

> This place had been on the market for years....At the time, no one planted grapes on hillsides.
> —Doug Shafer

EF: What he's said is that he had read books about what a great vineyard should be, and it should be on a hillside.

DS: This place had been on the market for years. Heitz had looked at it, [Joseph] Phelps [Vineyards], no one wanted it. So he bought it. At the time, no one planted grapes on hillsides—Elias grew up here, he knows it better than I do—because it cost too much to farm.

Doug, did you graduate from UC Davis?

DS: Yeah, in viticulture. But I decided I wanted to teach school, so I got my teaching credential, and in '79 went to Tucson and taught junior high. Didn't stay; realized I couldn't change the world, and decided to come back to wine. Dad said, "Great. But I don't have a job for you." I said, "Fine, I don't want to work with you." I got a job as assistant winemaker with Randy Mason, over at Lakespring Winery. Dad had a winemaker, but when he moved on, Dad said, "You want to be the winemaker at Shafer?" This was 1983. And I said, "No. I don't know enough," because I was just hauling hoses, you know? And he said, "Well, I have a problem. Napa's a small valley, and if I hire somebody else, a Ken Deis [of Flora Springs Wine Company] or Craig Williams [of Joseph Phelps], they all know that Doug Shafer's over there, learning, and will probably be coming back." Dad was using Chuck Ortman as a consultant, so he said, "We'll just up Chuck's time, and you can work together." And that's what we did.

When was the first Hillside Select?
DS: That same year, '83. What happened was, I inherited the '82s, and they were all separate lots, and there was one from our Sunspot vineyard that was really good. I told Dad, "I think we should keep it separate. Let's have a Reserve," which at the time everybody was doing reserves. So that was our '82 Reserve, the precursor to Hillside Select.

And Sunspot vineyard is—?
DS: Right behind us, a block.
EF: A true southwest exposure.
DS: Always the backbone of Hillside Select.
EF: Sunspot gets that morning sun and also the late sun, just seems to always have intensity. It's also the Eisele clone.

Why did you change the name to Hillside Select in '83?
DS: Because I got tired of explaining: "Why is it Reserve?" "Well, it's our best lots from the hills that we select," blah, blah, blah. So we came up with "Hillside Select" to describe it.
EF: Also, at that time *reserve* started to become a common name. There was a $3.99 Chardonnay with "Reserve" on it—it didn't mean anything, so that's why.

What is the elevation of the vineyards?
EF: Between five hundred and eight hundred feet.

Has your canopy management changed over the years?
EF: From the California sprawl when I got here, early in 1984, Sunspot was no wires, all over the place. Today it's all vertical [shoot positioning].

What is the oak regimen on Hillside Select?
DS: A hundred percent new French oak.
EF: Medium toast to medium-high toast, thirty-two to thirty-four months.

Do you toast heads?
EF: Some of the coopers, yes.

Why do you put on that much oak?
EF: Well, yeah, that's a lot of oak. In the early days we used around 30 percent new oak. But the wine didn't taste very oaky, it was still very fruity, so

we opted for 50 percent. And as we developed the new trellis system and got smaller berries, the wines got more intense, so they could handle more oak. We feel 100 percent adds to the whole package, the power, the elegance, and the barrels have very sweet tannins.

Elias, when did you meet the Shafers?
EF: My last year at UC Davis. I graduated in 1984.

Why did you go to Davis?
EF: My parents brought me to Napa Valley; they were farmworkers. I was born in Stockton, so they worked in the San Joaquin Valley and migrated with the crops. Napa Valley at that time was walnuts and prunes, in the early '60s, when we moved here. I graduated from St. Helena High School in 1979. I was planning on attending college and happened to get a Fulbright Scholarship in music, actually, to the University of Nevada–Reno. I played jazz trumpet. But I didn't want to be a starving musician. So I asked around: "What can I do to come back to the Napa Valley?" and it was either construction, real estate, or this wine boom that was starting.

> I played jazz trumpet. But I didn't want to be a starving musician.... It was either construction, real estate, or this wine boom that was starting.
> —Elias Fernandez

Were you personally into wine?
EF: No. But in college I worked at Louis [M.] Martini [Winery], in summer on the bottling line, so I kind of saw the inside. After that first year I transferred to UC Davis's enology program. Once I got into that, I never looked back. In 1984, when I was about to graduate, on the job board at UC Davis there was a posting for someone to interview at Shafer. Doug was the only one working here at that time.
DS: It was lonely!

So you got the job as assistant winemaker?
EF: Cellar rat!
DS: At that time, everyone knew "assistant winemaker" was a glorified cellar rat.

When did you become winemaker?
EF: In 1990, and in 1994 he [Doug] was gracious enough to give me the title.

What is the collaboration between you guys?
EF: It's probably unique.

DS: It's very unique. When I started in '83, I was trying to figure out how to make wine, helping Chuck Ortman. I needed a cellar rat, so I hired Elias. He was as green as could be. And so there we were: Dad with no real wine knowledge, I'm green, Elias is even greener. And the way it happened was, it was a group effort.

EF: We were all for the same cause.

DS: It wasn't like, "I'm the winemaker, do it my way." It was like, "What do you think?" We'd sit in the lab, go back and forth on blends. In our twenty-two years together, there's never been some type of rift or uncomfortable situation.

Does Hillside Select have a specific Stags Leap character, or a Hillside Select character?

DS: Both. The Stags Leap standard line is soft tannins, velvety texture, nice mouthfeel, tannins there but not harsh. Hillside Select is all that, just the concentration's turned up three or four notches.

How much does Hillside cost?

DS: The 2001 is $175. It was $150 for four years. Costs go up. Supply and demand. If it was $175 and it wasn't selling, it wouldn't be $175 next year. Count on it.

Do you feel you have to have price parity with other superexpensive Cabernets in order to be perceived on that level?

EF: He and I would say no, but John Shafer would say, "You're damned right!" *[laughs]*

What else do you own in Napa Valley?

DS: Red Shoulder Ranch, which is Chardonnay in Carneros, and moving up into the Oak Knoll area, about seventeen acres of Merlot, twenty-five acres of Syrah and Petite Sirah, and twenty acres of Cab. And just north of there, we have another twenty-five acres of Cab.

What do you do with the Syrah and Petite Sirah?

DS: Put them together and make Relentless, which is 80 percent Syrah and 20 percent Petite Sirah. The name is an honor to Elias, for over twenty years of relentless pursuit of quality.

What was the first vintage of Relentless, and why did you do it?

DS: Nineteen ninety-nine. He and I would go out for dinner, have a cold beer and a steak, and we'd always be ordering Syrahs and going, "Gosh, this is good." We just were digging it.

Why put Petite Sirah in there, too? Syrah's a noble variety, while Petite Sirah isn't.

EF: Well, it has a lot of history in Napa Valley. We knew there would be a lot of Syrahs coming out, and we wanted to be different, to add a little bit of the old-time Napa Valley and then the Syrah from Europe.

When did you start making Red Shoulder Ranch Chardonnay?

DS: Nineteen ninety-four. We'd been making Chardonnay from the start, wallowing in that Chardonnay ocean, and we started buying fruit from Larry Hyde, down in Carneros, and seeing how much better it was than up here, and that got us thinking. So we bought that ranch, planted Chardonnay—

EF: Tell him about the scores.

DS: Oh, God, the scores.

EF: And John, you know—*[laughs]*

DS: Well, we asked our distributors, "Give us your take on Shafer," and they'd say, "Look, Shafer: nice people, great red wines, white wines suck." In '84, '85, we had the same [Chardonnay] score in the *[Wine] Spectator,* 68, just brutal. That's when I thought about retiring! So we had this Carneros vineyard, hadn't really gotten the fruit yet. In '94, Elias had been promoted to winemaker, and Dad comes in and goes, "Doug, I'm really happy. We're succeeding, we're making money, we've got a good reputation, but I'm pissed off about the Chardonnay!"

EF: Yeah. *[laughs]*

DS: "So fix it!" And he gets up and leaves. So Elias walks in. And I say, "Hey, sit down. You remember we got you that promotion to winemaker? You got a raise, but, you know, more responsibility [too]. So Chardonnay, fix it." And Elias says, "Okay, this is what I need."

What did you need?

DS: Well, fruit from Carneros—

EF: Different clones, new barrels. Our standard procedure with Chardonnay was aging eight, nine months in barrel. But we said, Red Shoulder, we've got to hit it. So we tasted it and the wine was still so fruity, we thought, "Let's let it go through the harvest and bottle in January." So it ended up fourteen months on *sur lie,* stuff like that. Today, that's standard procedure, with 50 percent new oak. But no malolactic [fermentation]. That's one thing we held from the old days.

Why no malolactic?

EF: Malo destroyed that fruit Chardonnay character. It gets dominated by the buttered popcorn produced by the malolactic. And it drops the acid.

What else do you make?
DS: Firebreak.

That's your Super Tuscan?
DS: Yes. It's less than 10 percent Cab, from this estate. The Sangiovese is from the Oak Knoll vineyard.

Sangiovese is an awfully difficult wine to make, isn't it?
[both laugh] EF: And to grow!

Whose idea was it to plant Sangiovese?
DS: Dad's, in 1988.
EF: He'd gone to Italy, and that's where he got—
DS: —hooked. He just fell in love with it.
EF: He [John] just came and said, "I want to make Sangiovese." He [Doug] goes, "Sanjo- what?" *[both laugh]*
DS: I did say that. Dad looks at Elias and goes, "I paid for his college education."

Tell me about your heartbreak of Sangiovese. You must have had some difficult times.
EF: The first one, boy, were we surprised. It was like Kool-Aid, so we had to add a lot of Cab, 39 percent.

What was the problem?
DS: The acid was incredibly high, screeching—
EF: Higher than Chardonnay in Carneros.
DS: The tannins knocked you right on your butt. Nasty wine.

So is your Sangiovese where you want it now?
DS: Yes. Over the years, Elias and the guys in the vineyard have learned what to do, when to do it, to get good color and lower acidity. But it's going away. We're going to stop making it. No more Firebreak; 2003 is the last vintage.

Why?
DS: We've done very well with it, even though the [Super Tuscan] category isn't that great. But why hang out in this category that no one cares about? So we pulled the Sangiovese out and planted to Syrah and Petite Sirah.

Elias, did you ever have a hankering to go out on your own?
EF: Mmm, not really. Making wine here, I'm very happy, and it's a great organization to work for. It allows me to express myself.

One last thing, the whole late-picked—
DS: Oh, yeah—

—riper, higher-alcohol, long hang time thing.
EF: Hang time! *[laughs]*

Are you picking at higher Brix than you were fifteen years ago?
[both] Yes.

How much?
DS: [In] '90 we were picking at 24—
EF: Maybe anywhere between 1 and 2 Brix [more].
DS: So maybe 26.
EF: But there are people going way beyond that. It reminds me of the early '80s, everybody was like, "No sulfur is best." And then all these wines got spoiled and the pendulum swung back. We were actually one of the first that started picking riper, the flavors were better.
DS: I remember people saying, "I heard you guys are picking at 25. What's going on?"
EF: We used to pick Cabernet at 23 Brix. It was veggie—
DS: Ugh!
EF: Asparagus. Do you want that, or do you want blackberry and, you know, a little more jammy? But we didn't go beyond that other step, which is what is happening now. People are picking at 29, 30, and then watering back or using reverse osmosis.

What do the alcohols run on Hillside?
EF: 14.9, 15.5.

You're not bothered by 15.5?
EF: No. It's a balance of the acid, the amount of fruit that can handle that alcohol.

What do you make of the suggestion that when you get these high alcohol levels, there's an internationalization of flavors?
EF: Well, what if they were all 24 Brix? That's still international. I mean, I don't get it.

The implication is that high alcohol and late picking eliminate terroir.
DS: There are wines around the world made like Hillside Select, but do they taste like it? No. So I think it's more important to focus on "What does each area bring to the wine table?" and maximize that. In Napa Valley, the best thing we bring is big, fat, rich, voluptuous wines. Russian River Valley, South

Africa, Sancerre, New Zealand, they bring something else. That's what's so cool about wine.

Where do you guys see yourselves in ten years?
[both] Retired!
EF: And he can teach me how to play golf! *[laughs]*

KATHY JOSEPH

FIDDLEHEAD CELLARS

Kathy Joseph is a self-made woman. The odds were never much in her favor, but through sheer tenacity and smarts she mastered not only the winemaking skills, but the business savvy to succeed in a field that requires an enormous amount of cash—money she didn't have when she started. Today she's one of the most respected vintners in Santa Barbara County, and Oregon too, for her Fiddlehead Cellars crafts wines from both regions. We met up in 2006 on a windy late spring day in San Francisco, where she was visiting her parents.

How did you get into the wine business?
I thought I'd go to medical school. But when I tried studying humanities, it was a complete flop! So I dropped out and worked at Crate and Barrel, in Chicago, where I blossomed socially and honed my marketing skills. Then in 1981 I moved to California and applied to grad school at Davis in enology and viticulture.

That's a pretty big leap, from Crate and Barrel to UC Davis.
Not really. I'd been encouraged to go to professional school, and it didn't matter in what. And I had studied microbiology and biochemistry, so I had the prerequisites. I just dove right in and learned how winemaking was related to what I already knew.

Did you graduate?
No. I got a job, and I loved working so much that it diminished my interest in finishing.

Where was the job?
At Simi. There was no work in the cellar, so it was in public relations. I interviewed with Zelma Long, and she thought I might be an ideal candidate. I announced to my husband I was moving West, and if he was interested in coming, great! *[laughs]* He did, and here we are, twenty-six years later, still married.

What was doing PR at Simi like?
The great thing was, I was giving the VIP tours, so I learned to relate to educated consumers and distributors. And most importantly, I was invited to taste with Zelma.

You once said, "Zelma taught me how to taste wine and appreciate the layers of enjoyment in the glass."
And not only the artistic layers. She taught me the technical aspects, how sugar and acidity play off each other, how aromatics and tannins play off each other.

How long did you stay at Simi?
Five months. Every vintage, I worked for another producer. In '82, Joseph Phelps. [In] '83, for Bob Long [of Long Vineyards]. Each place I went, there was a little bit of education to be had.

When you went to Phelps, that wasn't PR, was it?
No. I worked with the cellar rats. I learned to hook up pumps, and about wine transfers, and filtrations, and fining, and driving the forklift and the dump truck.

The unromantic stuff.
Actually, it depends on how you look at it. I *love* that stuff. Even what some consider the cruddy jobs I find romance in!

Then you went for five years to [Robert] Pecota [Winery]. Was that your first long-term job?
It was. I started as assistant winemaker and quickly became winemaker. Bob was brilliant at business, and there was a lot to learn from him about negotiating a small winery operation that was underfinanced and had big goals.

You worked with, as you once said, "every varietal under the sun."
True. One way Bob survived in business was that he had a custom-crush operation. So I made, gosh, probably eight Chardonnays, ten Sauvignon Blancs, Zinfandel, Merlot, sweet Muscat, Cabernet.

Did you have a favorite?
Well, I grew passionate about Sauvignon Blanc. Pinot Noir, it's a different story, because I made very bad Pinot at Pecota. The fruit was from Carneros, and I made it like Cabernet, in a closed, cylindrical tank, pumped over, and kind of macerated quite a bit. It was a lean wine with very little aging potential. But the great thing at Pecota, I was offered an opportunity to do marketing. Bob couldn't get out on the road, so I was thrown to the wolves. I met a man who represented almost all of the wineries in Oregon, and I started tasting Oregon Pinot Noir. At the Steamboat Conference [an annual gathering of Pinot makers in Oregon], I was able to taste hundreds of unfinished Pinot Noirs before I ever made my own Pinot under the Fiddlehead label.

You would find wines you really liked, and then you would—
—translate how they were made. Yes. It was a very honest discussion. Not what you talk about with your distributor, but talk about with your cellar crew, trying to figure out, What size vats do you use? Do you want indigenous yeasts? Some years, stem inclusion was a hot topic, or SO_2 addition, or malolactic fermentation in a barrel versus in a stainless vat.

What about stem inclusion? It's still a hot topic.
I've played around with that. In my first years, I started with about 50 percent stem inclusion. Then I weaned myself to none. Santa Rita Hills fruit is big, dense fruit, and I just don't find that stems enhance the texture.

Greg Brewer loves stems.
That's correct.

He doesn't think of it as stem inclusion, he thinks of it as not removing the stems.
Right. Well, stems don't work well with the fruit I'm working with. But no commentary on someone else's approach.

How come you left Pecota?
I think I kind of topped out on my education there. I was a driven woman to constantly grow. Pecota was becoming a little bit normalized and routine.

Where did you go?
When I decided to leave, I was groping. I interviewed at a couple positions. At the same time, I started to write a business plan. The Fiddlehead concept

started to form in 1988, when I homed in on the two varietals that really excited me, Pinot Noir and Sauvignon Blanc.

Pinot was an interesting choice for the late '80s. It hadn't really—
—happened. That's right. Part of it was the passion created through this Oregon symposium. You taste enough wines that are delicious, you can really buy into what they're all about.

Who was making Pinot in California then that you liked?
Part of my mission was to zero in on where I should be making wine, so the districts that excited me were Russian River and Santa Barbara County. I set them in a different category from Carneros, because I found them to be more layered wines, spicier. They had greater intrigue for me. I knew I would be a small fish in a big pond in Russian River, and I could never afford property there. And Santa Barbara I just felt had tremendous potential. I approached Chuck Ortman, who was working at Meridian, and Beringer [Meridian's parent company] had just expanded that whole production, and he facilitated access to fruit from Sierra Madre vineyard. I bought the equivalent of about 150 cases.

Where did you make it?
I can't even remember the winery, because it doesn't exist anymore. It was in Paso Robles.

Where did the name Fiddlehead *come from?*
I groped for two years with what would be a great symbol of the brand. It's the fiddlehead fern. I decided, when I left Napa, that I did not want to name my brand after my family name.

When did you start doing Oregon?
The business plan had it written in right away. In '89, '90, I did exclusively Santa Barbara Pinot Noir. Then in '91 I added Sauvignon Blanc from Santa Ynez Valley and Willamette Valley Pinot Noir. In '90 and '91 I made the wine at Au Bon Climat; Jim Clendenen was incredibly gracious. And in '92 Talley built a new facility, so I made it at Talley. I moved around wherever there was opportunity to work at a place where I was the only additional custom-crush person.

And today you make wine in the so-called Lompoc wine ghetto.
That's correct.

How long did you make the Sierra Madre Pinot?
Through 1993. Then the partners in Sierra Madre were interested in selling the property, and the farming quality diminished. It didn't work well with

my objective, which was to make Pinot Noir in a reserve style that had great fruit and was meticulously farmed, whether I owned the vineyard or didn't.

Can a winemaker who doesn't own a vineyard have control?
I do think we have some great partnerships, where you buy the fruit by the acre and control crop loads. And many of the irrigation regimes and canopy regimes can be dictated by the buyer now. But it's never the same as owning, where you make every decision.

What happened when you lost Sierra Madre?
I didn't want to purchase just any grapes. Bien Nacido had quality fruit, but it wasn't available. So if I wanted to keep Santa Barbara Pinot in my portfolio, and I did, I would have to invest in a property of my own. I set out on a search for a location, and even though I was making Santa Maria fruit previously, my palate drove me to the cool, western part of Santa Ynez Valley, what is now Santa Rita Hills. The model was the old Sanford wines. I approached a farmer that was directly across the street from [the] Sanford & Benedict vineyard and made a proposal, which was ultimately accepted. That was in 1996.

Was it expensive? Because there was controversy over what you paid.
This was right at the beginning [of] when people started to expand Pinot Noir production, and I was part of the beginning of the wave. So was it expensive? It seemed like a reasonable value at the time. It was about 133 acres and probably about nine thousand dollars an acre.

A million dollars.
It was huge.

Did you have the money?
I didn't have the money to start Fiddlehead! To buy barrels! I mean, in 1989? No way! So I put together a limited partnership.

Who are your partners?
I have many. Family, friends, people I got excited about investment in this, quote-unquote, "opportunity." Because it's years and years before you see any sort of return.

What is Beringer's involvement?
I evaluated that if I only wanted to make about 3,000 to 5,000 cases off this large property [now called Fiddlestix vineyard], that I would have to spend a lot of time selling grapes, and that concerned me. So I explored other ways. It made more sense to break the vineyard into a separate company and approach a winery as a partner. The thinking was that a winery would be in-

terested in buying into the very high level of farming that I needed for Fiddlehead. So I wrote a partnership agreement. I established how the vineyard would be planted, to certain clonal material, and I wanted to live on the property, and to handle the daily management. My thinking was that a small winery would be best suited as a partner. But the problem was, number one, small wineries didn't have any money either; and two, they had their own ideas of what they wanted from a property. So I adjusted my thinking. I heard through the grapevine that Beringer was looking for a premium Pinot Noir property in this cool-climate part of Santa Ynez Valley.

Pinot was missing from their portfolio.
That's correct. So I approached Beringer. My lawyer thought there was no way they would express interest, but we closed the deal in a couple of weeks—on my terms. It offered them to buy in on a fifty-fifty basis. So that's the deal. I take what I want, first, and the other wineries right now receiving fruit are Taz, Hitching Post, Ampelos, Ancien, Arcadian, Bonaccorsi, Summerland, a small brand called RN Estate, umm . . .

What's the most expensive Fiddlehead wine?
It's a wine that was just recently created, Doyle. From Fiddlestix vineyard, I make three tiers of Pinot. One is named after the mile marker, Seven Twenty Eight, which is a tribute to the place. I do a barrel selection that highlights the best choices of the vintage, called Lollapalooza. And then, if in a given vintage there's a single barrel that is a stand-alone phenomenal wine, I give tribute to my husband, Tom Doyle, selling it for ninety-seven dollars a bottle.

I want to talk about alcohol levels.
Oh, good! *[laughs]*

You sound like you have something to say about it.
There's room for lots of winemaking styles. Not every bottle of wine is destined to age well, nor does the winemaker care if it ages. My winemaking is about balance, and my wines tend to age well because of that. But there are consumers who like big, giant, fruity wines and robust alcohol. I believe those tend not to age, but if you don't care, so what? Now, I do think one of the reasons there's a trend in high alcohol has to do with vine age. At Fiddlestix, when the vines were younger, flavor maturities seemed to happen at higher Brix, and that translated into higher alcohol. I believe that as the vineyards mature, there will be a trend in identifying that flavor maturity at lower Brix.

So are you picking at lower sugars as the vines mature?
Yes, but you also have to recognize that we're impacted by the vintage: 2005

allowed that to happen, relative to 2004, because it was a cooler year. So we need more history to test this theory.

Is your Santa Ynez Valley Sauvignon Blanc 100 percent varietal?
It is. My first, 2001, I tested the personality of Sémillon addition, but it overshadowed the Sauvignon qualities I was looking for, the fruit, the mineral components. And I also felt that in Santa Barbara County, at least, the Sémillon grapes I was working with are a little fat and flabby.

Are you doing any oak?
I make three styles of Sauvignon Blanc. One is Gooseberry—unoaked, strictly stainless. Another is all oak, almost 100 percent new oak with additional bottle age: Honeysuckle. And then the third is Happy Canyon, a blend of all the things I do, of stainless, of Sauvignon aged in older French oak, and a blend of newer French oak.

No interest in Chardonnay?
Nada! *[laughs]* None at all. It's not one of my fortes, and there's plenty in the market.

Cabernet?
No interest.

Syrah?
Well, the purpose of Fiddlehead was to be very focused and become quite good at working with two varietals exclusively. And we haven't talked about my late-harvest Sauvignon Blanc, Sweetie, and my rosé, Pink Fiddle!

> My thrill is that I design wine styles and decide where the grapes come from, and I make the wine and farm the grapes, and then I get out and sell it.

So what's next?
I'm happy with what I have. My thrill is that I design wine styles and decide where the grapes come from, and I make the wine and farm the grapes, and then I get out and sell it, and I write the point-of-sale material. There's a lot to manage. And I love the educational aspect, the interaction with the public. In Chicago I addressed a group of a hundred women who manage companies valued over one million dollars. So there's lots of different types of things I get involved in, and it's the diversity of what I do that keeps it very exciting.

Do you think women in winemaking have achieved parity with men?
No. You just can't get away with as much. And maybe because we're in a minority, we're forced to be that much better at our jobs. But I never recognized limitations to what I do because I'm a woman.

MARK AUBERT

COLGIN CELLARS, AUBERT WINES, OTHER WINERIES

He speaks of "the myth of Aubert" unpretentiously. Indeed, it would be pretentious if he pretended such a myth did not exist. With a list of consulting winery clients, current and past, as prestigious as that of any winemaker in California (as well as his own eponymous brand), Mark Aubert is like some wine god perched on a vinous Olympus, acutely aware of, guardian over, and surprisingly forthright about his image. We met up in August 2006 at Laird Family Estate, in Napa, where he makes his Aubert Chardonnay; he crafts his Pinot Noir at Colgin, where he is winemaker.

Did you always want to be a consulting winemaker?
No. I just wanted to be a winemaker for myself, but there were people who wanted my services, because of all the accolades.

Accolades for Peter Michael [Winery bottlings]?
Yeah, my ten vintages there. Critics, and then consumers, went hog wild. The energy was incredible. I was gainfully employed and happy, but people started asking, "Would you consider helping us?" I still get requests.

You recently said you rely more these days on the vineyard and precision farming and less on winery technique than you used to.
That's right. We do very, very complex farming on these grapevines, and we are incredibly anal-retentive about getting the exact amount of clusters per

vine, the nutrition of the soil, the row direction, all these things working together to get an intensity of that grape to reflect the site. I just capture that and exploit it in the winery by what we call neoclassical techniques.

Does precision farming trump location, so you can grow great Cabernet wherever the weather's right?
Certainly Napa's climate is conducive to getting it to a spectacular level of ripeness. So are parts of Santa Barbara, Lake County, Mendocino, Sonoma.

So is Paso Robles.
So is Paso Robles. It could be Mexico. And there's some great wines coming out of Washington State. So there are other places, but it also takes the mindset of the whole team of people to exploit the grapevine, not in the sense of high yields but of flavors. And that's very expensive, very time-consuming. A lot of people don't have that depth of knowledge. I mean, you can't just go out and expect to learn this thing overnight.

On the consulting side, you've worked for Peter Michael, Monticello, Rutherford Hill, Freemark Abbey, Sloan, Colgin, and others. Have you run into situations where you were overruled by a client?
Yes. I've never been terminated, but I have terminated clients because I feel the fits aren't right.

Give me an example of something that didn't fit.
It could be like new marketing people who are taking the brand in a different direction. You know, winemakers are pivotal in images of wineries, especially at this level I'm at where it's ultraluxury labels, and I think I know the market better than most people: what the consumer needs, what you guys in the press need. I certainly don't want to butt heads with bean counters. That would be one situation where I don't want to have my name associated with it, because image is very important to me. It's never about money. But marketing guys, bean guys can get in the way.

You told an interviewer in 1999 that when you went to Colgin, you wanted to get the alcohols higher.
[laughs] Did I say that?

I'm quoting, "14.5 is achievable." Now, I went and looked at the alcohol on the 2003 Colgin IX Estate and Cariad. They're both 15.6.
A percent higher! [laughs]

What happened?

[still laughing] Let's see: '99, yeah. A lot of the Cabs that Helen [Turley, Aubert's predecessor at both Peter Michael and Colgin] made were mid 13s. There was a change going on in the marketplace between, I'd say, '94, '95. Ripeness, ripeness, ripeness, we want to get riper tannins, riper skins. So what we were seeing is the need for longer hang time. And with the new clones and rootstocks that were used, the tannins were more aggressive, and we were on a learning curve. So the alcohols go up and up.

What was the role of wine critics in higher alcohol? You've been putting it on new clones and rootstocks, but people say it was driven by the media.

Actually, I should back up. There's one other innovation that happened in the early '90s: better phenolic analysis of wines. It seems like every five years we go through a revelation about phenolics. We study them and research and travel and taste and do all that stuff, and then a laboratory comes out with a really great over-the-counter analysis.

> We don't necessarily require scores to validate our work, but it is nice to have what I call my report card.

Explain phenolics.

Phenolics are constituents in tannins that give color, body, and ageability to wine. The advent of tannin analysis is what led us to [think], "If it tastes like this now, if I wait a week and reanalyze the grapes, they're going to taste even better." We basically get a chart of concentration of flavor.

How do you avoid waiting too long, with these heat spikes we get during harvest, so you get raisins or residual sugar? There are problems with waiting.

That's right. And that comes with a long tenure of the person working with the same vineyard for many years. Harlan [Estate]'s a great example. They keep learning and applying, and thus their wines get more and more concentrated. You can see they've hit a crescendo where they know they can't pack any more flavor into these bottles, and they're happy with that, so now they're just maintaining their image, their quality level. It's the same thing I'm doing.

Are scores important to you personally?

Yes and no. We don't necessarily require scores to validate our work, but it is nice to have what I call my report card. I've always strived to work hard and be awarded. That's ingrained in my mind since childhood. Work hard, keep your nose clean, and good things will follow. And a report card from wine writers is great validation.

You said in '99 you would make enough wine at Aubert "to get out to the right hands." What does that mean?
The right hands are, and this is true today, a mix of 50 percent restaurants and 50 percent direct to consumer. So we're balancing about 50–50 of a mailing list–type vehicle for our wine, across all states that are reciprocal.

Do you have to market, or are you so famous that you don't have to market yourself?
We don't have to market ourselves, but we are very in tune with the restaurant scene. I've often said that restaurateurs and their hard work and my hard work go together. We align ourselves with a distributor in a certain market that will authenticate the myth of Aubert and keep it parallel with what restaurants are doing and having an ambience. So we spend a lot of time studying and reading and cooking ourselves and traveling to these markets to make sure we're being supported and we're supporting them.

Who's we?
Me and my wife.

Do you have a staff?
No. I have an assistant who protégés with me, but my wife and I do all the marketing.

So restaurants are more important than wine shops?
Yes. By far. We don't sell to wine shops any longer. It's the hand sell, the story. We have all these ambassadors for our wine label out there, the restaurant staff, servers, sommeliers, chefs.

What are you making now at Aubert?
Chardonnay, Pinot, and soon to be a Bordeaux blend, from Howell Mountain. It's the culmination of twenty years of experience, the interest I have in Burgundy and Bordeaux, making wines that are classic single-vineyard bottlings. We have four single-vineyard Chardonnays, all Russian River and Sonoma Coast, either-or. The largest cuvée is Ritchie, at about 1,200 cases. The next one is Lauren, our estate Chardonnay, named after my daughter, at 1,000 cases. Then we have Quarry [vineyard], which is from Peter Michael. That's about 300 cases.

So he's still selling you fruit.
Well, 2005's the last vintage. Might be a moot point now. And then we have Reuling, about 450 cases. So that equals about 3,000 cases of Chardonnay. Then we have two single-vineyard Pinot Noirs, one from the Reulings, about 350 cases, and a new one, first vintage in '04, it's called UV, named after Ulises

Valdez [Aubert's viticultural manager]. That's on Laguna Road, right over the hill from Kistler, wonderful area.

What Merry Edwards calls the Golden Triangle.
That's exactly right.

And the Bordeaux blend?
Is from Howell Mountain. It's [vineyard manager] David Abreu's daughter's vineyard, called Lucia Abreu. The 2005 is the first vintage. It's in barrel now.

What will that retail for?
I have no idea.

It's got to break triple digits.
It'll be a hundred dollars, yeah.

Is that an imperative, that unless you charge a lot for your wine people won't take it seriously?
We have to put a value on the image, and since I'm making a $250 bottle for Colgin, if Aubert was fifty dollars a bottle, they'd be, "Oh, this can't be Aubert."

Who is David Abreu?
David is a good friend of mine. He's the premier viticultural manager for Colgin, Harlan. He does Screaming Eagle now; he did Araujo, Bryant. He's definitely the best in the business.

Who is Ann Colgin?
Ann Colgin is a dear friend of mine. She's the founder of Colgin Cellars. I just love her to death. She's the most amazing person. She has such a colorful and complex demeanor, she knows great wine, she's been the best client I've ever had.

Who is Alain Raynaud?
Alain Raynaud is Colgin's Bordelais consultant. They've always wanted to reach out to Bordeaux, to try somebody who was sort of new and fresh in American eyes, the media and winemakers.

In other words, not Michel Rolland?
As an example, not somebody who's around a lot. And Dr. Raynaud, his family's been in the wine business for four hundred years

What does he bring that you don't bring yourself?
A very, almost like an emeritus palate. He was a medical doctor. Then he went back to winemaking. He's a master blender. And he was the president of the Union des grands crus [de Bordeaux]. Very in tune.

Do you guys ever disagree?

Oh, of course. Sometimes things that work in France won't work here. And vice versa. I have no pertinent examples, but . . . we love this interchange. The exchange of information between two consciousnesses is fabulous.

You'd been primarily a Cabernet guy before starting Aubert. Why didn't you start out with a red Bordeaux, instead of Chardonnay?

Well, you know, I felt I learned so much about Chardonnay, and that's a much smaller niche, that niche of high-end Chardonnay, than high-end Bordeaux. And I felt like I had enough experience to do everything. I can make mind-blowing Sauvignon Blanc, if need be. But that's the wonderful thing about being on both sides of these counties. You know, Sonoma, I go over there and make Pinot and Chard, come over here and make Cab.

Best of both worlds.

I've learned how to mix the two. I've often said that I will never do a Chardonnay from Napa, and I will never again make a Cabernet from Sonoma.

You think you could make a good Chardonnay from Napa Carneros?

I'm sure I could. I'd love to get some Hyde [vineyard] Chardonnay, or Hudson [vineyard].

And why couldn't you make a great Sonoma Cabernet, à la Peter Michael? Some of the Vérité properties, I love those wines.

Yeah, I love those wines too, but now I've become a specialist in Bordeaux blends in Napa, and I don't want to deviate from that. I don't want to wear two hats again on those varietals. And my wife and I have agreed that we will not make Chardonnay or Pinot Noir for any clients. That's going to be our line. If Ann [Colgin] wanted to make Chardonnay, I wouldn't do it.

You make your Pinot from Sonoma grapes, but do you have thoughts on the other Pinot Noir areas of California?

Oh, yeah. We drink all the appellations.

Is it fair to ask if one is best?

Well, I don't want to become a target for other winemakers, you know, but I loved Santa Lucia Highlands when I was doing Pisoni [vineyards wine] at Peter Michael, phenomenal. Santa Rita Hills is fabulous. Oregon has not been one of the places I wanted.

Maybe you have a California palate.

Well, I love Burgundy, and Burgundy and Oregon are much more similar. I just don't feel that, uh . . .

Do you have any criticism of California Pinot Noir, and particularly the knock that some are Rhône-like?

Yeah. Very, very ripe, *surmaturité*. You know, my knock is the proliferation of pedestrian wines. The crop levels are too high, the wines are shrill, they don't have the *gras* [textural qualities of weight and density]. And Sonoma has a lot of this.

> My knock is the proliferation of pedestrian wines. The crop levels are too high, the wines are shrill, they don't have the *gras*.

Your Pinot vineyard is not on the Far Coast.
No.

Do you wish you were?
No. I don't think the Far Coast is any more advantageous than being eight miles in. I've never farmed vineyards that are two miles from the ocean, and I'll tell you, I would lose sleep [out there].

Tell me about the use of whole clusters and stems in your Pinot.
I don't do it because, very simply, whole clusters are a lot harder to manipulate with my winemaking criterion. You have to really take the fermentations to very vigorous [levels], to open those berries up and ferment. Much more advantageous with Syrah rather than Pinot. I don't like a lot of stem contact. We've done up to 20 percent whole-cluster experiments and discovered the ones that are 100 percent better. So that's based on my phenolic material in the vineyards, clones.

Do you have plans to have your own winery?
In three to five years Aubert will have its own winery, next to one of our vineyards. Hopefully. It doesn't come without a heavy price, but it's very important that we have our own winery to hang our hat, to conduct even further our quality winemaking. There's no waiting for anybody.

What will be the production capacity?
About 5,000 cases.

So you'll stay small.
Oh, yes. There's no reason to get any bigger. We want to stay small. It's much easier to manage, less headaches. You can keep on planting, but you reach a limit of quality, of image.

Well, this is a good segue to talk about image.
[laughs]

What do you think your image is, and who is it that perceives you as that person?
Ah, that's a good question. I didn't know you were going to ask me that. The whole image thing, I sort of have to pinch myself. I'm in my twenty-second year of making wine, and sometimes I just think, "How did this ever happen to me?" I don't promote myself. I don't contact writers. I've never contacted you to "Please come visit." No. We've been working in the trenches for years, and I think it's been recognized by a lot of influential people that the work I've done does not go unnoticed. I make wines that I know people will like. A lot of winemakers are very dogmatic about "I make wine I like." Well, that's fine. I've just discovered that my way crosses over a lot of boundaries of people who, you know, say, "I never drink Chardonnay unless it's from Burgundy." Well, except for Aubert, or Marcassin, or Kistler. "I never drink Pinot Noir unless it's from Burgundy." Well, and then they drink Aubert. So I've obviously realized something, and I'm able to exploit it, and then people recognize me for these particular achievements.

But also, being with the right people is very important to me for image. Working with a high-end cult Cabernet like Colgin—the original of the original Cult Five, Cult Six maybe—working at Peter Michael for a long tenure, not just a short little stint, like the recent winemakers coming out of there. You know, Luc [Morlet] wrapped up after five years, he said that was long enough. Bullshit. You've got to really put in some time, not just pop in and out. And a lot of my friends in the restaurant and the trades, they're my ambassadors, they're almost, if I were working for a PR agency, promoting us. All the places where Aubert appears on these wine lists, and it's usually one of the more expensive, we spend a lot of time with edification. We're always educating people. I'm not into taking anything, I just want to show people what we're doing, cultivating relationships.

Do you think you could be happy making wine in Lodi?
[laughs] Oh, sure. It would be like a gulag, right?

Your word, not mine!
Like the Russian front for the poor soldiers. But I would say, I could elevate Lodi! I wouldn't want to, but if it was my destiny, I'd make wine there. I love a challenge. I seem to have a natural ability to elevate things and make them better, being a steward of the land. I walk a fine line. I like to think I have good karma. It's almost a cosmic belief.

Is there a downside to your reputation? The bigger they are, the harder they fall?
Oh, absolutely. All it takes is—I think the consumer and the media can accept a couple little bumps in the road, but if you become too egotistical, if

you're making wines that are overpriced and the value's gone, if you deviate from your philosophy, that's how you fall as a winemaker. My mother always said the meek will inherit the earth. Not that I'm meek, but you don't want to let it go to your head. Don't ever let your image go to your head. There are so many people who treat other individuals very poorly. If I treat you poorly, you'll never forget it. In this business, especially.

In February 2006, Colgin Cellars announced that Mark Aubert had ended his contract with them.

1990s

They were, in a certain sense, lucky. By the time the '90s arrived, California wine was a relatively mature industry. For a young man or woman, it offered a real career path as a winemaker, maybe even a lucrative one, not to mention a lifestyle that couldn't be bought. Pioneers no longer were needed to hack a path through the jungle, but instead specialists to develop the industry's burgeoning infrastructure. There are parallels with the simultaneous rise of the Internet. A winemaker could choose, with some precision, what to specialize in. Pinot Noir? All right, but from where? Santa Barbara County? Sonoma Coast? Russian River Valley? Anderson Valley? Carneros? If from Monterey, grown on which side of the freeway? Such a range of geographic possibilities had never before been available in California.

And what clones to use, what rootstocks? Both of these raw materials began to be available in greater quantities and types during the '90s. How should the vines be trellised, the rows oriented with respect to the sun? Was irrigation needed? Was there enough money to pay for developing hills, which sometimes had to be terraced? Overarching all these concerns, could or should the vintner own his own vineyard, or buy grapes from others?

The questions piled up. What kinds of oak barrels might be used, from which forests, which manufacturers, and toasted to what levels? Did only French oak suffice, or could the barrels be American, Hungarian, Russian? How should a brand name be decided on, what ought the image on the label look like, what kind of closure, foil, bottle color, typography, type size? What price point, in a complicated hierarchy of pricing, should be aimed at? What customer demographic? Making and selling wine had become as involved as making and selling automobiles or clothes. At every decision point, a mélange of choices awaited, or confronted, the vintner.

Nature itself seemed to propel even the most reluctant winemaker toward change. The decade's famously expensive development—the widespread onset of vine-killing phylloxera in the North Coast and elsewhere—after having been predicted by the pundits to be a catastrophe, proved instead to be an opportunity: once all those vines had to be ripped out, they could be replaced with state-of-the-art plantings. Fortunately, the national economy during these years was healthy. Banks were eager to lend growers and vintners money. As a result, the '90s may best be remembered as the era when the near-perfect matching of grape variety and *terroir* was achieved, at least along the coastal areas, always the source of California's best wines.

More personally, winemakers of the '90s placed themselves on a fast track. They were not necessarily more ambitious than their predecessors, but perhaps they had honed their ambitions with greater calculation. They knew where they wanted to go, and the ones in this section of the book were determined to get there as quickly as they could. Some possessed highly polished PR and communication skills; others who didn't eventually developed them (however abashedly) on realizing that courting the wine press was almost as important as making great wine. And let there be no mistake: in the '90s the wine press became a behemoth. These winemakers understood the gentle art of making the behemoth work for them.

They came to understand, also, the importance of distinguishing themselves from the competition. It's not enough simply to have another product out there; it has to be special, or perceived as special. The entire developed world is one great big market now, and people willing to spend money on wine want something with panache. Everyone featured in this section of the book found a quality niche: John Alban's Central Coast Rhônes, the Pisonis' Santa Lucia Highlands fruit, the Lees' portfolio of vineyard-designated Pinots grown by others, and Gina Gallo's success at bringing her Sonoma winery to the point where upscale becomes affordable. These winemakers have had to be adroit in identifying and staking out their turf, and then in stamping them indelibly with their signature.

The winemakers in this section are true entrepreneur-artistes. They have pushed the wine industry in new and exciting directions, not only in production but in shaping our, the consumers', perception of what wine should be. And all of their careers are likely to evolve further in unexpected ways. These men and women have opened avenues that will long be exploited by the next generation of winemakers, who even now are studying in the V&E departments of colleges and universities or apprenticing at the wineries profiled in this book and others scattered across the globe.

ADAM AND DIANNA LEE

SIDURI WINERY

Siduri took the wine world by storm in the late 1990s after Robert M. Parker Jr. discovered its wines. The husband-and-wife team of Adam and Dianna Lee owns no vineyards; instead, the pair established a formula, now copied by other Pinot Noiristes, of buying grapes from well-known vineyards and then striving for *terroir* typicity. Siduri's wines (as well as Lees' Novy Family Wines brand), made in a rented facility in a Santa Rosa industrial park, are complex but easy to enjoy, much like the Lees themselves. Unpretentious and friendly, with two young children and a new baby in tow, they had a wonderful story to tell when I visited with them in May 2006.

How did you get into wine?
AL: I grew up Southern Baptist and never drank until college. Later, I started going to wine tasting events in Texas, and this retailer was opening a new store, Austin Wine & Spirits, and needed an assistant manager. It was a wonderful place to learn about wine.
DL: I grew up Catholic, so we had wine with dinner at times, but mostly beer, because of the Texas heat. I got a degree in business and then got a job at Neiman Marcus in Dallas, where I met Adam.
AL: I had gone from the wine store to a job in wine wholesale, up in Dallas. I didn't like it very much. I was calling on Neiman Marcus, and they needed

somebody to co-head their wine shop. So I started there the same day Dianna started.

DL: I was put in the Epicure department, with the gourmet food. I'm getting a tour, and the first stockroom I come to, Adam's sitting on the floor! We both got stuck working late-night shifts. Adam was one of the only straight guys there, and he also was surrounded by alcohol, and me being right out of college, those were two very attractive things. We started dating, and I got into wine. And we decided, after six months, that we wanted to move to California and become winemakers.

Just like that.

DL: So we were definitely nobodies moving to California with no winemaking experience. But as salespeople, we understood what consumers were looking for.

AL: Neiman's was a great place to take it to the next level, as far as—

DL: —clients.

AL: —developing a clientele.

So when did you move to California?

DL: Adam moved out before I did, in 1993.

AL: To Guerneville. It was the least expensive place I could find.

DL: We split up when Adam moved out. We kept in touch, though, because I started working in the wine department when he left.

AL: I'd moved out with the goal of getting involved in the wine business. I'd visited before, and it was amazing the number of wineries that said, "Oh, Adam, if you ever move out, come by, we'll find you a job." And then you got out here and called, and it's like, "Who are you?" When I couldn't find a job, I worked at Sterling, which was quite a commute from Guerneville.

Did you always have Pinot Noir in mind?

AL: That's what I'd discovered at Austin Wine & Spirits, Rochioli wine. They came out and visited, and Tom [Rochioli] said to me, "You ought to see these other guys, Burt [Williams] and Ed [Selyem], and get their Pinot in." So we got some Williams Selyem, and I really fell in love with Pinot. High-quality California Pinot was not known that well, and if you could find these Rochiolis or Williams Selyems, it was the kind of thing Dianna and I would drink, if we had the opportunity.

So, Dianna, when did you come out?

DL: January of '94.

Did you guys move in together?
DL: No. I moved to Healdsburg. Remember, I grew up Catholic, so we did not live together before we got married. I wouldn't have moved out, I wouldn't be in wine, I don't think, had I not met Adam. He opened the door for me. But Adam would never be a winemaker if I hadn't moved out.

AL: That's true. The wine end of things, I pretty much introduced her to, but the entrepreneur, the idea of starting your own business, she did that. We got our first grapes in the fall of '94.

Tell me about those grapes.
AL: Well, we had twenty-four thousand dollars saved up.

DL: Who did? *[smiles]*

AL: You had twenty-one thousand, I had three thousand! *[laughs]* I always told people I lived more life, and that's why I only had three thousand dollars! So we decided to make a little wine. At the time, it was incredibly frightening. But we both had day jobs in wineries—I ended up working at Lambert Bridge.

DL: And I commuted on weekends to Lambert Bridge and did shipping, until they offered me a full-time job. So we both worked there.

AL: We put an ad in *Wine Country Classifieds* saying we were looking for Pinot. And we read books, not UC Davis or Fresno publications, but just people's books, like *The Heartbreak Grape*

> We heard that Robert Parker was at Meadowood....We bottled up a sample and dropped it off with the concierge, with a handwritten note.—Adam Lee

[by Marq de Villiers], about the great Pinot. We realized that Pinot responded to lower yields more than other varietals.

DL: We decided on Anderson Valley, the reason being it's so much cooler, and yields are lower. We got grapes from Christine Woods [Vineyards], but we didn't want to use that name because nobody heard of it. So we came up with "Rose Vineyard," because the grower's name was Vernon Rose.

AL: They allowed us to make it at Lambert Bridge.

DL: The cellar guy, we paid his hourly wage, because we didn't know how to drive a forklift or use a destemmer. But we thinned the fruit ourselves. Adam and I would spend the night at a campground up there.

AL: That '94 turned out to be pretty nice.

DL: We thought very highly of it.

AL: We heard that Robert Parker was at Meadowood [Resort], so we were pretty drunk one night, and said, "Oh, Parker would love our wine." We bottled up a sample and dropped it off with the concierge, with a handwritten note. And the next morning we woke up, like, "Oh, my God, what did we do?" We called the concierge trying to get the bottle back, but it was too late.

DL: They told us, "Parker came out for coffee and his newspaper this morning, and we gave him the message and the bottle."

AL: We were like, "At least we still have our day jobs!" About three weeks later we came home and there was a message on the answering machine from Parker, saying he tasted the wine, thought it was terrific, but he lost the notes, could we fax them?

DL: It was really funny. We heard that message, how Parker thought the wine was "terrific." Adam had saved all his past issues of the *Wine Advocate*, and he's looking through them for the word *terrific* to see what score that was! Was "terrific" a 95?

AL: We got a 90-plus, and started getting calls. So we quickly got licensed and sold it as futures to customers, under [the] Siduri [name].

DL: [Siduri is] the goddess of wine, from Babylonian mythology.

What were your next grapes?
AL: Hirsch vineyard. That was Dianna's doing.

DL: Well, you discovered the fruit. A few years ago I asked David [Hirsch], "Why did you sell to us? We were unheard of." He said he'd been selling to Kistler—

AL: —Williams Selyem—

DL: —all these people, and they'd been making incredible wines, but they had a lot of experience, and he didn't know if it was the winemakers or the grapes. So he wanted to give it to a couple of inexperienced unknowns, to see what happens.

It's like he was saying, "Since you guys have no idea what you're doing—"
DL: Exactly. But it got us in there, and we didn't know that at the time.

Was it your plan to make only Pinot Noir, and to source from as many vineyards as you could?
DL: We definitely only wanted to make Pinot Noir. But we had no idea we would source from as many vineyards as we do.

AL: In '04, we made seventeen vineyard designates and six different appellation blends.

You often talk about letting terroir *express itself, but how do you know what the* terroir *of a particular vineyard is?*
DL: I get a lot of feeling from the vineyard, even without tasting the fruit. You get an impression just by being in that site. And, I think, also a part of *terroir* is the personality of the grower. With Pinot Noir especially, there are

some eccentric growers. Gary Pisoni is a very bold, out-there person; so's the wine. [Martin] Van der Kamp, he's an earthy, funky hippie, loves everybody, the wine's got that funky, earthy stuff going on. David Hirsch being such a free spirit out on the [Sonoma] Coast, and you definitely have that foresty, mushroom, free-spirit sea breeze blowing through the wine.

Are you constantly looking for new vineyards?
DL: It's changed a little. The more children we add to the mix, our priorities about travel are a little higher.
AL: We're not looking for more vineyards that are more far-flung. I mean, getting another Russian River vineyard is not difficult, given that we live here. Likewise, if we were offered another acre at Pisoni, that's not difficult because we're already there.
DL: It's easier to get to Oregon than to Anderson Valley! When we're going south to Cargasacchi and Clos Pepe [vineyards], we stop at the airport and fly up to Oregon. Anderson Valley's like in the wrong way, so we're not looking for fruit up there anymore.

What does each of you actually do? Maybe I should have asked that earlier.
AL: We share responsibilities. We're both winemakers, and if anything now, with children, I'm doing more of the trips to faraway vineyards, and Dianna is doing more local vineyards.
DL: With a little baby and the fact that I'm breast-feeding, I can't really go on a long trip, so I'm the local one.

Is there a vineyard out there you would love to have but don't?
AL: Rochioli would be the one I could say right off the top of my head.
DL: We talk to Joe Rochioli Jr. every time we see him in the grocery store. I don't think he knows who we are, other than a couple of pests that keep saying "Hi" to him! *[laughs]*

Are there any vineyards you've dropped?
AL: We dealt with fruit from Carneros in '96, and then decided we weren't enthralled with it.
DL: And honestly, I think, under the other label we started, Novy, there could be more interest in Syrah from down there than in Pinot.

From your statewide perspective, do you see distinctive differences between Pinot appellations?
AL: I think there are distinctive differences.

Is it getting more or less?

AL: That's an interesting question. A year like '04, which was really hot in California, the fruit looked the same, and there were more similarities. We had to be careful to make wines that tasted different; while in a year like '05, you had different yields in different areas, so '05 was naturally different. The real question is, with more people doing Dijon stuff, is there more similarity?

DL: I worry about Dijon clones being planted all over the place now.

> It's not our intention to make these high-alcohol wines. We're just trying to make the very best wine we can.—Dianna Lee

How did Novy start?

DL: Novy happened because we ran out of Pinot Noir in '98. We had a lot of barrels and not enough Pinot to fill them with. We had to come up with a plan on how to fill up our barrels so we could make more wine so we could afford this building we just moved into. It was the end of September; you are not going to find any Pinot Noir of quality. So we had to start looking at other varietals. We thought, "Okay, what's later-ripening than Pinot Noir—which everything else is—and that we liked?" We don't really drink Cabernet or Merlot. We like old-vine Zin, but where are you going get that? So Syrah was the next obvious choice. And Syrah wasn't—you know, Merlot was really popular at that time, so there was Syrah available.

Did you have to learn to make Syrah, after Pinot Noir?

DL: We read every magazine article and book we could on Syrah for the next few weeks, but still, what did we do? We made it just like our Pinot. And the wine was pretty decent! Not great by any means, but a good first try.

Why did you call it Novy instead of Siduri?

DL: Because Siduri had been dedicated as a Pinot Noir brand. That was our dream, to have a Pinot house. Novy is my maiden name.

What are your highest-alcohol wines right now?

AL: Let's see. In '04? Maybe, oddly enough, Sonatera Vineyard, which is Sonoma Coast. 15.8 percent? And Novy, one of the Zins, probably in the 16½ range.

DL: There's just been a lot of heat spikes at the wrong time, causing the grapes not to be ripe and not taste good. So they hang longer, and consequently the sugars are much higher. It's not our intention to make these high-alcohol wines. We're just trying to make the very best wine we can, and if your sugars are creeping up, you're going to notice that alcohol, unless the other flavors are mature and as forward as they can be. Because to make a wine balanced,

if one thing is extracted, it all needs to be extracted. If it's just one thing—
AL: If it stands out, that's where the problem is. If alcohol stands out, that's where the problem is.

You say it's not your intention to make high-alcohol wines, but there's a theory that some people are doing it to curry high scores from certain critics who like these bigger wines.
AL: Well, back in '95, we made the Hirsch Vineyard Pinot, which is one of the best we've ever made. And we made our Oregon Pinot, and '95 was a difficult vintage in Oregon, and that wine, we thought, was pretty modest. We lowered the price, compared to our other wines, by 60 percent. That Hirsch Vineyard Pinot from the *Wine Spectator* got an 87, and the Oregon Pinot got a 91 or 92, and it never deserved anywhere near that rating. That was the year we came to realize that as far as reviews go, we're going to get things we don't deserve, both positive and negative. So we make wine for ourselves.

Is there a Siduri style across all vineyards?
DL: A common denominator in our wines? I hope it's in the area of texture, of mouthfeel, that silkiness that makes the wine go down easy, where no one thing really stands out.

Do you think the greatest California Pinot Noir has to be a single-vineyard?
DL: I think it could be a blend.
AL: It could be, but one of the things that's most important to us is that the wines are distinctive. Our goal is to make the best Pisoni Pinot, or the best Hirsch Pinot, that we can.
DL: And just to make a California appellation? You can't sell it, and we do have to consider that. Besides, we've tried taking our best barrels from Santa Rita and blending them with our best Russian River. It hasn't worked; we haven't been blown away.

GREG BREWER

BREWER-CLIFTON, MELVILLE VINEYARDS AND WINERY

Brewer-Clifton's rented production facility is in an industrial park in Lompoc, a drab agricultural town beyond the western edge of the Santa Rita Hills appellation. On the early February morning in 2006 when we met, a cold wind from the Pacific, only a few miles away, was sweeping in—the same winds that cool the Santa Rita Hills during summer. Greg Brewer is an intellectual, assertive, ambitious, articulate, and sometimes pugnacious young guy. His own winery is Brewer-Clifton, which he runs with his partner, Steve Clifton. Brewer's day job, however, is as the winemaker at Melville. Both wineries have come to define the red-hot Santa Rita Hills appellation.

When did you meet Steve Clifton?
In 1995. He was assistant winemaker at Beckmen and I was at Sunstone. We saw a real kinship—that our age, our passion, our drive were really in synch. We put together the concept of Brewer-Clifton in 1995.

What was the concept?
We were enamored by this appellation, which wasn't an appellation yet, Santa Rita Hills. We wanted to work with Chardonnay and Pinot Noir as vehicles for place. Obviously, no matter what you do, you're going to impose some style or thumbprint. But we wanted that to be subtle and consistent across the wines. No stylizing comes into play. It's a very nonbiased exposition of

place. But at the time there wasn't much fruit available, so we bought time by working with Santa Maria sites. Starting with the 2001 harvest, we were completely Santa Rita Hills, which was always the plan.

You had been a French teacher?
Right, at UC Santa Barbara. I loved teaching, but my supervisor and I clashed. The course work was mundane, and French was being phased out of schools, unfortunately, so the jobs were pretty slim.

How do you and Steve divide the responsibilities?
Fifty-fifty. If he's doing cellar work and I'm on the road or tied up at Melville, that's great. If he's somewhere and I'm here, then I'll handle production.

Where did you guys get your training?
On the job.

You didn't go to enology school?
No. If there's a situation, a chemistry issue or something beyond our scope, we have dear friends, people who have the training, and they're happy to offer whatever they can. And I've done translation work [for them] where [French] coopers come out. We all do our thing.

Has there been a learning curve for you with Pinot Noir?
Of course! There always will be.

What were your early blunders?
Well, we do Pinot different than most. We do everything whole-cluster, no stem removal at all, and there are aspects of that which are risky. The results can be phenomenal or disastrous. And we've fallen. It's a question of the farming: there are times where the stems aren't ripe, where the stem inclusion aspect protruded, and became a distraction in our wines.

Why do you retain stems?
Because when they're ripe, the wines are on a whole different plane from wines that are destemmed, from a holistic, textural way. People see stems as something that's added; we see it as something that hasn't been taken away.

What are your grape sources these days?
For Chardonnay, we make five or six: Mount Carmel, which is a vineyard we've taken over, our *monopole,* if you will. Then Sweeney Canyon, Rancho Santa Rosa, Ashley's, and Sea Smoke [vineyards]. And Melville Chardonnay we've also worked with. We used to make Clos Pepe Chardonnay, but starting with '05 our Clos Pepe shifted into a new project, Diatom, which is my third arm, if you will.

We'll get to that later. And Pinot Noir?
Pinot Noir is Ashley's, Clos Pepe, and Melville, but at Melville there are two wines: our Melville, and then a particular block that we planted for a cousin of mine, Kim, who was murdered ten years ago, and all the proceeds are donated to the local rape crisis center. And then there is Ampelos, which hasn't come online yet; Rio Vista; Rancho Santa Rosa; and Mount Carmel.

Brewer-Clifton owns no vineyards?
No.

These vineyards are the grands crus *of Santa Rita Hills. How did you manage to get that fruit?*
Really good question. Steve and I are products of this area. Collectively, we've been here over thirty years. We've done our best to promote and be cool and just do our own humble thing. It's funny: when we started, we're struggling, trying to procure a ton here, a ton there, and thinking, "Gosh, wouldn't it be cool someday if people came to us?" And now, without sounding presumptuous, they do. They know we'll pay anything, we'll pay before they pick. We stay out of the way. We don't micromanage growers. We don't blend things away. We always vineyard-designate, and their name is almost as big as ours on the label. So it's in everyone's best interests to provide cool fruit to us.

You say you don't micromanage, but you must give growers parameters.
Mostly for leaf removal, which we like done more aggressively than most, for stem ripeness. Yields, we're pretty cool about. It's such an extreme area that yields rarely get out of control. We pick very, very ripe, but we're not having growers hang out for months of rain, saying, "Oh, you told us to wait!" And because we're so cool about that, in my eyes, and so calm, and we like things so ripe, when other colleagues get frenzied, and more imposing on growers to "You gotta pick mine tomorrow," we're like, "You know what? Take care of everybody else, and when the dust settles, pick on your next available morning that's convenient." We don't care.

That can be dangerous, can't it? Like in 2004, where two days can make a huge difference in Brix?
It can, but things respond, things come back. Two thousand four, we're more proud of our work than we were in '03.

What do you look for in a vineyard? Is there inferior ground in Santa Rita Hills, or all grand cru?
That's a slippery slope to talk about. There are vineyards that are more conducive to our style than others. Pinot Noir in a sandy environment makes

wines that are more ethereal; they don't quite have the bottom-end and voluptuous core of dense fruit that more clay–sandy loam soils have. That, cou-
pled with stem inclusion, oftentimes goes in an awkward direction. You have
this ethereal, spicy, non–fruit-developed wine, no matter what ripeness, because it's grown in sand—that, with stems, can backfire.

Define your Pinot Noir style.
We love exploring dynamics with both Chardonnay and Pinot Noir. So we
pick very ripe, because there's ferocious acidity out here. Let's speak of
Chardonnay. We get a really developed lemon-lime, tequila, agave-esque min-
erality. You get weight and drive and mouthfeel from alcohol, and you have
this mouthwatering acidity to counter that. So that's the game we play, that's
the juxtaposition we explore. With Pinot Noir, similar trend—picked ripe,
the fruit is very pure, very round. It can be jammy, and that can go too far,
so instead of taking that to this jammy, over-the-top fruit-bomb direction—
and I'm not saying that as a negative, even though it sounds that way, it's really just that style—we like that core-rich roundness, anchored by the stem
inclusion, which hardens it, grounds it, distracts the palate from alcohol and
fruit. So that's our thing, in a nutshell, that dynamic pull to two extremes.

What are bottle prices?
Usually forty to seventy dollars, that range.

What is case production?
In 2004, just over 3,000 cases, and that was thirteen wines. From '05, all our
sites crept up by a ton or so an acre, and more importantly, as we took over
Mount Carmel we now have a twenty-two-acre estate, for lack of a better
term. So that really fueled our growth, pushing us just over 7,000 cases.

> I'll do whatever I
> can to get as close
> to place as I can…
> to produce wines that
> transcend grape and
> place.

*Your alcohols are high. You've alluded to the rea-
son for that—you pick ripe. Are you getting any
blowback about 15.7, 15.9?*
Every day, yeah. It's a complicated issue, and
there's a lot of writing about it. It's a twofold
story. One is, we disclose to the tenth what the
alcohol is [on the label], and by law we don't have
to. If you're under 14, you have 1.5 percent lee-
way. Over 14, you have 1 percent.

Why tell the truth?
Why tell a lie? We approach it from that perspective. If people are hung up
by a number, or critique the wine because of that, fine. Maybe our wines

aren't appropriate for that person, that critic. If someone reads a label and says, "Oh, 15.9, that can't go with food, that can't age, I won't like it, it'll be hot," then great. If you're going in with that mind-set, then please don't buy it. If you've got acidity and fruit substance and everything else is in check, who cares? I've had Muscadet at 9 percent that's hot because there's no stuffing.

Have you ever used any alcohol-lowering techniques?
Never considered it.

Why not?
Why? Why?

To get alcohol down.
I don't see that as a need. I have no problem with these alcohols. I have no problem with the wines, and no problem disclosing what the alcohols are. Beyond that, a compelling wine story, for people like you who are sent samples all the time, would be to send 100 milliliters of everything to Vinquiry [testing lab] and spend fifteen dollars in analysis and write a story about ethics, or the truth of that. You know, I've had Montrachet, the label says 12.5 but the wine is unctuous as hell! It's not 12½! I'm sorry!

What is your relationship with Melville?
Melville is my primary job. Ron Melville had a business on the Pacific Stock Exchange, and was looking to diversify. So he purchased land and started planting in '97.

Just nine years ago. It shows what a young area this is.
It's amazingly young. What's staggering is that whole list of vineyard names I rattled off for B-C, none is older than seven years. When Melville planted, there were only about four hundred planted acres out here. Now there's fifteen hundred. It's been a very fast evolution. Anyway, I learned that Melville was going for it. It wasn't a mom-and-pop, three acres—I love those vineyards too—it was more like, there's money here, and he's going for it. So we approached him, looking for an acre of Pinot Noir for B-C. We secured that, and the two of us hit it off, Ron and myself. Eventually, he said, "If I built the winery, would you be interested in coming on board?" And I said, "Sure."

Is B-C making money?
Yes. But it's a very expensive business. We pay a phenomenal amount for fruit, and to grow a business like this, from basically nothing, and never take on loans, is very rare.

Is it difficult to spread yourself between Melville and B-C?
Harvest is hard. When the chips are down, my priority goes to Melville. That's one of a myriad of perks to having a partner. When I'm under the gun at Melville, Steve's here. When he's feeling pressure from Palmina, which is his brand, I compensate at Brewer-Clifton. And our schedules are disparate. I'm a morning person, and he's a night owl.

Do you make the Melville and B-C wines the same?
I'm not like some Jekyll and Hyde. At the same time, I take more risks at Brewer-Clifton because if something goes south, it's just Steve and me. I'm not answering to anyone else. I make more conscientious, deliberate, thoughtful decisions at Melville, and at times B-C can be a little irrational.

Could you identify blind your different Pinot Noirs?
Uhh, not year-to-year. I could take a stab at it! *[laughs]*

Could you identify blind Santa Rita Hills from other Pinot appellations?
I usually could. The area where I feel most familiar is the true Sonoma Coast, way out on the water there. When I've tasted Flowers or whatever, it's like, Whoa, in an eerie way, it's reminiscent of home. There's a raw purity and extremity for those wines that feels natural for me. I could see being stumped by those other wines, but I don't know.

Tell me about Diatom.
Diatom is my new thing. Just me. Chardonnay only, done in a very serene, solitary, pure Asian style.

Asian?
Well, in the sense it's the ultimate expression of raw material and zero intervention.

Where's the fruit from?
Clos Pepe and Huber [vineyard], which is across the street from Clos Pepe.

Why are you doing Diatom?
Because I need to, emotionally, irrespective of financial gains or whatever. It's Chardonnay done in a very naked, very unadulterated, very—

—unoaked?
It's not oaked, but if it were, that would be okay, too. There's more to it than "Oh, this is Greg's stainless [steel] Chardonnay."

You have an unoaked Chardonnay at Melville, don't you?
Yes, Inox, and that's one of my favorite things I do there. Diatom is the next
step in my exploration of that.

What's Diatom's price?
The Clos Pepe will be thirty dollars and the Huber is thirty-six.

So they're—excuse this word—cheaper than Brewer-Clifton.
Yeah. There was a part of me that wanted to push them way higher. Deep
down, I didn't want the wines to be seen like, "Oh, let's have a tasting of unoaked California Chardonnays." And for that reason, I almost put the pricing ridiculously high.

But you might oak it at some point?
I'm going to do what I'm going to do. Maybe it will be 90 percent stainless
steel and 10 percent old barrels. I don't know. I'll do whatever I can to get as
close to place as I can, to work with a single grape
within a very small sphere, geographically, to
produce wines that transcend grape and place.
Steve and I had the good fortune to blind-taste
at [Domaine] Raveneau, and if you opened up
a textbook on Chablis, it's like, boom! That's
what Chablis should be. It went beyond Char-
donnay, beyond Chablis, to a very serene, driven, precise model. I'm not saying I want to do that, that's too trite and weird, but that visit made a huge
impact on me, and made Diatom come into being.

> A lot of the inspira-
> tion for thinking
> about wine… is born
> out of music or art.

*On Melville's Web site you say, "When discussing wine production, conversations
revolve around such banalities as type of barrel, time in barrel, yeast and malolactic fermentation." Why do you call these very important things "banalities"?*
They're important as tools, but it bores me to talk about them. Do you talk
to a carpenter about who makes the saw? You need to go beyond that. If you
confine yourself to that, you're confining yourself to just wines that are kind
of fettered by the same control. In the wine business, you have to look beyond for inspiration, to provoke and challenge yourself. Restaurants are far
beyond where most wineries are; art and fashion and design are beyond restaurants. A lot of the inspiration for thinking about wine, my understanding
and clarity about that, is born out of music or art. For me, it's where some-

one has pulled off that extreme. That's what I meant: whether I use Sirugue as a cooper, or if the wines go through malo, who cares?

Do you have plans to build a winery?
No. This is it. We have no aspirations of a winery. At a certain level, it becomes counterproductive, as far as perception goes, at a culty level. Here, when buyers come, it's very real, no-frills, very pure. It's all about the wine.

JUSTIN SMITH

SAXUM VINEYARDS

Summer had finally arrived along the Central Coast in May 2005 after a wet spring when I sat down with Justin Smith on a terrace overlooking the steep, bowl-shaped James Berry vineyard. Part of a cadre of Rhônistes on the west side of Paso Robles, Smith crafts complex and appealing red Rhône-style wines that have achieved cult status, and are priced accordingly. Saxum seems destined to be one of those coveted brands that will never be produced in quantities great enough to satisfy demand. We talked about all this as his blond Lab, Annabella, nuzzled his knee.

When did you start Saxum?
Saxum's first release was the 2000. I'd started making wine in 1998 under another label, Linne Calodo. When my former partner and I went our separate ways, we divided the inventory. I took some of the 2000 and 2001 in barrel, so the first Saxums were those. The first Saxums we did by ourselves, entirely at the winery, were the '02s.

When was the vineyard planted?
In 1980. My father's name is James Berry Smith, which is why we call it James Berry vineyard. He was a veterinarian. He and my mom wanted to get back to the rural life, so they bought fifty-five acres of bare land here and planted thirty-two to Chardonnay and Pinot Blanc. These soils are very Burgundian,

we're only ten miles off the ocean, so they made a gamble on those being the varieties. But the Chardonnay that comes off here is so steely and minerally, the total opposite of what happened to Chardonnay in the '80s. It never really shined. Then, in '87 or '88, John Alban approached my dad with the intent to plant a few test blocks to see how Rhône varieties would do. John was looking for property and wanted to experiment, to get an idea where he wanted to make his home.

He obviously decided not to come here.
Yeah. We planted Viognier and Mourvèdre for him. But he felt this area was too warm, so he settled in Edna Valley.

What's growing here now?
We pulled the Pinot Blanc. We still have the Chardonnay, but the Rhônes are all we've planted, Syrah being the biggest, then Grenache and Mourvèdre, falling behind with Roussanne.

Why no Marsanne or Viognier?
I haven't been a big fan of white Rhônes out of this area. I like searing acidity, low alcohol, crisp whites, and that's not what we do here.

What had your father been doing with the grapes before you started Linne Calodo?
The Chardonnay has been long-term contract with Fetzer. The biggest planting of Rhônes went originally to Wild Horse. They did some James Berry vineyard designates.

How many wineries designate James Berry vineyard today?
Besides Saxum, it's Wild Horse, Villa Creek, Copain, Garretson. Then we've got a block for Carlisle that's coming online this year.

What does it cost to buy James Berry fruit?
Well, you're definitely paying a premium. If you're paying twelve thousand dollars an acre and you only want two tons an acre, then you're paying six thousand dollars a ton. That might not be high for North Coast, but for Paso Robles it's top end.

What percent of your fruit do you sell?
Out of the fifty-five acres planted, Saxum keeps only about ten acres. I want to grow Saxum slowly, keep the demand higher than I have product, being as I don't want to be a marketer and hit the streets. And it's fun to work with other winemakers, as their viticulturalist, find out what they're doing, taste their product. It allows me to learn.

Do you have quality control over the wineries you sell grapes to?
Yeah. In our contracts, we specify that we have to approve the wine before
they can put "James Berry Vineyard" on it, to make sure it's up to par.

Have you ever said to someone, "No"?
Not yet. We've been lucky enough that the wineries we're dealing with are
doing a good job.

Well, I've tasted some James Berry wines—not yours—that weren't very good.
It might have been before these new contracts, where we just redid that clause.
We were unhappy with some previous producers that carried our name.

Tell me about this western part of Paso Robles.
It's the coolest corner. When people think of Paso Robles, they think of one
entity, but it's huge. Some areas are nine miles off the coast, and some are
closer to the Central Valley. Sometimes we'll get more influence from inland,
sometimes from the coast. In a cool year like '98, we're a Region I, and in a
warmer year, we're a low III.

Why not grow Bordeaux varieties here?
Bordeaux varietals do well. Justin [Vineyards & Winery]'s had success with
them. But it's nice having our own niche. Even if we did the best Bordeaux,
we're still going to be competing with Napa, and we'd always be second—
where with the Rhône varieties we can be, "Hey, if you want great Syrah/
Grenache, Paso Robles is doing excellent ones."

Why don't you make a 100 percent Syrah?
We could, but it always seems like pure Syrahs benefit from a little Mourvèdre and Grenache. I think we probably have more in common with the
[southern] Rhône than we do for the northern Rhône. It's possible to get a
great Syrah and a great Mourvèdre and a great Grenache, all out of the same
season.

*Do the westsiders want to distinguish yourselves from Paso in general or the east
side in particular?*
I'm sure it won't be long before there are subappellations out here.

Is anyone working on one?
Maybe.

Why the coyness?
Well, because it's off the record. But, yes, there are a couple in the works.
[Ed.: Early in March 2007, Paso Robles growers and winemakers submitted
petitions to the federal government for the creation of three new American

Viticultural Areas within the existing Paso Robles AVA. Another eight were expected to be filed within weeks after that.]

What would they be called?
That's one of the problems. There's actually two of them. One would be centered around the Templeton Gap influence, and one around the hills of Adelaida. We would be Templeton Gap.

What's the difference between the two?
There's a ridgeline where the Adelaida Hills are, so there's much less of a marine influence. Templeton Gap would be cooler than Adelaida Hills.

What is Bone Rock?
When we first bought the vineyard, that hill had been cleared for barley, back thirty-some years ago, and the farmer attempted to farm it, but it was so steep he gave up.

That's this higher part here?
Yes. It's all part of James Berry, and Bone Rock is the block. We knew it couldn't be farmed conventionally, so we had engineers draw up plans for terracing, and we cut these steps into the rock. All the terraces catch the water and drain it down to culverts, because erosion's a big concern. It's all planted to Syrah.

Why do you call it Bone Rock?
This whole westside area is sitting on top of the Monterey shale formation, this ancient seabed. With the fault line, it lifted out of the ocean five to twenty million years ago. And for some reason, there's a high proportion of whalebones littered into the shale. So when we cut this block, we cut right through these bones.

And what is the bottom part?
As you get down to the valley, you'll find a deeper topsoil. There will still be shale beneath it, but typically, you've got the clay and loam on top of it that can be eight feet deep.

Is there a difference between Syrah from the lower part and from Bone Rock?
Oh, yes, not only from the soils but from the aspects. Bone Rock is a southwest slope, so it gets a lot of heat. Some of the lower parts are almost north, they're away from the sun. So you've got the difference between the heavier clay that holds on to moisture better and stays colder, and the top of the hill where it's solid rock and catching a lot of sun. We'll have a six-week difference between the time we harvest Bone Rock and when we harvest our lower

Syrah. A warmer year, the lower stuff does well, and a cooler year, Bone Rock is better. Bone Rock Syrah is actually a blend of the two. Typically, it's about 80 percent Bone Rock, but in warmer years like these last three, it's dropped down to around 50 percent.

We'll also blend Mourvèdre and Grenache in. One of the nice things about Mourvèdre, and why it makes its way into almost all my blends, is we get a nice ripeness at the lowest alcohol of any of the varieties we're playing with. I don't like to water down or dealcohol, I like to pick things when they taste best, when they're physiologically ripe; so I end up blending instead of manipulating. Mourvèdre works great for that. You can put in 10 percent and knock your alcohol down.

And Grenache adds what?
It's very bright and uplifting. You put in a touch and it lifts up the aromatics.

> We're picking at where we think the flavors are, and when you get a hot, dry year like these last three years, the alcohols are going to be up there.

What else do you produce?
We also do Saxum Broken Stones. That's a Syrah-based blend, like Bone Rock, but it's part James Berry—mainly the Syrah that doesn't go into the Bone Rock, whether it's a little of the Bone Rock or a little bit of the lower, and then we have two other vineyards we manage that also go in.

What's the price difference?
Bone Rock is fifty-six dollars and Broken Stones is thirty-eight.

How do you set the price on Bone Rock?
We're trying to keep it reasonable, so we're making some profit. I probably could charge seventy-five or eighty dollars, but I don't like to gouge.

What are alcohol levels on the wines?
Fifteen-five, 15.9. It's something we're aware of, but we have chosen to show respect for the season and let it be what it is. We're picking at where we think the flavors are, and when you get a hot, dry year like these last three years, the alcohols are going to be up there. It's just something you have to deal with. You have the choice of watering down or spinning cones, or you can let it show what it is. We show what it is. I'm not superhappy about high alcohol, but this fruit does a good job of hiding the alcohol on the palate. You're going to feel it in your head, but it's not often that someone tastes a glass of James Berry vineyard and says, "Wow, it has high alcohol."

You seem a little uncomfortable talking about alcohol.
Well, it's a hot topic. Paso Robles is warm climate, and there's definitely a lot of high-alcohol wines out there. It's touchy.

Who has made it touchy?
You just hear consumers and critics—well, not so much critics, I mean there's been some writers saying there's this big trend for all the wines to be riper and more alcohol. I think that's true, but it's also true that we're coming off three of the hottest, driest seasons. Give us another '98, and they'll be back down. It's not something we're consciously doing.

Why are you loath to dealcoholize your wines? Lots of people do.
Because we work hard in our vineyard, and it's more respectful of your season and your vintage. If there's a problem, then yeah, fix it. But for me, I don't think our wines have a problem. You know, there's a problem with a little part on the label that says 15.9, but I think the wine doesn't have a problem. So I'm not going to fix it if it's not a problem.

What's total production?
We've got 1,000 cases being released of the '02s. As we get more plantings on-line, we will nudge our way up to 2,000. We've designed the winery to be 2,500.

Is that enough to make a good living?
It can be.

Are you making money?
Saxum hasn't started to make money yet.

How does a winery stay in business and not make money?
We originally financed it. And we had our foot in the door by not having to buy fruit. We started very slowly, with 300 cases, at a custom-crush facility where there's not a huge overhead. So each year we've taken the profit and rolled it back. I think when we top out, yes, we'll be able to turn a profit. And what helps is, I do consulting for a number of vineyards and wineries.

Where did you learn your viticulture and enology?
From my dad. I went to Cal Poly San Luis Obispo, but I studied ecology.

When you were growing up, did you always know you'd be involved in this?
No. No.

What made you decide to do it?
In college, I hadn't decided yet. I loved being here, but it wasn't until I moved away and realized how special it is here, being out in the field, doing your

sweat labor and hard work, and then to see the happy consumer and the outcome.

What are your main challenges nowadays?
In the vineyard, the biggest challenge with these new plantings is to figure out what variety we're going to put here, what rootstock. There's many more choices now, and clones. And then we've got all those different aspects of hills. An east slope will have a completely different aspect than a south slope, and so it will need to have different varieties.

Have your canopy management techniques changed over the years?
Yes, they have. They're continually changing. Like stuff we planted in 1980 was, at the time, state-of-the-art, AxR[#1] rootstock, a trellis with a high thirty-two-inch cordon with a T a foot and a half above that, so the vine had a lot of canopy, what they called California sprawl. And our planting after that, we did a lyre, which is taking a wider spacing but dividing your canopy into two. And then we've done some head-trained stuff, and now we're going more towards a high-density vertical shoot positioning. But we're finding with some varieties in this climate, where we have these heat spells, that having a canopy with some shade is ideal.

> We're not here to just make and sell wine. We live it, and it's fun.

So what goes around comes around.
Yeah, something like head-pruned that provides a little shade, especially on varieties like Grenache or Mourvèdre, might be ideal.

And in the winery, what are your challenges?
We're experimenting with different oak regimes, and different oak levels, where our coopers will give us six different forests, all the same toast level, and we'll compare them all, or they'll give us all the same forest but five different toasting techniques.

Does that make a difference in the wine?
Not much. Our fruit is so overwhelming that it's not a huge difference between, say, a heavy toast and a medium toast. It's hard to pick out the difference.

When does it stop, all this tinkering?
Well, I think we're not here to just make and sell wine. We live it, and it's fun, it's playing around. Maybe we'll never find the best technique, but for now, there's just too many things to figure out.

Do you taste with the other westside Rhône guys?
Yeah. All the time. Typically, we'll go to Villa Creek [restaurant, in Paso Robles], where [owner] Chris [Cherry] has a great wine list. We'll pick out McLaren Vale Syrah, whatever. It's not like a formal tasting, it's more of a party. Everybody will bring four, five bottles of something they found lately, just trying wines and talking about them.

Is there anything else you wish you'd done instead of owning a winery?
No. No. This is it here. If I could change anything, I wouldn't. It's a great spot to be in, and everything has worked out well.

MICHAEL TERRIEN

HANZELL VINEYARDS

Michael Terrien had been at the helm of Hanzell less than a year when we spoke in November 2005, and I sensed a tentativeness in him, as though this dream job—winemaker at one of California's most venerable small wineries—might disappear as unexpectedly as it had come. It had been daunting. At Hanzell, tradition reigns supreme; things are done very differently than at Acacia Winery, where Terrien had worked for nine years. We talked at the Hanzell château, high on an outcrop of the Mayacamas Range. On this clear November morning, the view of the Sonoma Valley was surreal and inspiring.

How did you get into winemaking?
I came west after college and worked in a San Francisco restaurant, learning about wine. On my way to becoming a marine biologist, I was sidetracked by the UC Davis program.

How did that happen?
By accident. Scanning through the course catalog, I stumbled on the enology program. I remember thinking I didn't know that one could choose to be a winemaker! I thought you had to have the right parents.

Now that you are a winemaker, was your idea of it back then close to the reality?
Yes, although there have been shocks along the way. The grower is not always interested in making good wine. I thought that was the goal of humanity. I

I was so naive, but
it seemed surprising
that some growers
are more interested
in making money
than quality wine.

was so naive, but it seemed surprising that some
growers are more interested in making money
than quality wine.

What was your first winery job?
Acacia Winery. I was living in San Francisco, and
one requirement was to be able to commute to
the winery. Pinot Noir was evolving as the variety that spoke to my soul, and I wished to pursue. So Carneros made sense.

How long were you there?
Nine years. It evolved each year to the next step up, through serendipity. I
became chief winemaker in 1999.

Who owned Acacia at the time?
Chalone Wine Group [in those days called Chalone, Inc.].

Did they always own it?
No. Acacia's reputation in the early '80s was glorious. It was one of the first
Pinot Noir "cult" wineries, and helped to pioneer Carneros. Then Chalone
acquired Acacia in '86. At the time, you were seeing a decline in the status
of Carneros as a darling. It was no longer a new appellation or hyperquality,
it was transitioning to a larger, industrial era.

What do you mean, "industrial"?
Well, you had Acacia growing larger, but you have Mondavi there, and
Beaulieu, Buena Vista. Saintsbury is larger, too, so there's less room for the
small boutique producer in Carneros.

Did Acacia's wines become, quote-unquote, "industrialized"?
We were able to make wines that were honest and capable of delivering personality at a fair price. That's the point of pride I have during my tenureship
at Acacia, to make an ever-increasing amount of wine at, frankly, an ever-
increasing quality level.

What's the problem with increasing production?
When a winery begins to chase diminishing margins by increasing production, quality tends to fall. We saw an influx of money from larger players
who found Carneros's proximity to Napa Valley as an opportunity, and that,
combined with zoning characteristics, meant a limited number of small
parcels where a young guy can set up shop.

Did you feel pressure to increase production?
It was a mandate to increase production.

How much did production increase?
You have vintage fluctuations, but I remember '98 being very small, 10,000 cases of Pinot Noir, and then 2005 the production is 50,000 cases. Of course, Diageo brought more aggressive growth to Acacia.

When did Diageo buy Chalone?
Late fall 2004.

When did you leave Acacia?
December 31 [2004].

What Pinot Noirs did Acacia produce?
The larger blend, and then single-vineyards, the historically important one being St. Clair, going back to '79, and Beckstoffer. The [Ira] Lee vineyard, which had a two-decade run. Iund also had a long run. And shorter-term ones, like Winery Lake.

What were you striving for in single-vineyard Pinots?
Expression of place, as defined by the piece of ground, as well as the person growing those grapes. In the case of Jim St. Clair, he tended those vines himself, and he has a distinct way of training the vines, which are virused and older. So those pieces of ground all have their distinct differences to showcase.

When you went to Acacia, did someone taste you through all these wines, so that you'd know what they're supposed to be like?
I understand the direction of your question, but no. My understanding of the vineyards grew out of walking them with [then-winemaker] Dave Lattin, and exploring the library of older vintages. I could see how these wines were made, but I had free rein to pursue winemaking how I would wish to interpret it, through intuition and respect for history. With distinct vineyards, the vineyard persists, the farmer persists, the flavors persist; and although a winemaker could obliterate the identity of a vineyard, it would be remiss and irresponsible.

Did you make all the wines the same?
I tried to apply the same recipe, to show it was not the winemaker's hand influencing these differences.

So Diageo buys Chalone in 2004, and you leave Acacia.
End of the year. I had begun talking to Hanzell a few months before.

Were you looking for a new job?
No, although the acquisition process that Chalone had started, with Constellation making a play, and then eventually being beat out by Diageo, made me think about other options.

Why?
In retrospect, even with Chalone, I would have had questions about my viability as a winemaker with dirty hands, and that's what I want, to do the work myself. As a winery gets larger, the natural progression for a winemaker is to become a manager of managers, rather than a manager of grapes.

Do winemakers always keep their options open?
Do we try not to burn bridges? Certainly. I think it's fair to consider one's options, and I don't believe that's disloyalty to your employer. It's a responsibility to ourselves and our families, as well as to keep your employer honest.

Did Hanzell approach you?
Yes. Jean [Arnold-Sessions] is the president of Hanzell, as well as the wife of Bob Sessions, who's been winemaker at Hanzell since 1973, recently retired.

How did the Sessionses know you were thinking of leaving Acacia?
Through the services of an employment search firm.

How did the search firm know you were viable?
I had talked to them on other inquiries.

So you were looking around.
I did not go to them.

They reached out to you?
Yes. They keep a database and they call you regularly to say, "Know anybody interested in a job that has five million cases in the Central Valley?" No, thanks.

What happened?
Went for an interview, first with the search firm, and they compiled the interviews and presented them to Hanzell. But I bungled it! It was videotaped, and I bungled the question "Why do you want this job?" I did not have a prepared answer, because I had not been looking for a job, and I did not know much about Hanzell.

What did you know?
It was, in my mind, a heritage winery, a place with great traditions, old roots, and I loved the label.

How did your interview with the Sessionses go?
Very well. I ended up having a half-dozen interviews. It was immediately evident that there was a humility and gentlemanliness about this estate and the people behind it.

Who owns Hanzell?
Alexander de Brye. He lives in London.

Is he involved in the business?
He spends his summer here, and visits quarterly.

So you gave Acacia notice?
Yes. It was a tremendous upheaval and transition at Chalone. It was difficult to get attention to tell someone I was leaving!

What was it like leaving after nine years?
It wasn't difficult. Even in a wonderful place, you get tired of seeing the same four walls. But what made me sad was the usual things. The people I'd worked closely with.

Were you surprised by anything at Hanzell?
Yes. To learn Hanzell has the oldest Pinot Noir vines in California, had the first French barrels in which the wines were made, the stainless steel fermenters installed in 1956, with the double walls so the jacket flows the coolant for temperature control. This was an advance that was introduced by Hanzell to the world.

Was there anything that gave you pause?
The respect for tradition here is profound. At first, my response to that was arrogant. I assumed what I would do with Hanzell would be similar to Acacia. I remember feeling, "Well, these [Hanzell] techniques seem old-fashioned." And I began to confirm that these are practices that are no longer fashionable.

Give examples of old-fashioned practices at Hanzell.
With Chardonnay, there's the stainless steel fermentation, for the majority of the wine, as opposed to barrel fermentation. And when it does go to barrel, it's a lower percentage of new oak than many higher-end Chardonnays. And malolactic fermentation is suppressed, which all result in a wine that is very elegant and refined, rather than about dominating flavors of barrel and butter. As for Pinot Noir, "old-fashioned" refers to the duration in which the wine is in barrel, twenty-four months.

Is that longer than Acacia?
It's sixteen months longer than Acacia.

Why do they keep it so long in barrel?
It's hard to figure out. One reason is that Hanzell has always prided itself on its difference. That goes way back to when Brad Webb made the wines. They decided this is the best way to approach Pinot Noir in 1957.

Did the Sessionses look to you to bring innovations to the winemaking?
I think they would like me to have a shutter-opening influence. Let the light in. In acknowledging that Hanzell has been doing the same thing for fifty years, there's implicit the understanding that Hanzell is out of step with the current industry.

So what are you doing differently?
Not much. Being out of step is an advantage. The population that drinks wine is maturing, and becoming tired of certain flavors that are dominant in California Chardonnay. It's a natural progression. With Pinot Noir and a new cellar, there's the acquisition of equipment that's more gentle on the grapes.

Are you expected to change the style of the Pinot?
No. The mandate is to make Pinot Noir that ages for decades. Ambassador [James D.] Zellerbach set this property up on the *grand cru* level for cellar-worthiness, and that mandate persists. I'm under direct orders by the weight of tradition, but also by Bob and Jean and Alexander, to make sure these wines do not break that tradition.

Are you looking for higher scores from the critics?
No. I would never sign on to a winery that said my compensation was related to scores.

Is there a Hanzell Pinot Noir character or personality?
Well, from the Hanzell [clone] vines we planted at Acacia, we saw extraordinarily thick, dark, tannic wines, and to me it correlates quite well with the size of the berry and relatively low yield these Hanzell vines produce. I think it's inherent to the selection.

Is there a terroir of this estate?
Well, it's only a mile from Carneros, two miles, but we're up here at eight hundred feet elevation.

In the Sonoma Valley appellation.
The soils are volcanic rather than [the] heavy clays that accumulated under the [San Pablo] Bay, so very different parentage. The difference in water-

holding capacity alone is tremendous. We don't have soils that retain moisture. Yields are necessarily low due to the soil, but also due to the fact that these Hanzell clone vines don't support much fruit.

What is the climate? One thinks of Sonoma Valley as a hot place.
We benefit from the Petaluma Gap to our west and San Pablo Bay to our south, so there is the cooling influence that is not felt further into the Mayacamas Range, or up in Sonoma Valley. So we have a certain amount of wind that keeps the heat off. But this is, granted, a warmer spot.

What does that say about the concept that Pinot Noir needs a cool climate?
It does need a cooler climate than the Central Valley. I think my skepticism, when I signed on, was quickly obliterated by tasting the wines, and finding Pinot Noirs from forty years ago that are not only intact, but have the structure to go another decade or more, and whose fruit is still alive.

What Brix did you pick Pinot at this year?
The average was, I believe, 25.

Are Hanzell Pinot Noirs, over the years, being picked at higher sugars?
The records are reflective of lower sugars and alcohols than today. The reputation, though, is for a very substantial, powerful wine. That's the interesting thing I've learned, is, people's impression of Hanzell is that it's a riper style.

Are you concerned with this tendency toward higher alcohol in wines?
I don't identify alcohol in the wines I taste from many of these producers that are making higher-alcohol wines.

> I am translator of a piece of ground to the bottle.

You mean because they're balanced, and you can't taste it?
Yeah. I think you get inebriated faster, but I don't believe the alcohol itself has a dominant impact on the aroma.

A lot of people knock this modern style of California wine as over-the-top.
I would in many cases agree. I think the use of extraction and oak and alcohol as an expression of a high degree of ripeness drives that fruit in a direction that is simple and not satisfying.

That won't happen at Hanzell?
I think we'll continue to make wines that are powerful, but it's the way it expresses its power that's different. The fruit, historically, and what I'll con-

tinue in the winemaking, is subservient to the tannic structure, the architecture of the wine.

So how's this first year been?
In some ways, I feel like it's an extended interview. I'm pleased with the developing relationship I have with this property, and I hope Bob and Jean agree.

You feel like you're still on probation?
That sounds somehow not quite right, but yeah, I'd say self-imposed probation. I want to be in a place that I want to be for a good long time. I feel like Hanzell is—well, there are older wineries in California, but there are no wineries as old as Hanzell that have continuity of vision from the beginning to now.

Tell me about Kazmer & Blaise.
K&B was begun in 1995. It's my partnership with Peter Kazmer Molnar—my name is Michael Blaise Terrien. Peter is the vineyard owner. He had fruit, I was learning how to make wine, and we hooked up. We make 400 cases of Carneros Pinot Noir.

And the Sessionses don't mind you making Pinot?
I think they're realistic about how difficult it is to find a winemaker who doesn't have a side project.

Your heart is in both wines?
Yes. The strictures of tradition that I am happy to work under at Hanzell help me to distinguish my two responsibilities. Competent winemaking can occur with very different styles of wine. So in both cases I am translator of a piece of ground to the bottle, and doing right by the grape in each case.

GARY, MARK, AND JEFF PISONI

PISONI VINEYARDS & WINERY

I had to reinterview the Pisonis in 2006 because the first time around, son Jeff (far left in photo) had been away and Gary (middle) had lost his voice; he'd been up all night partying. This is not an unusual thing for Gary Pisoni, *père,* to do. He is a larger-than-life figure, most of whose statements seem to end in exclamation points, and it is not for nothing that his sons happily describe Pisoni wines (and wines others make from Pisoni grapes) as Gary-esque. We met at son Mark's farmhouse, on a dirt road in a Salinas Valley lettuce field, where my car promptly got stuck in the mud. We soon settled down and started drinking—what else?—Pisoni Pinot Noir. The three men frequently laughed, something this joyous clan does easily and often.

———

Do you guys still farm?
MP: Yes, we have a thousand acres of lettuce, broccoli, celery, asparagus, cauliflower, your standard Salinas Valley crops.
GP: Pisoni vineyard is twenty miles south, on the Santa Lucia Highlands, on the south end.

Is there a temperature gradation between the north and south Highlands?
GP: Probably fifteen degrees. Jeff, tell him when the fruit comes in.
JP: There's definitely a temperature gradation. Dad's a partner in a small Pinot Noir vineyard, north of the Highlands right outside the border, and we harvest that three, four weeks later than Pisoni.

What is Pisoni's elevation?
JP: Most of the Highlands is about three, five hundred feet. Tucking back into Pisoni, at fifteen hundred feet, you really get into different soil. And a lot of mornings above the fog layer, so you have cooling effects from the fog, but you have the sunshine.

Is Pisoni the warmest vineyard in the AVA?
MP: Warmer in the sense that the highs are higher, but you have colder nights, too.
GP: This is the *papa*, Gary, speaking. And that's one of the reasons I wanted to plant the Garys' vineyard, because when I planted Pisoni, I thought, "Maybe it's too warm for Pinot Noir." It turned out to be just right, I believe, but I wanted another site.

When did you plant Pisoni?
GP: Nineteen-eighty-two, to Cabernet Sauvignon, Merlot, Cab Franc, Petit Verdot, Malbec, Chardonnay, and this special [Pinot Noir] clone I brought back from Burgundy, the Pisoni clone.

Do you still have the Bordeaux stuff?
GP: Only one and a half acres. We make a lovely Bordeaux blend, but it's just something we play with.
MP: We have forty-five to fifty acres, 90 percent Pinot Noir, and a young Syrah vineyard, which was planted in 2000.

Why did you plant the vineyard, Gary?
GP: Well, I started collecting wine in 1975, and I was drinking my collection so fast, I figured I better plant a vineyard and stay even!

How did you learn to make wine?
GP: Met a lot of winemakers. I'd talk to them about winemaking, get 'em drunk and learn their secrets. And I used to help my grandfather make wine, and my cousins, the Pisoni family in Italy.

Who bought the property?
GP: My father, Dad, in 1979, for cattle. We'd go to round up the cattle, and I'd want them to go one way, and they'd go another. I said, "Dad, I'm no cowboy, I'm a grape grower!"

What was his reaction?
GP: "What the hell's the matter with you? These grapes won't grow down here. There's no damn water!" I used to haul water up from the valley floor.

How do you get water now?
GP: Well, I drilled six wells, and finally we hit.

What did you do with the fruit the first years?
GP: It took four years before I got any because the deer were eating them, the pigs, the birds. I always tell the deer and the pigs, "If you eat my grapes, I will eat you." This morning we shot another deer. If you want a deer for lunch, we got one! Finally, the fourth year, I got a little fruit. I was selling it to a cousin of mine [who] had a winery, Cloninger. They didn't know what they were doing, they got a big batch of vinegar. Then I sold to Estancia, and they put it into a vat. I asked them to vineyard-designate, and they wouldn't. But I finally got people to vineyard-designate. I just basically copied Williams Selyem. It really started in '97, when I got Peter Michael, Patz & Hall, Siduri, Testarossa.

> I always tell the deer and the pigs, "If you eat my grapes, I will eat you."—Gary Pisoni

Why did they buy your grapes? You were unknown.
GP: Okay, I'll tell you why. I called 'em up, invited 'em down, and told 'em, "I have blue-ribbon Pinot Noir." They tasted barrels that I made, and I knew it was very, very good. Their tongues hit the ground! I said, "I'm just an amateur, think what pros like you can do!" So they looked at the grapes, and they saw it was textbook Pinot Noir bunches, like little pine cones, and they said, "Pisoni! You really got it!"

You once told me that before you launched your brand, you let other people make the name famous.
GP: I figured, get some people that had reputations, and they would get a good score and shoot us to stardom! And then I had my son Jeff going to college, ready to work.

Who else was growing Pinot in the Highlands back then?
GP: Nobody. Well, there was some funny clones of Pinot Noir, Gamay Beaujolais, at Vinco [vineyard]. But no real good-growing Pinot Noir.
MP: We were the first that went for quality. There was a very farmer mentality here, because they're row-crop guys, not grape guys.

When was the first Pisoni wine?
GP: 1998. Mark Aubert helped me. I was tasting the fruit and, like, "Man, it's delicious!" But I didn't know what to do with it, so I called Mark up, at Peter Michael, and said, "Mark, I have this special field, it's my favorite, my pride and joy, I don't know what to do with it." And he says, "Gary, bring 'em up here, we'll start your first Pisoni label."

How did you know him?
GP: He was buying my fruit. Peter Michael did a '97. I didn't ask him, he just did it for a favor.

Is there a character to a Pisoni Pinot Noir no matter who makes it?
GP: I like to think it's identifiable, that there's a thread, that common denominator, of the *terroir*, the *typicité*, through every winemaker who makes the fruit there.

Can you describe it?
GP: Big!
JP: Outside of specific flavors, there's a core of fruit that can be really dense and powerful, but not overdone. And it's cool enough to have a lot of acidity.
MP: I'm a firm believer that these wines really represent Dad's flamboyant, larger style.

How many wineries do you sell to?
MP: Ten.

If you don't like their wine, can you tell them they can't put "Pisoni" on the label?
GP: We taste the barrels, and if they cannot make the cut, they have to bulk it out.

Has that ever happened?
GP: Well, we haven't had any problems with anyone yet. But we've come close. Anything you can say, boys?
JP: We've got three rules.
GP: Three rules! To make the cut, you have to be our friend, make good wine, and pay the bill! The third rule is the hardest. *[all laugh]*

Is there a long line to get Pisoni fruit?
GP: From here to Napa, and from here to Santa Barbara, both ways.

How many people do you have waiting?
GP: Ten, fifteen? Twenty?
MP: At least.
GP: Jeff wants to bring in another winery, I won't say who, but we had a little family meeting before you got here, if we're gonna let this dude in or not. *[all laugh]* And I approved it, but Mark's not quite sure, he has to think about it.
MP: I'm the most cautious.

JP: What's neat is that we have all these different personalities. It's not like a board where we sit and have formal meetings.

GP: We do it over a bottle!

JP: A couple bottles, and we still get along.

Now you also have Garys' vineyard.

GP: That's Gary Franscioni. He's a wonderful partner of mine. I've known him all my life. I taught him how to plant grapes, 1996. He planted seventeen acres of Chardonnay and three acres of Pinot at his Rosella's vineyard. I told him to plant Pinot, but he didn't plant what I said! He planted Chard, and then later he wished he planted Pinot! But no big deal, he budded over, it was just a little mistake. And then we planted Garys', which is forty-two acres in Pinot, the next year.

And Jeff is now winemaker—

GP: And he's good!

And Mark is—

MP: The farmer.

And Gary is—

GP: Pop. *Papa.* Let me say something about Jeff. He's been making wine since he was three years old, so it's about time he figured it out!

Where is your production facility?

JP: We started out at Peter Michael. We're now up in Cloverdale, at the Peay facility.

Why don't you make it down here?

JP: We just kind of started north with that first vintage, and sort of stayed up there, I guess.

Any plans to build a winery?

JP: We're trying to put something together.

How much would it cost?

GP: Five million bucks!

The average person would think you guys are making a lot of money.

GP: No, no, we're very broke. *[all laugh]*

You referenced another Pinot vineyard, north of the appellation.

GP: Yeah. Silacci. I'm a partner.

Would that be colder than—?
GP: Oh, very cold. Like Oregon.

Why that far north?
GP: I want to test the limits of the Santa Lucia Highlands. See, it's outside the Highlands, and when my friend [Robert] Silacci said, "Gary, we're not in the appellation," I said, "You know what we're going to call it? Don't call me Santa Lucia Highlands, don't call me Monterey County, call me Silacci!" Like the Mouton[-Rothschild] saying. [*Premier ne puis, second ne daigne, Mouton suis:* "First, I cannot be. Second, I do not condescend to be. Mouton, I am."]

Have you made wine from there?
GP: Oh, man. Tell him.
JP: Yeah. It does struggle to ripen. We haven't decided what to do. It could be where one in every ten years, it's great. The other years, it's mediocre.
GP: We just have to learn about it. So I want to do the whole flavor profile, from the warmest tip to the coolest tip.

Describe that profile.
JP: Pisoni vineyard is the deepest fruit, the richest, spicier. Up north, towards Garys', it's cooler, so more aromatic, more delicate, with more lush, velvety palate. Where the palate at the Pisoni vineyard, being in the mountains, is more coarse, more tannin. As you go north, where the Silacci is, so far what we've seen is, it's a little green. But again, it's a young vineyard.

What is total production of the brands?
JP: We make about 3,000 cases of Pisoni, and 2,500 of Lucia [a second label].

Will those numbers stay steady?
JP: Probably. For the most part, we're out of land. We'll pick up a little more from special projects. Like the other day, Mark planted an acre and a half of vines on this little block that he terraced.
GP: Beautiful spot. It was so difficult to decide which way to go with row direction. I said, "I don't want to get near this, man!" And then, when I saw the way he designed it, it was so beautiful and perfect. Mark, I'm so proud of you.
JP: So little projects like that are how we're going to grow. And also, if a winery said to us, "We no longer want Pisoni grapes," we'd say, "We're happy to have 'em back!" But at the same time, these are relationships, like Adam Lee [of Siduri], great friends. We'd never say, "Adam, we need another 500 cases of Pisoni, we're going to take your grapes back."
GP: I'd kill these kids if they did that.

What's the secret of making a Pisoni Pinot Noir elegant and refined, with such explosive fruit?

JP: A lot rests on the harvest decision, when to pick. Mark's in the vineyard every day, and Dad has twenty-five years of harvesting, as far as knowing what stage the grapes are in ripeness, and when these flavors have developed.

MP: Of course, there are different producers, so each decides when they want to harvest. But we give them suggestions.

GP: I tell them, "You don't know shit! You can't pick yet!"

You mean, you tend to want people to pick later?

MP: Each winemaker has their own style, and some don't coincide with the style Dad wants. A classic example is Arcadian [Winery, run by Joe Davis]. He's regularly the first to harvest, going for a leaner style.

GP: He's trying to make a Burgundian wine in California. You can't do it! So let's express the California sun! Let's grasp it, kiss it, love it!

Are you the latest to pick?

GP: I'm always pretty late. I may have been a little too late. I'm backing off. *[laughter]* I'm going with the kids on this, a couple days earlier.

What Brix—?

GP: Don't ask Brix! *[laughter]*

Why not?

GP: That's why I like Silacci. Because when Silacci's ready, in October, it's 24 Brix. Pisoni would be 29 then! Ask more important questions.

Well, this is important.

GP: We don't go by Brix, we go by flavors! I taste 'em when they're ripe! But some people—I want this machine [the tape recorder] to hear this. When we were in New York for the Pisoni extravaganza, and people were talking about our wine being too hot in alcohol, Adam Lee said—which I love Adam Lee for—"There was a man, in the late 1800s, who made a wine that was 13 percent alcohol, and he asked people, 'What do you think of that wine?' And they said, 'Very, very good.' And 14 through 14½ percent, 'What do you think of that?' 'Outstanding.' And 14½ to 15 percent alcohol, 'What do you think of that?' 'Absolutely outrageous wine!' Who said this? The owner of Romanée-Conti, in the 1870s."

> Our wines are identifiable! They're showing what the vineyard wants to produce. And that's what I want: *typicité!*
> —Gary Pisoni

MP: That was from Richard Olney's book *Romanée-Conti.*

GP: I'm getting it wrong, but those high-alcohol wines were wonderful, because they had the sugar! They had the sunlight. They didn't put sugar in.

MP: Dad's referring to those great years.

GP: And we have—every year's a great year!

So this is a phony issue that writer/critics—?

MP: I think it's overly debated. Of course, there are hot wines that are out of balance, but there are other wines that can handle alcohol very well.

JP: Our harvest dates and alcohol levels are the same as ever. We haven't shifted because of market trends.

MP: And now, in the wine press, like five publications in the last three months have [said], "Are wines going too far? Are they overextracted?"

GP: Our wines are identifiable! They're showing what the vineyard wants to produce. And that's what I want: *typicité!*

JP: I think trying to force a style onto a wine from our vineyard would not work.

GP: It's got mouthfeel! It's got expansion! I mean, you put one drop in your mouth and it explodes.

Did either of you boys ever think, "I'm going to kick the mud out of my boots and go to the city and be a lawyer or an Internet guy?"

MP: No.

JP: We're just so fortunate to be in this situation. I mean, our job is so easy compared to what Dad did twenty years ago. To be planting grapes in the middle of nowhere was something! We just don't want to screw up what he did.

GP: I'm gonna cry!

JP: I don't want to knock him, but he didn't know much when he started. He just did things, and if he screwed up he did something else, and he was smart enough to ask [for] people's help.

MP: And I think we're going to be the same people doing it in ten, twenty years. It's not like my brother Jeff is going to jump to another high-powered winery that's offering him more money!

JP: I'd work here for free!

ROLANDO HERRERA

MI SUEÑO WINERY, BALDACCI FAMILY VINEYARDS, OTHER WINERIES

He was one of the only winemakers I interviewed for this book whom I didn't know beforehand. But Rolando Herrera forced himself, or at any rate his talent, on me with a bottle of wine (Baldacci 2003 Brenda's Vineyard Cabernet Sauvignon, Stags Leap District) that blew me away. That made me want to know more about him. We met up on a paradisaical June morning in 2006 at his own winery, Mi Sueño ("My Dream"), located—like so many others in these pages—in an industrial park, this one in the southern suburbs of Napa. There, Rolando recounted his remarkable story.

You were born where?
Mexico, in the state of Michoacán, in a small village called El Llano. My father brought us here to the States in 1975. He was the manager for a nursery in St. Helena.

How did he get that job?
It goes back to the '60s, in the bracero era. He would come here and work, and then go back to Mexico. He worked one harvest at Schramsberg, and Mr. Schramsberg [Jack Davies] liked my dad, so he referred him to Jack Chandler, who was starting his nursery, and Jack Chandler hired him.

Was wine a part of your parents' life?

No. My dad drank beer. All I knew about wine was that Jack Chandler drank it. My dad would say, "I don't know how you can drink that, it's sour." Then in 1980 my father retired, and brought us all back home to Mexico. That was even harder than coming to the U.S., because we left our home and all our friends. But three years later, I said to my dad, "You know what? I want to go back to St. Helena. I have no future here. I don't want to work in the fields, I want to go to school." I came back with some older friends of my dad. We got a coyote, who got us to the border. It was a night of adventure.

What did you do in St. Helena?

I said to my parents, "I promise when I go back, I'm going to work, support myself, and I will graduate from high school and go to college." My older brother, José, was already here, working at Auberge du Soleil, with Masa [chef Masataka Kobayashi]. He found me a job as a dishwasher there. But I already had been working at Stag's Leap [Wine Cellars].

Wait. We're getting ahead. When did you start at Stag's Leap?

In 1985. Let me back up. When you're young, restaurants are great to work in. You get out of school at 2:30, go to work, get back at midnight. And I had no other options where else to work. I worked at Mustards [Grill] for a while, and then I decided, for a career, it's not for me. So I went to my cousin, who was working in the grape fields, and he said, "Come work with me." So I went there. Hard work, shovels, I loved it. Manny Gomez was managing. One day Manny said, "Okay, I need three guys to help at a winery." My ears stuck up. I'd never been to a winery, but I was very interested because of the stories my dad told about Schramsberg, the big barrels, the smell. So I'm hoping to be one of the three. And Manny says, "You, you, and you," and I was one of them. I was like, "Yes!" I got in my 1970 Volkswagen and followed him up to the winery. But Manny passed the winery and went up the hill, and I said to myself, "This doesn't look good. I thought we were going to the winery." Manny drives all the way to the hillside, and there's this beautiful home, lots of construction. [Stag's Leap winemaker] Warren [Winiarski] is remodeling. Manny hands me a pair of gloves, goggles, and a hammer.

You're in a construction crew!

"Here's your new job." So I said, "Okay, I don't care, no problem." That's where I met Warren Winiarski. We had great respect and got along well. He liked my work ethics, and soon I was some sort of little foreman there. Come September, I go to Warren and say, "Thank you, it's been great, but I have to go back to school."

I'm walking down the hill, and Manny catches up to me and says, "Hey, Rolando, where are you going to work?" I said, "In a restaurant." I had a résumé, Masa's, Mustards, and I could walk in almost any restaurant and get a job. Manny said, "Would you like to work here at the winery?" I went, "Yeah, but I need a job from 3 P.M. 'til 11, so I can do my school." He said, "We're picking grapes, would you like to be part of the night crew?" So I got the job.

As soon as I opened those winery doors, walked in, saw the dark, casks, barrels, smell, the first thing that crossed my mind was, "This is my home." I washed tanks, barrels, I was a true cellar rat for three harvests. I was learning a lot, really liking it, proving myself, getting more responsibilities. When I decided this is what I want to do for the rest of my life, I went to Napa Valley College, taking the winemaking course. In 1989 I was promoted and offered the cellarmaster position.

> As soon as I opened those winery doors, walked in, saw the dark, casks, barrels, smell, the first thing that crossed my mind was, "This is my home."

Had you started drinking wine?
No. For me, drinking was really bad. Alcohol, drugs, all that stuff. But 1989, I'm sitting there having lunch, and Warren asks—I think he was already planning on giving [cellarmaster] to me, but he knew I didn't drink. He says, "Do you like wine?" I go, "No, I don't drink alcohol." He said, "How would you expect to be successful in your career if you don't like or appreciate the product that you are working with?" Well, that was a big blow. He made me think. I didn't have an answer. I said, "Señor, you're right. I probably should start tasting." So from then on, I would go to the tasting room, get educated—that's how I got started.

So you become cellarmaster!
Yes, a great honor. I'm a twenty-one-year-old kid running a crew of eight, everybody's older than you, and you're hiring UC Davis graduates. But they would teach me, too. I didn't know what pH was, all this stuff, I had no idea. But they did. But they didn't even know how to clamp a hose. Those were great years, but in 1994, I was close to leaving Stag's Leap and going to UC Davis as a full-time student. I needed more education. I consulted with my winemaker friends, and they said, "Rolando, you don't need to go to Davis to learn what we know." So I said, "Okay, what I'm learning in the winery, Davis can't teach me." So I made a decision: "I'm going to continue my school at night, and stay here and grow."

When did you finally leave?
Nineteen ninety-four. I had to choose: Am I going to be complacent and work in my cellarmaster position, or do I want to explore new opportunities?

Did you want to be a full-fledged winemaker?
Well, I wanted to prove myself, to be part of blends, be in the vineyard. I wanted just to be involved.

And you couldn't do that?
No. I wasn't given that opportunity. So I had to quit. It was the biggest decision, the hardest, because I thought I was going to retire at Stag's Leap. I started when I was eighteen and left when I was twenty-seven.

Where did you go?
Chateau Potelle, as assistant winemaker. I wanted a place where I could prove myself. No fancy toys, a place that's starting up, very small, where I can do everything. I didn't know who Chateau Potelle was, but I saw an ad. So I meet them, and it's exactly what I'm looking for. I stayed at Chateau Potelle three harvests, then I went to Napa Wine Company, in '97, as assistant winemaker. I left because I wanted to continue learning.

Chateau Potelle was a tremendous experience. I felt like I was in Burgundy, but back then is when all these new boutiques—[Jayson] Pahlmeyer's, Paul Hobbs's, [Ann] Colgin's, [the] Bryant [family]'s—Helen Turley and Heidi Barrett were at Napa Wine Company. I felt, "Okay, after Chateau Potelle, I can make wine."

At Napa Wine Company I could meet the winemakers, see what everybody's doing, and prepare myself to be a winemaker. I applied, and it was a long process. I was qualified from a practical experience, but not from the educational background. Finally, Randy Mason, the GM, made the decision that "we need someone like Rolando to put this team together, we don't need another educated person," because they had plenty of that. So I got the job. I was so excited! But it was a very short-term job. The head winemaker, Jack Ryno, leaves two weeks after I started. And one of the main reasons I wanted to work at Napa Wine Company was Jack Ryno. So I was bummed, like, "Man, what's going to happen now?" But I guess Randy Mason saw enough of me that they promoted me to winemaker.

Wow.
Head winemaker at Napa Wine Company. I was thirty.

How did that work? What was your role vis-à-vis, say, Heidi Barrett?
Well, it's mainly more a coordinator. I was head winemaker for Napa Wine

Company's label, but basically, Heidi Barrett comes in and says, "Rolando, here's a work order, I'd like to do this to my wine." But then, two weeks after I got promoted, Vine Cliff offered me the winemaker position. And I'm like, "Oh, man, another big decision. What should I do?" Napa Wine Company, Randy Mason, they were great to me, but I had to remember, What's my goal? Why did I come here? I came because I wanted someone to offer me to be their head winemaker. So after consulting with great friends, the best thing for Rolando was, here's a huge opportunity knocking on your door, just take it!

What was Vine Cliff making?
All Cabernet from the estate vineyard, and Chardonnay.

Did you consider yourself a Cabernet specialist?
You know, when I left Chateau Potelle, I knew I could make good wine from any variety. What I learned there, from [winemaker] Marketta [du Fourmeaux]'s philosophy, was the art of making wine. I didn't learn a protocol of how to make Cabernet, or Zinfandel, or Gewürz. I learned the art of winemaking.

How long did you stay at Vine Cliff?
Three years. And from there, got an offer from a friend and mentor of mine, Paul Hobbs, to come and be his director of winemaking. Warren had hired Paul Hobbs as a consultant, so I met him there, and we kept in touch. When Vine Cliff hired me, they said, "Are you okay if we hire an outside consultant?" And I'm like, "Of course, just hire a *good* one." I said, "I know someone very good, Paul Hobbs." So they called Paul Hobbs and hired him. And when I was ready to leave Vine Cliff, Paul was in need of someone to manage his winemaking production. I said, "I will take your offer, with one condition. My full-time job is working for Paul Hobbs. But I need the freedom to work on Mi Sueño."

Because that was your dream.
Right. "So I need to be able to work on Mi Sueño with your full knowledge." And he said, "Okay."

When did the idea of doing your own thing happen, as opposed to being someone else's winemaker?
At Chateau Potelle. It was one of those feelings. I experienced this anxiety, frustration. I was already in the industry eleven, twelve years, and I said to myself, "I'm making wine under other people's direction, not making the decisions. I can't do that. I want to make wine. I don't want nobody to tell me

anything." I was also realistic. Who's going to trust me with grapes, two thousand dollars a ton? That's a lot of money. No vineyard is going to trust someone without any experience with those financial responsibilities. So I went to my father-in-law and asked him to sell me some grapes.

Who is your father-in-law?
Reynaldo Robledo. He's been here since the early '60s, growing grapes. In the '80s he started his own vineyard management company, buying land. So I told him, "Listen, this is how I'm feeling. I want to buy four tons of grapes from you." He said, "Sure." I asked Vine Cliff, and they were happy to let me make the wine there. And boy, I felt like a little kid in a candy store.

> Stags Leap is still my favorite, preferred appellation. It was very personal, that's where I started. So when I left Stag's Leap, I said to myself, "I'll be back someday." And here I am.

How long did you stay at Hobbs?
Three years. When I came, I already had some clients. When my father-in-law said he wants to make wine, I said, "Okay, I'll be your consultant." And he had friends who were starting up who were interested. So at that time I had three wineries come to me to make wine, and I said, "Great, I'm going to start my own consulting company."

Then you quit Paul Hobbs?
Well, Mi Sueño was growing, my consulting was growing, I wasn't able to give him the best of me.

Let's go through Mi Sueño. How many cases?
About 3,500. We make three Chardonnays, a Pinot from Russian River, a Syrah from Napa Valley, Cabernet from Napa, and my new baby is a blend of Syrah and Cab I named El Llano, after my hometown.

Do you own vineyards?
No. I have leases.

Whom are you making wine for now, besides Mi Sueño and Baldacci?
Robledo, Longfellow, Sharp Cellars, and a small label, Pugash, from Sonoma Mountain.

And all these wines are made here?
Yes, except Baldacci, who has their own production facility.

It's interesting, I wanted to meet you because of the Baldacci Cabernet, but it turns out Baldacci is only one little piece of the Rolando empire! When did you go there?
May 2004, after I left Paul Hobbs [Consulting], I got a call from Tom Baldacci, the owner, a developer. That call from Baldacci, it made me very happy. Stags Leap is still my favorite, preferred appellation. It was very personal, that's where I started. So when I left Stag's Leap, I said to myself, "I'll be back someday." And here I am. So I felt like I was coming home, but with more experience, more knowledge.

When you first looked at the Baldacci vineyard, did you think, "I can make great Cabernet here"?
Yes. I knew Stags Leap. I knew the wines they were making, with Warren Winiarski and [John and Doug] Shafer. I knew the potential.

But Warren and Shafer are on the foothills side. Baldacci is on the river side. It's not the same terroir, *maybe not as good.*
Right. It's not. It's more challenging. You have good-quality soil under you at Shafer and Stag's Leap. But Stags Leap [AVA] is Stags Leap, and with the vineyard management techniques, I feel comfortable we should be able to make great wine.

Do you want to grow Mi Sueño?
I'd like to get to five thousand cases. And I have a new project, a small label under my family's name, Herrera, a selection of the best of the best, kind of like my reserve, and every year I want to dedicate a varietal to one of my kids, my babies.

Do you see yourself owning a vineyard or building a winery?
I'd like to. You know, *mi sueño* means "my dream," and I would like to say, dreaming is free, you know? So my ultimate goal, I would like to own some vineyards and have a winery out in the countryside, in Napa.

Do you ever get back to El Llano?
Oh, yes. Not as often as I like, because of all the responsibility. And I have four kids.

Are they drinking wine?
Yes. Unlike me, they're definitely going to know wine!

JOHN ALBAN

ALBAN VINEYARDS

John Alban is one of those grower-vintners who is not well known to the public, and his wines, produced in quantities usually below six thousand cases, are mostly sold out in advance. But among his winemaker peers, both in California and abroad, Alban is regarded as a minor deity. His name crops up time and again in conversations with vintners for whom he has been both role model and inspiration, particularly for the Rhône-style varieties he pioneered in the Edna Valley of San Luis Obispo County. We covered a wide range of topics during several visits I made there during 2005.

Where are we?
At the southeast tip of the Edna Valley, six miles from the beach. We get a strong coastal influence.

When did you plant the vineyard?
In 1990, to Syrah, Roussanne, and Viognier. In 1991 we planted Grenache.

Who was in Edna Valley then?
The vast majority was and is controlled by Edna Valley Vineyard [now owned by Constellation Brands]. Back then, nobody gave a rat's rear about these Rhône varieties. Everything was Chardonnay and Cabernet, chocolate and vanilla, and I thought, "My goodness, California is such a tremendous state, with a tremendous range of latitudes, there has to be an opportunity for other

varieties." At UC Davis they had a program that enabled me to get to France, and I went to the Rhône Valley to do research. I got forty years of climate data, did the number crunching, and lo and behold, the northern Rhône turns out to be a Region I, just like here in Edna Valley.

What's the source of your Syrah cuttings?
That's a good question. . . .

What was your first commercial wine?
Nineteen ninety-one Viognier and Roussanne, but neither from this vineyard. The first from this vineyard was a Roussanne blend, 1992. The first Syrah from this vineyard was 1992 Reva. In '93, there was estate Viognier, Reva and Grenache. Lorraine Syrah was 1995 and Seymour's Syrah was 1998.

Why was there a gap between Reva and Seymour's?
That's a great question. I was so new to farming, I took one look at the hillside that's Seymour's and thought, "I need to learn a whole lot more about farming before I even try to plant there." It was years before I knew how to terrace a hillside.

Couldn't you hire a terracing expert?
You could, if you had the budget. We've been very much a self-built, bootstrap experience.

Is there a curve when your Syrahs hit their peak?
That's a very individual question. Personally, I would rather drink reds on the young side, while I find old whites fascinating. So I'm upside down from most people. But there's no question they're fifteen-year wines. Whether or not they're twenty-five-year wines, I don't have a wine that old!

How much vintage variation is there here?
Not as much as France. There's no probability of hail or torrential rains in August, so those things that are blights on a vintage are virtually unknown. But if you taste wines from a vintage like, say, '99, which was cool, with a small crop, and then compare that with a very warm year, like 2003, you'll see remarkable differences.

Do you think cool-climate Syrah is better than warm-climate?
It's not about "better" to me; they're different. A lot of people like the forward, gooshy fruit you get from warmer-climate Syrah, and others like the higher-toned, more layered notes you get from a cool-climate [wine]. And I can understand someone wanting to blend them. It all makes sense to me.

How do you decide when to pick?

That's the single biggest question. It's so funny that people have arguments over ripeness, when *ripeness* is a word we can't define. Since we can't define it, I don't see how anyone can argue it. In the end, though, one does have to make a personal determination of what is ripe. And I like when people add the term *physiological,* because we can no better define *physiological ripeness* than *ripeness.* They're the same thing. Either you're ripe or you're not.

So how do you decide?

I certainly follow certain numbers—not because they represent ripeness, but because they represent true limits. For example, you can't make good table wine out of something that's 33 Brix. So anyone who says, "I don't care about the numbers," what they mean is, the numbers don't make the decision. But hell, yeah, they care about the numbers, because there are just certain limits to the cosmos. But also we found that here, where we tend to retain so much acidity, following the pH and TA [total acidity] are much more telling than anything. We'll see a sudden drop in TA and a substantial rise in pH, and if we pick before that happens, we are making a mistake.

As a Rhône pioneer in California, do you see the public embracing these varieties?

I think the consumer today is the best educated, most passionate, most committed wine drinker the world has ever known. That group wants more and more great wine, and they're willing to support that pursuit.

So are we still locked into Cabernet and Chardonnay?

I don't think we are. It used to be like that, but now it's breaking down.

What is responsible for it breaking down?

It's a natural evolution. Once upon a time we didn't recognize varieties, and gave wines goofy names like "Chablis." Then we got varietal consciousness, but we became varietally myopic. We decided, "If variety's important, what are the most famous varieties? Chardonnay and Cabernet." But we grew out of that and said, "It's not that simple." When I first made Grenache, I met what I call varietal prejudice. People said, "Well, that's delicious, but I wouldn't pay that much for a Grenache." That's like saying, "I wouldn't pay that much money to a woman, because a woman shouldn't earn that much." We all know that's ridiculous. There are some Grenaches that cost as much as any wine in the world. So to answer your question, Syrah has become mainstream. Grenache

> Once upon a time we didn't recognize varieties, and gave wines goofy names like "Chablis." Then we got varietal consciousness.

is only held back by virtue of the lack of high-end production. But when it kicks in, it will do it; the doors are open.

Do you see consumer acceptance of Rhône whites?
[laughs] I used to want to buy a life insurance policy on every person who bought a bottle of my Viognier, because there were so few of them, I thought I'd go under if they passed away. Viognier sells; it's on restaurant lists. But Roussanne and Marsanne are the last orphans.

It's frequently said that some overseas markets don't care for California wines because they're too sweet and alcoholic.
I don't find that to be true. Export market has a lot to do with our having survived. In the early years, we had a lot more acceptance from Europe than we did locally. If we wanted to sell every bottle of Syrah we make in Europe, it would be very easy.

Why don't you have a Web page?
I'm not a computer guy. I only recently became Internet compatible.

You don't have a tasting room either. Both are considered de rigueur for marketing. Are you so in the catbird's seat you don't have to market your wine?
No. Everybody has to market, one way or another. It's just not the way we do it. I built the winery through beautiful sommeliers and wine buyers who, for whatever reason, embraced Alban Vineyards.

> I think biodynamic is really more of a religion than a farming technique.

Have you hopped on the organic bandwagon?
I farm organically, but it's not a bandwagon, nor do I label my wines "organic" or pursue organic certification. I have no interest in being rubber-stamped. I have neighbors who farm organically and biodynamically, and I have neighbors who don't. I think biodynamic is really more of a religion than a farming technique. And I wasn't born into a family of *biodynamiques,* I was born into my own family.

How do you see the role of wine critics and writers?
I think they're catalysts. A catalyst makes a reaction go faster, but it cannot make an impossible reaction go. So if all you guys got together, in cahoots, and decided, "We're going to take a crappy wine, give it a big score, and make it popular," you'll sell out the first vintage. But do you think you'll keep selling? The consumer is unbelievably smart. I have seen them gobble up good wines that didn't get critical attention, and I have seen them puzzlingly look at wines that got big scores but did not live up to their expectations.

Do you think a wine writer should have a technical background in viticulture and enology?

That's an interesting question. I never pondered it before. Off the top of my head, it may be a detriment. It depends. As far as evaluating a wine, I don't think you need to know anything about winemaking. You simply need to conclude that it's good, bad, or otherwise. Now, having said that, I don't think it's unreasonable when someone says, "Hey, I really like *your* wines, and that's why I'd like to know things you do." I'm sure you've had this same experience, where you can travel to a region where you love numerous wines, and then you visit these producers and find they all do different things, even some that are diametrically opposed. The guy who says, "We learned you have to destem everything," and the neighbor who says, "Oh, we never destem."

Tell me about how Hospice du Rhône, which is the biggest tasting of Rhône wines in the world, began.

Well, Mat Garretson started the Viognier Guild, and he called me up asking if I could sell him some wine, because he had to buy it for a tasting he wanted to have of all these Viogniers. I got so captivated by this very unique idea, and this very quixotic person whom I'd never heard of or met, that I went to Georgia to the tasting.

Georgia!

Georgia. The very first Viognier Guild, involving thirty-two wines and twenty-two people, was in Georgia. As Mat drove me back to the airport, I said to him, "That was fantastic, but it's ridiculous to have it in a non–wine-producing area. If you want to do it next year at my place, we'd attract a who's who of California wine, because it's such an avant-garde idea." This would have been 1992. In 1993 Mat moved out here, took my truck, moved into my parents' home. I wrote letters of introduction for him to all the various wineries, and we held the event here.

Who came?

The Araujos, Manfred Krankl [of Sine Qua Non Winery], Josh Jensen [of Calera Wine Company], Bob Lindquist [of Qupé Wine Cellars], [Joe] Phelps [and] Craig Williams [of Joseph Phelps Vineyards], Gary Eberle, Bill Smith of La Jota, Pete Minor of Ritchie Creek, on and on.

Was there a sense then that this Rhône thing was reaching a tipping point?

You know, long before a phenomenon can take place with wine, it first has to take place on a nursery level. Next, it has to happen on a viticultural level. And then you have to have wine for anyone to get interested in it. This was very much in the fundamental stages where people were getting interested in these varieties and working with them, kind of a very innocent and idealistic stage, because they didn't have anything to sell yet, so it was all about speculating what would be.

If you think about it, there hasn't really been anything big and new in California since, has there?
You know, the Italian varieties were introduced in pretty close proximity to the Rhône varieties.

But they didn't go anywhere.
Well, I'm just saying, because you asked me what else was out there. And people have dabbled in Spanish varieties. But as far as something that really sparked a revolution or a renaissance, very few of those happen in wine in a hundred-year period. That's the nature of wine; it doesn't tend to change that fast. And the Rhône thing is unbelievable; it really is remarkable what came of it. The first Hospice was twenty-two people, on no one's radar screen. Now it's thousands of people from all over the world, and the most celebrated producers pouring unbelievable wines.

Do you think the average consumer knows the difference between Syrah and Shiraz?
Oh. *[laughs]* That's an interesting question. I'm not sure that I do anymore, and that's a subject I *am* an expert in! So I definitely don't think the average consumer does. Obviously there is no legal difference. *Shiraz* is simply a synonym for *Syrah.*

What do you hope to achieve in the next ten years?
Speaking candidly, I've never thought like that. I really do, every day, think, "What can we do better? How can we continue to improve? What can we do in our vineyard?" So it's a daily process, to be able to learn something and apply it and move forward. I have been overwhelmed by the realization that we—and by *we* I mean California wine producers—have the opportunity to go so high, and how good the quality of these wines is going to be.

When you say "California vintners," you can't mean all of them. I mean, you're not talking about Central Valley Syrah.
I don't know the limitation of Central Valley Syrah. I really don't. I'm not that involved. By *we,* I'm talking about people who unreservedly are pursuing the greatest quality that they can from these varieties. What that means to me is, if tomorrow I woke up and thought there was a better place to do this than where I'm doing it, I'd find a way to get grapes from that place.

Do you think you're in the best place for these varieties?

I think I'm in one of them. I don't think it's so quantifiable. That's more a matter of style than of quality. For example, if people in [Rhône Appellations d'Origines Contrôlées] Hermitage or Côte-Rôtie waste their time thinking about which one is better—which I don't think they do—then they've lost touch with reality. Because they're simply different. So often, years ago, when I spoke about trying to do things better, I would read an article about "young California winemakers still finding their way." I thought, "Someday it will be 'ancient California winemakers still finding their way.'" Because I don't care if you've been making wine in the Rhône Valley for six hundred years! If you don't wake up every day thinking you can do something better, what's the point? Why consider what your father was doing to be the limit of what can be done? And when my kids take over, I hope they'll have the same attitude.

JAVIER TAPIA MEZA

CEÀGO VINEGARDEN

In August 2006 we sat and talked on the beach at Ceàgo Vinegarden, the winery on Clear Lake that Jim Fetzer had begun five years earlier. I had known Jim when he ran Fetzer Vineyards, before the family sold it, and I knew of his interest in organic and biodynamic grape growing. Thus, when I wanted to include a biodynamic winemaker in this book, I thought of Jim. I did not at that time know Javier Tapia Meza, Ceàgo's Chilean-born director of viticulture and winemaking, so I traveled up to Lake County to meet him. Javier had approached biodynamics skeptically, and he described it in a homely way that made this vast topic, of which we were able only to skim the surface, a little more understandable.

How did you get into wine?
My grandfather on my father's side was cellarmaster for [Viña] Santa Rita in the 1940s, and on my mother's side, my grandpa was a vineyard manager. So wine was an everyday thing. It's normal, because I was raised in that condition.

Did you always want to make wine?
No, but I knew I wanted to fall into the agriculture. My father didn't agree. His experience was cleaning pigs, feeding cows, going in the mud in winter, so he was, "I pay your private school not to be back in the mud, I don't feel

like wasting my money, you want to kill me?" *[laughs]* So he was against it. One summer I worked in my uncle's farm, picking watermelons, and I liked it. I was skinny and weak, and that summer I grew up, got a nice tan, "Oh, man, you got muscles." I was a totally different person. I knew what I wanted.

So I studied agribusiness, finished my degree, and started working in Santa Rita, in grower relations. I met the cellarmaster, Alvaro Espinoza [Durán]. After three weeks, he goes, "Hey, you want to join me?" So I quit grower relations and start working with him. He went to VinExpo [in Bordeaux] that year, and he didn't have anybody to leave in charge, so he goes, "Okay, you're the cellarmaster." So I'm cellarmaster at Santa Rita! Twenty years old! Alvaro's taken to the airport, and he goes, "Don't say your age to anybody! I don't want [the owner] to know he's leaving his investment in a twenty-year-old kid's hands."

So I start from there. Alvaro teach me everything. He was my first mentor. I work for five years there, but it was a big corporation. They say, "This is your occupation, and this is how far you're going to get." So I was questioning if that was really what I wanted. But Alvaro was still there, and we make such a good team that I was afraid to take a new position. But then I had the chance to come here, in 1996.

How did that happen?
Brown-Forman [Corporation] was selling our [Viña] Carmen wines in the U.S. And they offer, once a year, one winemaker to do a little internship in any winery owned by the Brown-Forman Corporation. So in '96, it was my time. I came to Fetzer. And I go, "Where is the Fetzer people?" They go, "There's no Fetzers here, it's owned by Brown-Forman [which had bought the company in 1992]." The guy who drove me from the airport, Ken Beck, the hospitality guy, said, "Javier, you really want to meet a Fetzer? I'm a good friend of Jim Fetzer. He's building this biodynamic ranch, McNab Ranch, and you can see it." So I went and met Jimmy. I saw him a couple more times, and then I went back to Chile. When I got back I told my wife, Claudia, "How about we do some crazy stuff?" We just got a baby. "How about we sell everything and move to the U.S.?"

And do what?
Anything. I was just looking for coming here and get a job in a winery. The U.S. was my dream. Imagine a kid who had never been anywhere. The only thing you know is Chile. You never imagine you'll see anything else. I just wanted to cross the mountains and explore. My dad was like, "You know, you got to go to immigration, it may be difficult, they may kick you right

back here. Why you don't stay at Carmen? If you're not happy there, you should tell them to give you a [better] position."

So I talked to the same lady who hired me. I really wanted to be production manager. And she goes, "You have to study, you have to get that degree." And I already had five years! I get so pissed off, I just walked out the door into Alvaro's office and said, "I quit. I'm going to the United States."

Alvaro looks at me and goes, "Are you for real? What are you going to do there?" "I don't know, work in McDonald's. Somebody will hire me to make wine." Alvaro goes, "Man, I'm supporting you. I'm going to call [then-Fetzer president] Paul Dolan." So he did call Fetzer, and he got me a job, six-month contract.

I worked at Fetzer, got to the end of the season, and they go, "Okay, Javier, your contract is over, it's time to leave." It was difficult. It was approaching the time that my visa expired, so I really needed a sponsor to be able to stay. I beg for a job. I really beg. And nobody needs anything, basically they just let me go.

I'm sitting in my house all depressed, like, "What am I going to do now?" My dad's on the phone saying, "I told you so." And then Ken Beck, the same guy who pick me up six months ago, stop by. "Oh, Javier, don't get depressed, come to my house for dinner. I'll cook you some chicken. You're going to be happy by the end of the day, it's going to be okay." So we're cooking, and the phone rings, and it's Jimmy. He says, "Hey, Javier, how you doing?" "Oh, I'm doing okay. I just got fired." "So what are you doing now? Man, your English is getting good. You want to come work for me?"

Where was Jimmy at the time?
At McNab. He offered me $5.75 an hour, minimum wage for a farm laborer. I was shoveling weeds and compost.

Take me from McNab Ranch to Ceàgo.
Okay. Then Jimmy's vineyard manager got in some stuff with him and got fired. My wife was like, "Give [Jim] a résumé. He knows you, he may give you a chance." I go, "There's no way. I'm not good enough." "Give him a résumé!" So I walk upstairs, give him a résumé, and then I pray. And then he offered me a position of vineyard manager. That's how everything started. I worked with Alan York, the biodynamic manager.

Who is Alan York?
A biodynamic consultant, one of the important people in my life. Like when Alvaro let me take decisions in the cellar, Alan gave me opportunities. He's unbelievable with plants.

Was that the first time you heard of biodynamics?
Yes, when I was working for Jimmy.

Coming from traditional agriculture, what was your reaction?
It was weird. I don't think anybody, not even my grandfather, would ever tell me, "Let's fill this horn with cow shit and bury it, take it out six months and spray it on your vineyard." Nobody would tell me something like that. If he tell me about the moon, I could probably get it, because my grandfather did everything with the moon. The potatoes, the artichokes has all this moon thing going on. But the horn part? I was, honestly, very skeptic. But when I got hired as manager, I had to face the problems, like mildew, pruning, the whole thing.

Did they tell you why grapes grown with that method are better?
For Jimmy, I think because he was worried about what he was doing to his land. For him, like the feeling I had when I was a kid, that everything is clean and natural, and then at some point, everything becomes synthetic. His dad, they had rattlesnake hawks and animals all over the farm, and then they start spraying, and there's nothing alive on the farm, and they're scratching their heads: "We've got to do something, everything's dead."

Is that the main reason for biodynamics, to preserve the ecology, or to make better wine?
I think it's also to pick up the flavors. Somehow, you lose the flavors when you're doing everything that [traditional] way. Everything tastes the same. To try a tomato from my grandfather's garden, then to try a supermarket tomato?

Most wines from California are not biodynamic. You're not saying they don't taste good?
No, I'm not saying biodynamic's the best. There's nothing proved. I made a speech in Sacramento and I got bombed with that kind of question. "Why are you doing this? Makes a better wine?" I don't know. To me, it may be better; to another person, maybe not. I'm not saying it's any better, healthier. I don't talk about my wine like that.

If you had your own winery, would you do biodynamics?
Of course. I live here on the farm. I don't take my car and go back somewhere else and let some guy spray all night. My house is here, my kids grow up here, Jimmy lives here. So you have to have the commitment.

Let's talk about the elements of biodynamics. What is cow shit in horns about?
That's one of the preparations. You take fresh cow manure, pack it in cow horns, and then bury it, maybe thirty inches deep, on September 21. You leave it there six months, until it becomes compost.

Why on September 21?
Because at that time, leaves are falling, the forces are concentrating in the soil, everything's going down. There's two main forces: levity and gravity. That's our main concept.

Then you dig it up in the spring, when levity's starting? What do you do with it?
You make this tea. Mix it with hot water, stir for one hour with this machine, one way, then the other way. That's the activation process. You put it in a little sprayer and spray your vineyard floor. It's a ground application.

What does it do?
It will increase the microbial life in the soil. That's the only way for nutrients to get into the root system of your plants.

Can't you just add nutrients to the soil?
Yeah, but it's about flavor. Why if you want calcium, you don't just take calcium pills instead of drinking milk?

Good question. How do the microbes help the nutrients into the soil?
Well, there's a whole program. You do your cover crops, and when they decompose, they release

You're going to have insects no matter what…but they won't be in enough numbers to kill my plant. I can pull my harvest through.

nutrients. But the nutrients are in what we call a raw state, unavailable to the plants. The microbes break them down for the root system to absorb them. Like you were saying, you can do that directly, with chemicals, so the plant doesn't have to do anything, not even maybe grow the roots, because it goes right into the mouth. But it makes a difference when you have to chase your own food, than when somebody's feeding you like that.

You're healthier.
Yeah. Obviously. You want the vines to develop their root system, and the microbes will be doing their job, and the worms will be doing their job, and everybody will be working and healthy.

What about insects, fungi, mold?
There are sprays you use, like silica, which is ground-up quartz. You fill up the horns, lay them in the ground at the spring solstice, until September 21.

And that comes up as compost, too?
No, it's like rock. You grind it up and dry it, and it's a really fine powder. And you spray that on your canopy, first thing in the morning, in early spring, when things are cold. It's really successful against mildew. It's crystals, so it

has this prism effect, the magnifying glass effect on the canopy. It increases the temperature and the light. That's the reasoning behind it.

Does that protect against insects as well?
No. Insects, then is when you have to play with your plant health. Then is when the effect of the farming practices shows and you raise your plant strong by this method. You're going to have insects no matter what, leafhoppers and stuff, but they won't be in enough numbers to kill my plant. I can pull my harvest through.

So these methods increase the plant's immunity?
It's not immune, you know? It's going to get attacked, they're going to come and bite the leaves anyway. But you're also making sure your cover-crop program is in place so you have a strong beneficial insect program.

You mean good insects eat the bad insects?
Yes. Ladybugs, green lacewings are the two main good ones for mites and leafhoppers.

What about phases of the moon?
It depends if you're tilling, pruning, cultivating. For example, when it's the full moon, everything's coming up, there's levity forces going around, all the water's up in the plant. If you make a cutting, the sap will come right out. Let's say you have a really vigorous [vineyard] area. You want to prune in the full moon, to release some of that vigor, you want that plant to bleed. Then if you have a weak area, you want to concentrate the plant, you don't want to decrease it, it's barely making it. So you prune in a dark moon, concentrating it so it doesn't bleed to death. And in the winery, we do all the racking not by calendar, [but] by moon cycles. We rack in the dark of the moon, when everything is lightweight. My grandfather used to say you should never rack wine with a full moon, because you will pick up all the lees, so you want to go in a dark moon, when everything settles.

> The wine was made the way my uncles and aunts used to do, no temperature control, no lab analysis, no nothing. And it turned out really good!

How did Jimmy make the transition to Ceàgo from McNab Ranch in 2001?
In '98, we had a block of Petite Sirah and Merlot, we were selling grapes, and these winemakers didn't like the grapes, they thought it had botrytis on it.

Even with your biodynamic grape-growing?
Even with my biodynamic grape-growing, I got botrytis. I had the courage to go and say to Jim, "What do you want to do with these bins?" "What do *you* want to do?" "Make some wine." He goes, "Well, go to Mendocino Cooperage, get two barrels, and make some wine." The wine was made the way my uncles and aunts used to do, no temperature control, no lab analysis, no nothing. And it turned out really good! Then is when we decided to make wine under the Ceàgo label. I took the position of winemaker, because I made the wine. In 2000 we get bonded, and moved here in 2001. Now I am director of winemaking and viticulture, and CFO by default, because I do the financial part.

And after fourteen years in the wine industry, do you believe biodynamics works?
Oh, yeah. I've seen it. I do it. You ask me for proof. I mean, at the Sacramento thing, this one guy stands up and goes, "Why don't you show me some proof? Why don't you do one part of your vineyard chemical and the other part biodynamic and see what happens?" And I go, "Why you don't do your vineyard chemical and I do my vineyard biodynamic and then we see what happens? Why do I have to prove something to you? Why don't you prove it yourself?"

GINA GALLO

GALLO FAMILY VINEYARDS

After a series of postponements—she's a busy woman—we finally met in spring 2006, not in a vineyard or winery, but in the modern offices of the Wine Institute in downtown San Francisco, which Gallo was passing through on her way to Burgundy. Tall, slender, and fashionable, with an engaging frankness, Gallo—granddaughter of Julio, grand-niece of Ernest—talked about her role in the family business and what it's like to have what is arguably the most famous last name in American wine.

Are you a hands-on, get-wet-in-the-cellar winemaker?
Definitely. That's where my passion is. But I also enjoy people, so I balance it. I travel, to share the family story, make the history reality.

What was your first job in the winery?
Every summer you'd work at the [Modesto] winery, and we all had our chores. I remember starting out in the mail room, shuffling the mail. Then, after college, I started out in sales.

Were you schlepping samples?
Oh, yeah. You have a big box with your little duster for dusting shelves, and your little cut-cards so you can make your displays. I had San Francisco and Modesto. I'd go to mom-and-pop stores, take orders, and when the wine was delivered, put it on the cart, bring it out, put it on the shelves—because

once the wine gets to the back room, you don't just leave it there, you bring it out.

Gallo practically invented the science of shelf management.
Absolutely. You look at my grandfather, very progressive. And Ernest loved wanting to understand the consumer. A lot of wine companies used the strategic things he came up with.

How did you get from sales to winemaking?
When I was selling, I had no clue about how the grapes turned into wine. I really wanted to understand more of the science. So I went to UC Davis and took winemaking courses. I'll never forget, my first one was with Ann Noble, Sensory [Evaluation], and also Linda Bisson, basic 101 on wine. I sat through my Sensory, and I was so intrigued. Loved it! It was like, "Wow! It's much more than just food." So I was selling, and at the mom-and-pop shops they were like, "Can I pay next month?" And [I'd say], "Okay!" *[laughs]* And my DM [district manager] would say, "Gina, we can't keep doing this. You know, COD means 'cash on delivery.' There's an issue if they can't pay!" So I loved that side of it, growing the business, but it wasn't my love. There had to be something else. And it came very quickly.

> When I was selling, I had no clue about how the grapes turned into wine. I really wanted to understand more of the science.

Do you report to a production facility?
Where I go is Dry Creek [Valley], the old Frei Brothers [facility]. I work for Marcello Monticelli. He's head winemaker, the vice president of winemaking, in Sonoma, Napa, the North Coast, basically. He's my boss, my mentor. As far as balancing winemaking, I'm on the road roughly four to six weeks a year. People think I travel a lot more than I do, and I don't know if it's some of the [magazine] pictures I do or what.

How many different brands are there under E. & J. Gallo? Everything from your jug stuff to—
Exactly. The Carlo Rossis, Ballatore . . .

There must be scores. You don't have much to do with most of those?
No.

Just Sonoma County?
Well, not just. I'll focus my energy from Santa Barbara all the way to north of Sonoma. But a lot of it is Sonoma County, because with [Gallo] Family Vineyards, the ones I'm working on, it's all Sonoma.

So when we say "winemaker," it's really for Gallo Family.
Vineyards. Yeah. That's where it's been the last two years.

What's production?
The estate's at about 500 cases apiece. The single-vineyards vary from about 2,500 cases to 500 cases. And then the full Sonoma Reserve you could say is about 400,000 cases. And then the big transition, we brought Twin Valley into it. That would be California [appellation]. Roughly, [Twin Valley is] almost five million cases. That's made in Livingston [in the Central Valley], actually.

How can Twin Valley be part of Gallo Family Vineyards?
Why not?

I thought Gallo Family Vineyards was—
You have the Sonoma Reserves, single-vineyard, estate, which I work on very closely, and then California [Twin Valley] just came under the umbrella of Gallo Family Vineyards, which is California.

Are you involved in Twin Valley?
This year I will be.

What's production of just Gallo Family without Twin Valley?
It's 420,000 cases.

Do you aim to make wines under Gallo Family that can compete with the best wines in California?
The world. Absolutely. But it's not about competing. It's about the appreciation of style, it's about quality at a certain price. If I taste a $70 Cabernet and a Bordeaux that's $150, is the quality there? Where is the quality, where's the character, where's the personality?

Do you think you can make a Cabernet that's the equal of a Cabernet from Napa Valley?
Are you asking, Am I making, is our family making, the best Cabernet in the world? I mean, what's the best? I look at wine very differently. I look at wine as art. Could our family wine on the estate stand up against the best Cabernet? It has, and it's beat 'em. Could it in Bordeaux? It has. Could it stand up with that pack? Absolutely. But I would never say ours is better. I

mean, I love Harlan Estate. I am a super-big fan of some of the wines. So I would never say "better." That would not be my personality at all. But could it stand in the same pack? Yes.

Back in the 1980s, there was this media buzz that Gallo was going upscale. It was a huge story in the wine press.
I believe your timeline's right. Absolutely. We launched our first estate in '93.

Were you part of that? Do you remember discussions where the family said, "This boutique thing is happening, and we need to see what we can do"?
Yeah, but it wasn't about the boutique thing. It was being close to the consumer, and seeing how food was taking another evolution in California, and where food goes, wine's going. We saw that very soon the consumer's palate was going to start evolving. They started with jug wines, then moved to white Zin, then Chardonnay. So we saw the pattern. Definitely saw the trend happening and wanted to be part of it. But it doesn't happen overnight. I look at myself making wine today, and thank God we have all the different vineyards in Sonoma, because now it's going into varietals, understanding the land more. It's continuous involvement, continuous improvement, continuous quest of wanting to understand more. But they definitely saw the trend moving, and that's why we moved into it. But you can't forget about everything else [i.e., the lower-priced brands], because there's still a huge percentage who enjoy [that].

> Could our family wine on the estate stand up against the best Cabernet? It has, and it's beat 'em.

Are you working with new varietals?
We're working with almost a hundred different varietals.

What does it take to decide to take a new varietal and increase production and sell it?
For us right now, the land drives it. Going back, the consumer drove a lot of it. But when you really get down to it, how's the consumer going to know a Tempranillo if he's never seen one? So you have to go and say, "Okay, what is this site? What's it going to do best?" Because the thing is, you could do anything.

It seems to me—correct me if I'm wrong—that Gallo does a great job of—don't take this wrong—
No, just hit me hard! *[laughs]*

A great job of letting others take the risk of developing a new variety, and then you guys jump on it, and with your power and clout, you market it. You make it good at whatever price level you decide to put it at. But do you think that Gallo is innovative?

Absolutely.

How?

My grandfather was the biggest, you know, he started our research winery back in the '50s with our grower relations program, giving them the chance, saying, "We'll give you money if you can get this in the ground." So grapes got put in with that research.

But Gallo didn't get serious about high-end Cabernet until other people proved that there was a future in it. Same with Pinot Noir. You guys play catch-up in a certain way.

What year do you think the cult wines started? When you say high-end wines.

Heitz was probably the first, with Martha's. But that was early. The real cult thing started right here [points to Benson's book] with the Chappellets, Freemark Abbeys, people like that. So I think of Gallo as recognizing trends that other people start, and then developing them. In terms of new varieties, is there one you're really getting behind now?

Well, if you go to our family tasting room, in Healdsburg, we have a Tempranillo. I would say, as far as innovating, one simple little example would be Sonoma Coast. When we were there, Flowers was the only one, and they were way out on the coast, so there was no one, very few.

That's your Two Rock vineyard, in the Cotati area of the appellation. How come you didn't go out to the far coast, where Flowers was?

Because of the warmth. When you get up on those hilltops, you have a lot more warmth. My dad [Robert, co-president of E. & J. Gallo Winery] was a diehard lover of Pinot Noir, and he knew you really have to push the envelope. Might be a year you have a vintage, might be a year you don't. So I'd say that definitely was pioneering. And if you look at the Laguna vineyard with my grandfather: '77, Russian River wasn't an appellation. How many vineyards were there in '77? You had a lot of apples and prunes. When he went in, there was probably, definitely nothing on that road. So '77? That was pretty early for Russian River, but that's when he started investing.

I take your point.

But I think it's interesting that you would feel [we're] not pioneering. I think you might see more of the sales and marketing side, but as far as the farming, the agriculture, I see my grandfather as being an amazing pioneer, and a leader of different areas.

Would Gallo ever go public?
No way. We have too much fun. There's too many third-generations that are involved.

You're not married.
No.

No kids.
No.

Any plans?
God willing, absolutely. I love family.

Is it hard to be in your job and get married and have a family? I mean, you seem like you're very, very busy.
Well, the last three years definitely have been busy, as far as the traveling, but I wouldn't say it's hard. I learned from my grandfather. At the beginning, he was very much a workaholic, and it hit him—I don't know when, but he had to step back and say, "You know what? This isn't life. Life is about God, family, and the health of the family is the health of the winery." I think about that every day. You have to have balance. It's not all about the wine.

You mentioned magazine covers. Do you think of yourself as a public figure?
No! *[laughs]*

I mean, your last name is Gallo; you're in the public eye. Do you like that part of your job?
Well, I feel like I have an opportunity to make a difference, and be responsible, and use it respectfully. I love this industry. What I'm about is creating wine. But what's most important is back to what I grew up with. Back to the table. When someone tastes that wine, they're like, "Wow." Makes a difference in them. And more importantly, that wine adds a dimension to the table, the relationships. I sometimes think that being able to touch more people with your family wines is a greater value than making the most iconic wine that only three people in the world can have.

What do you think of the wine media?
We're lucky to have them. Absolutely. Without the wine media, we'd never be where we are today. So there's a lot of pluses. Can it hurt? I think it helps more than it hurts.

What do you think about the hundred-point system?

Well, *[laughs]* in some ways it doesn't matter what I think! Obviously, it works, because we all grew up with A, B, C, D, or F, you're out! So we all understand it. We don't have the time to be reading some of these descriptors. But people are wanting to know more, they want to understand; so if someone says, "This got a 90, it's going to be okay," that gives them confidence, they try it. I don't think it's a bad thing, because then at least they bought that wine. Hopefully they thought about it, understood it, and they said, "Ah! I never would have tried this wine. Maybe I'll try the same wine from a different region, or maybe . . ." You know, so a lot of positives. But descriptors I love to see. Because that's what it's all about.

Why has Gallo succeeded for the past seventy-five years when so many others from that era don't exist anymore?

Oh, it's the founders' philosophy, for sure. My grandpa Julio and my great-uncle Ernest both evolved into their respective areas so well. And the philosophy is continuous improvement. You feel it, you live it, you believe it. Never stop. It's that inquisitive mind, asking questions and evolving to where we are now. There came times when I'm sure they debated, and I know stories that they didn't have an agreement. But they made a pact that, if they didn't agree, they would go home, sleep on it, and when they came back, they came to a greater decision. So it was that learning to work together, and respecting each other. I was talking to my great-uncle Ernest just the other day, and he said, "Julio was my greatest partner in the world." You know, he must miss him so much. They were so—it's powerful. [Ed.: Ernest Gallo died on March 6, 2007.]

What's it like working with your father?

Great. Not to sound like madness, but I have a great closeness to my father. He could be strict, so it takes a commonality, and I think wine was that commonality. We talk a lot about work, but we talk about other things, too. So it's good. I see in his eyes, he's proud that Matt [her brother] or any of his kids are doing things that they love. You know, that's a good thing to see.

Where do you see yourself in ten years?

Well, I want to be making wine, by far first and foremost. Staying focused on this. And the key is really having that love and that passion, and never to lose that. So still creating wines, with hopefully greater depth, greater understanding of the land. It's just that continuous improvement, wanting to be better, professionally and personally.

GLOSSARY

ACIDIFICATION   Wines deficient in acid have a flabby, flat structure. Acidification is the addition of natural acids (usually tartaric or citric) to fix this problem.

ACID LEVEL   The total acid content of the wine, usually measured in grams per liter.

APPELLATION   Informal term, borrowed from the French *appellation,* for a grape-growing area. In the United States, the legal term is "American Viticultural Area," or AVA. An AVA must be approved by the Alcohol and Tobacco Tax and Trade Bureau (TTB) of the U.S. Department of the Treasury, a time-consuming and expensive process.

BARREL-AGING   See *oak.*

BARREL SELECTION   See *wine naming protocols.*

BÂTONNAGE   The act of stirring the lees (spent yeast cells; see *sur lie*) in the fermenting vessel, using a long stick, in order to impart lees character to the wine.

BENCH TRIAL   Term referring to the experimental use of various additives or procedures administered in the laboratory to small amounts of wine for purposes of adjusting flavor. For example, a little potassium carbonate could help lower a wine's acid level.

BIODYNAMICS   A farming system developed by Austrian Rudolf Steiner (1861–1925) that combines organic farming with practices derived from folk tradition, such as packing cow manure in cow horns and burying them in the vineyard; the use of herbs in compost material; and performing viticultural practices according to the phases of the moon.

BLIND TASTING   A way of tasting wine for evaluative purposes in which each wine's identity is concealed, often by placing the bottle in a paper bag. There are many variations on blind tasting, most of which allow the taster to know at least something about the wine (its price, variety, appellation, and so on). In a "double blind tasting," the taster knows utterly nothing about the wine except its color.

BOTRYTIS   Short form of *Botrytis cinerea,* a fungus that can attack grapes on the vine, mainly in humid conditions. Often destructive, in certain circumstances (especially with Riesling, Sauvignon Blanc, Sémillon) it can produce balanced, sweet dessert wines.

BOTTLE PRICE FORMULA   Nonlegal term, used by some growers, referring to a formula for determining the sale price of grapes based on the ultimate bottle price of the wine.

BRIX   A term referring to the measurement of dissolved sucrose to water in a liquid, i.e., a measure of a grape's sweetness; named for Adolf Brix, who invented the scale.

CALCIUM CARBONATE   One of several basic substances (another is potassium carbonate) that, added to wine, can chemically lower the acid level.

CANOPY MANAGEMENT   See *trellising.*

CAP MANAGEMENT   The cap (from French *châpeau*) is the mass of stems, twigs, and other solid material that rises to the top of the tank during fermentation. Various forms of "managing" the cap (such as punching down or pumping over) all strive to make fresher, cleaner, more stable wine.

CENTRIFUGING   A technology primarily applied to winemaking to remove yeast cells or other colloidal particles suspended in wine, in order to clarify it. Yeast cells left behind may also result in spoilage or secondary fermentation in the bottle. See also *dealcoholization.*

CLIMATE REGIONS I–V   A system developed by UC Davis researchers in which California was divided into five grape-growing regions, based on accumulated degree days (each degree a day averages about 50 degrees Fahrenheit, the coolest temperature at which vine shoots grow) during the growing season. See also *heat summation.*

CLONES   Among grape varieties, slight genetic variations, often arising spontaneously, make for a vine with distinct characteristics. Copies of that unique vine made by taking cuttings or grafting are clones. The laboratory development of new, highly purified clones was a signal development of the late twentieth century.

COLD SOAK   Winemaking process in which the must (prefermented grape juice) is chilled to under 50 degrees Fahrenheit. With white wines, this process delays fermentation, allowing solids to separate out. With some reds, especially Pinot Noir, cold soaking helps extract color and phenolics from the skins and pulp (chemical compounds important in wine mouthfeel, quality, and palatability).

CRUSHER   Any device used to crush or press harvested grapes, yielding fresh juice. There are many kinds. See also *destemmer-crusher.*

DEALCOHOLIZATION   The process of deliberately reducing the alcohol level in a finished wine before bottling. There are several ways to do it: the simple addition of purified water or rainwater, or reverse osmosis (RO; also "spinning cones"), a centrifuging application that can be used to remove alcohol or, alternatively, to remove water from must that has been diluted by rain. Anecdotally, winemakers are said to be loath to admit to dealcoholizing their wines.

DECLASSIFICATION   An old term, from France, referring to a winery owner bottling a certain proportion of his estate wine under a less-expensive brand (often called a second label) or selling it off because it is of inferior quality. Declassification generally is seen as a noble act and can boost a winery's reputation.

DEGREE DAYS   See *climate regions I–V.*

DESTEMMER-CRUSHER   Technology that removes stems and leaves from harvested grape bunches, in addition to crushing. Destemming—wholly, partially, or not at all—is a winemaker's aesthetic decision. It can help to remove tannins, which may make wine harsh. Whole-cluster, or whole-berry, fermentation refers to leaving all stems in during the fermentation of (almost always) red wines, in the belief that doing so adds structural and aromatic elements, and possibly longevity, to the wines. See also *crusher.*

ENZYMES   The use of commercial chemical proteins that act as organic catalysts to initiate or speed up desired reactions in must or wine. For example, certain enzymes bind to tannins and then drop out as precipitate matter, thereby reducing tannins in finished wine.

ESTATE WINE, ESTATE BOTTLED   Used on a label, a precise, legal term. The TTB defines it thus: "Estate Bottled means that 100 percent of the wine came from grapes grown on land owned or controlled by the winery."

FERMENTER   Any vessel, of any size, used to ferment grape juice (must) into wine, including wooden barrels and stainless steel tanks. "Jacketed" refers to stainless steel fermenting tanks that can be refrigerated through their linings in order to control fermentation temperature.

FILTRATION   Any winemaking process by which suspended particles resulting from fermentation are removed from the wine through a finely meshed filter. Filtering adds to clarity and chemical stability, but is thought sometimes to strip qualitative elements in the process.

FINING   Another process, often used in combination with filtering, to remove suspended particles from fermented wine. In this case, various materials (egg whites, bentonite) attach to the particles and then fall to the bottom of the fermenter. Some wineries use the terms *unfined* and/or *unfiltered* to suggest higher quality.

GONDOLA   Archaic; sometimes used to refer to a container into which grapes are placed after picking, so they can be transported to the winery for processing.

HANG TIME   Informal term referring to the length of calendar time grapes remain on the vine before being harvested. More controversially (as in "long hang time"), it refers to the modern practice of allowing grapes to ripen to historically un-precedented levels, which results in fruitier flavors but also higher alcohol.

HEAD-TRAINED VINES See *trellising.*

HEAT SUMMATION After winter dormancy, grapes start to grow in the spring as av-erage daily temperatures reach about 50 degrees Fahrenheit. During the growing season they require a certain minimum amount of heat, as measured by an aver-age daily temperature over 50 degrees; this is the "heat summation." If the heat summation is insufficient, the grapes will not ripen. See also *climate regions I–V.*

LEAF-PULLING Leaves are often removed from grapevines to bring grape clusters out from the shade of a heavy leaf canopy so they will be exposed to sunlight and ripening will increase.

MACERATION TIME The length of time must or fermenting wine is allowed to re-main in contact with grape skins, which influences the extraction of phenolic com-pounds (see *cold soak*), especially in red wine.

MALOLACTIC FERMENTATION The chemical process whereby malic acid, a natural component in wine, is converted to lactic acid. The process can be natural and spontaneous, induced, or prevented entirely, depending on the winemaker's aes-thetics. Usually it is desired because lactic (from Latin *lac,* milk) acid is softer, creamier, and more buttery than malic (from Latin *malum,* apple) acid.

MICRO-OXYGENATION The addition of small amounts of oxygen to wine by means of a device that distributes the gas in the vessel. Said to make wine (especially red) softer and lusher in texture. Somewhat controversial, MO's long-term effects—on ageability and stability—are not fully understood.

MUST The blend of unfermented grape juice and solids that results from crushing harvested grapes.

NÉGOCIANT From the French, an old term referring to a wine merchant who buys bulk (finished) wines from smaller producers, blends them into a final product, and then sells it under his own brand. In California, the term is used informally to describe such individuals, who thrive especially when large grape crops result in an abundance of bulk wine.

OAK Wine was traditionally fermented and aged in oak barrels before bottling. Today, regardless of how they are fermented, high-end wines often benefit from an extended period of aging in oak (anywhere from six months to four-plus years), which imparts desirable aromatic, flavor, and textural qualities. Consumers, es-pecially in the New World, seem to enjoy these notes. As the price of oak barrels rises, vintners sometimes (controversially) use substitutes, including liquid oak flavorings or charred oak staves. See also *toast.*

ORGANIC Organically grown grapes are grown without the use of chemical pesti-cides or fertilizers. This practice is increasingly favored by growers, for both envi-ronmental and, to a lesser degree, marketing considerations. Several organizations vie to certify grapes as organic. Organic wine is produced without added sulfites, but the practice is rare in California due to winemaker fears of bacterial spoilage. The use of the term *organic wine* on labels is prohibited by the U.S. government.

OVERCROPPING   Term used pejoratively to describe a grapevine allowed to produce too much fruit in order to increase the grower's production and thus profits. In theory, overcropping vines results in diminished fruity essence in the grapes.

pH   A measure of the acidity or alkalinity of a liquid. In general, the higher the pH number, the lower the acidity, and vice versa.

PHENOLICS   See *cold soak.*

PHYLLOXERA   A louse *(Phylloxera vastatrix)* that lives below the surface of the soil and attacks the roots of grapevines, causing gradual death. Most famously in California, a widespread outbreak of phylloxera in the 1990s cost growers billions but resulted in newer, better plantings.

POTASSIUM CARBONATE   See *calcium carbonate.*

PUMPING OVER   A procedure in which liquid from the bottom of the fermenting tank is circulated over the cap. This helps to add color and phenolics to the wine, and also to prevent bacterial spoilage. See also *cap management.*

RACKING   A very old term for a method of clarifying wine. Refers to the practice of sequentially moving wine from one vessel to another; with each move, more undesirable solid matter is left behind.

RESIDUAL SUGAR   The amount of unfermented sugar remaining in a wine after fermentation is halted. It is desirable in dessert wines, but can be problematic in table wines, and is a persistent problem in the warmer areas of California.

REVERSE OSMOSIS   See *dealcoholization.*

ROOTSTOCK   Refers to the root material onto which grapevines are grafted. After the phylloxera infestation (see above), desirable clones were grafted to rootstocks that are resistant to the louse. Rootstock choice can also be important in matching to specific soil conditions.

SULFUR DIOXIDE   The most common form of the element sulfur, long used in grape growing and winemaking as an antifungal or antibacterial agent.

SUR LIE   From the French (especially Burgundy); literally, "on lees." Lees are dead yeast cells that fall to the bottom of the fermenting vessel. Lees may contaminate wine but, properly utilized and stirred (usually with white wines), can give them added richness, flavor, and complexity.

TANNINS   An absolutely essential element of wine, especially red wine. Tannins are found in grape skins and pips (seeds); they are also imparted from oak barrels. They contribute to the aroma, structure, mouthfeel, balance, and longevity of the finished wine. The tannins in certain properly aged red wines will solidify and fall out (precipitate) to the bottom of the bottle. The punt (indentation or nipple at the bottle's bottom) helps to capture this muck.

TERROIR   French; from the Latin *terra,* "earth." This impossible-to-translate term is subject to endless angels-dancing-on-pins debates, always without resolution.

Most generally it refers to the climatic and geophysical aspects of a wine region, vineyard, or section of vineyard. The French term *cru* is sometimes used to describe the inclusion of the human factor with *terroir*.

TOAST   The act of firing, or charring, any portion of the inside of a wine barrel, including the head. Toasting caramelizes the wood, adding unique, desirable aromatics and flavors. Precise toast levels (light, medium, heavy) are determined by house style.

TRELLISING   Trellises are complex vineyard systems of posts and wires used by grape growers to train and guide growing grapevine tendrils along desired paths. There are great numbers of such systems, and every few years seems to see a rethinking in approach. Trellising is one part of the grower's overall system of canopy management, including pruning. Probably the most popular trellising system in California is vertical shoot positioning, which maximizes exposure to the sun. Prior to the development of modern trellising systems, grapevines traditionally were head-trained in California, i.e., allowed simply to grow in their natural state, like bushes.

VARIETY, GRAPE   See *Vitis vinifera*.

VINE SPACING   The precise distance between vines in a row, and between rows in a vineyard. A recent development in California (but old in Europe) is to cluster vines closer together; called *close spacing*, this is said to improve grape quality. Close spacing also maximizes the economic value of the land.

VINEYARD DESIGNATION   On a label, the naming of the vineyard from which the grapes were sourced. Federal law requires that at least 95 percent of the grapes come from the named vineyard for it to be vineyard-designated.

VITIS VINIFERA   Originating somewhere in or near the Caucasus, *Vitis vinifera* is the source of all the world's greatest wines. Probably the wines of the Bible were made from it. Also called the European grapevine, this species of grape has mutated into thousands of different varieties, such as Cabernet Sauvignon and Pinot Noir. Varieties, in turn, usually have different clones (see above). Wine can be made from grapes of a different species (e.g., *Vitis labrusca*), but true oenophiles do not consider them to be of the same quality.

WHOLE-CLUSTER FERMENTATION   See *destemmer-crusher*.

WINE NAMING PROTOCOLS   Every commercial wine must have a name. Usually, the front label on a wine bottle will contain numerous identifiers. The TTB mandates very strict parameters for some of these identifiers: variety, appellation, vineyard designation, and so on. Other terms, however, are left to the winemaker's discretion, and it can be difficult for the consumer to know what if anything they mean. Examples of the latter are "barrel selection," "private reserve," "reserve," "special selection," "vintner's reserve," and so on. Proprietary names are nonregulated, fanciful ones often used when the legal minimum quantity to label a specific variety (75 percent in California) has not been reached. See also *estate wine, estate bottled; vineyard designation*.

YEAST   A microorganism, classified as a fungus, responsible for fermentation in wines. *Natural, indigenous, resident,* or *wild* yeasts—all casual terms—are those occurring in the vineyard and/or winery, which spontaneously initiate fermentation in grape juice. Some winemakers believe natural yeasts produce better, more honest wines. Others prefer not to leave things to chance. For them, there is a wide selection of commercial yeasts available. Wine made from commercial yeasts is said to have been inoculated. Some winemakers lately refer to "superyeasts." Developed in the 1990s, they result in dry wines with alcohol levels higher than previously believed possible.

YIELD   Most simply, the amount of crop, usually expressed as tons per acre, produced by a vineyard. Anecdotally, low-yielding vineyards are said to produce the best, most concentrated wines, high-yielding ones wines of diluted quality. Exceptions, however, abound. Increasingly, *yield* has come to refer to pounds per vine, since the yield within a constant acreage can vary dramatically, depending on vine spacing among other factors.

INDEX

grape contracts, 51, 71, 85, 149, 205
grape prices, 71, 204, 237, 266
grape varieties. *See* varieties; *specific grapes*
Graves, David, 21
Great Valley Sequence soils, 106–7
Great Winemakers of California: Conversations with Robert Benson (Benson), 1, 2, 3–4, 5, 147
Grenache, 25, 204, 205, 207, 209; Alban, 241, 242, 243–44

Hampton, Dale, 12
hang time, 21, 73, 130, 160, 173, 190, 267–68. *See also* Brix/Brix levels; harvest timing; high-alcohol trend; ripeness
Hanzell Vineyards, 8, 213, 215–20
Happy Canyon, 17
Harlan, Bill, 3, 105–6, 108
Harlan Estate, 3, 61, 105–12, 173, 175, 260
Hartford Court, 137–38
Hartford Family Winery, 138
harvest labor availability, 14, 53
harvest timing: Alban on, 243; Edwards on, 52–53; Foxen, 14; Gary Pisoni on, 229; Hanzell, 219; Harlan Estate, 110; Janssens on, 35–36; Longoria on, 44–45; for Mondavi Cabernets, 35–36; for Morgan Chardonnays, 20–21; Peterson Barrett on, 128; Rosenblum on, 86; for Seghesio Zinfandels, 81; Shafer, 160. *See also* Brix/Brix levels; high-alcohol trend; ripeness
Hawk's Roost Ranch, 140
The Heartbreak Grape (de Villiers), 187
heat summation, 268
Heitz Wine Cellars, 154, 261
Hellenthal vineyard, 140
Herrera, José, 234
Herrera, Rolando, *232,* 233–39
Heublein Corporation, 69–70; purchase of Inglenook/Beaulieu, 67, 68–69
high-alcohol trend, 5, 267–68; Aubert on, 172–73; Beckstoffer on, 72–73; Brewer on, 196–97; consumer demand and, 35–36, 87; critics/ratings and, 36, 62–63, 64, 72–73, 173, 230; Edwards on,

52–53; Janssens on, 35–36; Joseph on, 168; Peterson Barrett on, 130; Pisonis on, 229–30; Shafer and Fernandez on, 160–61; Smith on, 208; Soter on, 62–64; Talley on, 121–22; Terrien on, 219–20; van Staaveren on, 95; Wathen on, 15. *See also* alcohol content; Brix/Brix levels; ripeness
Highland Estates, 145, 148, 149–50
Hirsch, David, 188, 189
Hirsch vineyard, 140, 188, 189, 191
Hitching Post Wines, 168
Hobbs, Paul, 71, 236, 237, 239. *See also* Paul Hobbs Wines
Home Ranch vineyard (Seghesio), 78, 79
Hospice du Rhône, 16, 245, 246
Howell Mountain, Aubert Bordeaux blend from, 175
Huber vineyard, 198, 199
Hudson vineyard, 176
Hyde, Larry, 158
Hyde vineyard, 176

image, 53, 93, 131, 172, 178–79. *See also* branding
INAO (Institut national des appellations d'origine), 3
information technology, at Kendall-Jackson, 147–48
Inglenook Vineyard, 8, 67, 68–69
Institut national des appellations d'origine. *See* INAO
inventory management, 147–48
Ira Lee vineyard, 215
irrigation, 69, 73, 78
Italian Swiss Colony, 75, 80
Italian varieties, 80, 129, 132, 151, 159, 246
Iund vineyard, 215

J. Carey Cellars, 40
Jackson, Jess, 13, 145, 146, 147, 150
James Berry vineyard, 203–5, 206–7
Janssens, Geneviève, *28,* 29–36
Janssens, Luc, 31
Jekel, Bill, 20
Jekel Vineyards, 19–20
Jensen, Josh, 245

McNab Ranch, 250, 251–55
Melville, Ron, 197
Melville Vineyards and Winery, 193, 194, 195, 197, 198, 199–200
Mendocino grapes/vineyards, 70
Meredith Estate vineyard, 48, 52
Meridian Vineyards, 94, 166
Merlot, 48, 64, 97, 108
Merry Edwards Wines, 47–54
Merryvale Vineyards, 105–6
Merzoian, Edward, 95
Merzoian, Robert, 95
Metallico, 24
Michael, Peter. See Peter Michael Winery
micro-oxygenation, 268
Minor, Pete, 245
Mi Sueño Winery, 233, 237–39
Molnar, Peter, 220
Mondavi, Robert, xii, 32, 34, 36
Mondavi, Tim, 31, 32, 33, 34, 35, 125
Mondavi Winery. See Robert Mondavi Winery
Monterey vineyards and wineries: Chalone, 12, 21, 48; Morgan, 19–26. See also Pisoni Vineyards & Winery; specific appellations
Monticelli, Marcello, 258
Monticello Vineyards, 172
Morgan Lee, Dan, 18, 19–26
Morgan Winery, 19–26
Morlet, Luc, 178
Moscato Azul, 129
Mount Carmel vineyard, 41, 42, 43, 44, 194, 195
Mount Eden Vineyards, Edwards at, 48–49, 50, 52, 54
Mourvèdre, 204, 205, 207, 209
Muscat Canelli, 129
Mustards Grill, 234

Nabokov, Vladimir, 137
Napa, Peterson Barrett on, 131
Napa grapes: appellation variations, 128, 153; Cabernets, 98, 128, 132, 154, 172; Chardonnay, 176. See also specific appellations, vineyards, and wineries

Napa soils, 106–7
Napa Valley Agricultural Preserve, xiii
Napa Valley College, 235
Napa Wine Company, 125, 236–37
Napa wineries: Baldacci, 233, 238–39; Etude, 57, 58–59, 60–64; Harlan Estate, 3, 61, 105–12, 173, 175, 260; Mi Sueño, 233, 237–39; Opus One, 31–33, 78, 137; Robert Mondavi, 2, 8, 32–36, 78, 214; Shafer Vineyards, 59, 153–61, 239
natural yeasts. See wild yeasts
Nebbiolo, 151
Niebaum-Coppola Winery, 59
Nielsen vineyard, 13
Novak, Mary, 59
Novy Family Wines, 189, 190

Oakford Vineyards, 127
Oak Knoll vineyard, 157, 159
oak regimens, 119, 209, 268; Hanzell, 217–18; Harlan Estate, 108–9; Longoria, 43, 44; Saxum, 209; Shafer, 155–56, 158; Talley, 119
Oakville grapes and wines, 58, 106, 127, 128, 132, 153. See also Etude Wines; Harlan Estate; Robert Mondavi Winery
old-vine Zinfandels, 77, 78, 79
Oliver's vineyard, 118
Olivet Lane vineyard, 48, 51
Olney, Richard, 230
Opus One Winery, 31–33, 78, 137
Oregon wines and wineries: Fiddlehead, 166; Pinot Noirs, 61, 165, 176; Siduri Pinot Noir, 191; Soter, 61
organic viticulture/organic wines, 54, 244, 268–69; biodynamics, 54, 244, 249, 251–55, 265
Ortman, Chuck, 58, 155, 157, 166
overcropping, 269. See also yields

Pahlmeyer, Jayson, 236
Palmina, 41, 198
Paradigm Winery, 125, 127
Paraiso Vineyards, 22, 24